WRITING THE SOUTH THROUGH THE SELF

Writing the South through the Self

Explorations in Southern Autobiography

JOHN C. INSCOE

Published in association with the
Georgia Humanities Council

The University of Georgia Press
Athens & London

© 2011 by the University of Georgia Press

Athens, Georgia 30602

www.ugapress.org

All rights reserved

Designed by Walton Harris

Set in 10.5 Garamond Premier Pro

Printed digitally in the United States of America

Library of Congress Cataloging-in-Publication Data

Inscoe, John C., 1951–

Writing the South through the self : explorations in southern autobiography /
John C. Inscoe.

   p.   cm.

Includes bibliographical references and index.

ISBN-13: 978-0-8203-3767-8 (hardcover : alk. paper)

ISBN-10: 0-8203-3767-6 (hardcover : alk. paper)

ISBN-13: 978-0-8203-3768-5 (pbk. : alk. paper)

ISBN-10: 0-8203-3768-4 (pbk. : alk. paper)

1. Southern States—Biography. 2. Autobiography—Social aspects—Southern States.
3. Autobiography—Psychological aspects—Southern States. 4. Southern States—
Social conditions. 5. Race discrimination—Southern States. 6. Miscegenation—
Southern States. 7. Social stratification—Southern States. 8. Segregation in
transportation—Southern States. 9. College students—Southern States—Attitudes.
10. Appalachian Region—Social conditions. I. Title.

F208.I67 2011

975—dc22   2010032652

British Library Cataloging-in-Publication Data available

Chapter 3, "'All Manner of Defeated, Shiftless, Shifty, Pathetic and Interesting Good
People': Autobiographical Encounters with Southern White Poverty," was previously
published in different form in Richard Godden and Martin Crawford, eds., *Reading
Southern Poverty between the Wars, 1918–1939* (Athens: University of Georgia Press,
2006). Reprinted by permission.

Chapter 6, "Sense of Place, Sense of Being: Appalachian Struggles with Identity,
Belonging, and Escape," was previously published in different form in the *Journal of
Appalachian Studies*, vol. 12, issue 2, Fall 2006, by John C. Inscoe. Copyright © 2008
by the Appalachian Studies Association. Reprinted by permission.

To my father and father-in-law,
both of whom have written beautifully about
their lives as southern boys who came of age
on the front lines of World War II

To know oneself is to know one's region. . . .
The writer's value is lost, both to himself
and to his country, as soon as he ceases to
see that country as a part of himself.
— FLANNERY O'CONNOR

CONTENTS

PREFACE

THIS BOOK EVOLVED from a course I have taught at the University of Georgia for the past two decades or so, called "Southern Autobiography as Southern History." It was inspired by a similar course John Boles designed and taught at Rice University called "Growing Up Southern," and by an initiative led by Bill McFeely in our department at Georgia to bring more biography and autobiography into our history curriculum under the general rubric of "American Lives." In designing and teaching that course since, my purpose has always been twofold: first, to use these works to explore the variety and complexity of the southern experience over time; and second, to allow students to examine in depth one of the most vital, yet often overlooked, of historical primary sources — individuals' accounts of their own lives. There's no course I teach with such relish or teach more often, and from these many years of lectures, discussions, and feedback by what now must be hundreds of students, I have shaped the essays that make up this volume.

Equally influential to my thinking on the pedagogical value of this work has been my involvement in workshops, symposia, and summer seminars with middle and high school teachers throughout Georgia, and on occasion in North Carolina, in which I have joined with other colleagues in pushing the great appeal — and age appropriateness — of so much memoir and autobiography as teaching resources. As coming-of-age narratives, many of these works deal with issues and concerns that young people can relate to; I have also found them an effective means of promoting character education, which was a major initiative of the Georgia Humanities Council for a number of years. In short, the more I've taught these works myself and discussed them with both students and teachers, the more convinced I've become that autobiography and memoir offer an exceptional window into the southern past and an accessible means of addressing that past on a variety of levels and to a variety of readers.

☆ ☆ ☆

I'm sure that part of my interest in autobiography stems from the fact that I come from a family of autobiographers — of sorts. My father has written and published two accounts of his early life, the first a vivid narrative of his experience as a fighter pilot in World War II who was shot down over Germany in the war's waning weeks; the second, a nostalgic account of his childhood and adolescence in the small town of Nashville in eastern North Carolina.[1] Both of these were written for other family members — especially his grandchildren. My remarkable father-in-law, Charles Hawkins, (who gave up teaching high school English at the age of eighty-two only a couple of years ago), has done the same as a legacy for his grandchildren in an engaging account of his Tennessee childhood, his college years at Vanderbilt, and his World War II experience in the Pacific.[2]

My aunt, my father's older sister, is a beautiful writer who produced an eloquent memoir of her early life as well, describing not only her childhood in Nashville, but also her war career as a WAVE, her marriage, and raising her family in 1940s and 1950s Washington, D.C.[3] All of these were designed, typeset, and beautifully packaged by my creative and resourceful twin brother Joe.

A generation farther back, my maternal grandmother wrote a wonderful account of her early years in the wilds of central Florida at the turn of the century, and of her education at Salem Academy and Salem College in North Carolina.[4] She later provided a rich, revealing history of her years as a teacher at two Presbyterian mission schools in the mountains of Kentucky from 1918 through 1921.[5] The newest jewel in this collection is a recently recovered partial memoir by my great-grandfather, Joseph Turner Inscoe, who in the early 1950s recounted his youth in rural Franklin County, North Carolina, in the 1870s and 1880s.[6]

In thinking of these memoirs, and in appreciating the tremendous value they have for me and my siblings and will have (I hope at some point) for our children as windows into our family past, I also wonder how much value they would have as southern history to anyone without an inherent interest in these people as kinfolk. So I have asked, what is it about my family members' early years, as they've recorded them, that is distinctively southern, and how do they — and we — distinguish what in their childhood experiences and family relationships is tied to a specific regional identity?

Much of what my father and his sister have to say about their early lives in Nashville, North Carolina, or what my father-in-law writes about being a "preacher's kid" in small-town Tennessee, could just as easily have taken place in early twentieth-century communities in the Midwest or New England or almost anywhere else in the country. Even my grandmother's account of life in turn-of-the-century central Florida, while very place-specific and full of revealing details about the turpentine business in which her father was engaged in the piney woods there, devotes far more attention to amusing anecdotes about the mischief she and her siblings got themselves into, much of which could have played out in much the same way in a little house on a prairie somewhere. Her narrative of her experience in Appalachian Kentucky is far more grounded in a specific place, culture, and moment in time that gives it historical relevance and southern context.

And yet almost none of these memoirist relatives of mine ever explicitly claim any sort of southern identity or offer even the faintest hint that their young lives are offered to their offspring as a way of better understanding the South. They never even acknowledge that they see themselves first and foremost as southerners. Only my great-grandfather sees his southernness as not only integral, but central, to the story he wants to tell. After pointing out that one of the most important events of 1870 had been the death of "the beloved" Robert E. Lee, he went on to say that "at the beginning of a new decade after the South had seen war and trouble and heartaches indescribable, and as the great leader of the southern cause was passing out, it happened to be my time to enter the stage." He went on to quip: "When I think of it, I am glad that I waited until the great Southern Struggle was over before I came on the stage, but I want to make clear . . . that I arrived as early as I could, and the fact that I did not arrive earlier was not my fault and was not meant as any act of disloyalty to my dear Southland for whose cause I would gladly have fought and which is not yet lost."[7]

Perhaps it is to be expected that one born in the Civil War's wake would grow up with a far greater consciousness of his regional identity — and loyalties — than those of later generations. And yet the fact that none of my other family members describe their lives as distinctively southern raises a question that becomes integral to this study and one that I constantly urge my students to consider in their own lives and those of their elders: what is it that makes a life — or, more relevant here, an account of that life — inherently southern, and therefore worthy of attention in a southern history class? Certainly some write with far more self-consciousness of regional context and identity than others. Indeed, what is perhaps most striking about the life stories of southerners is the sheer number of those who do explain themselves as functions of southern society, values, and attitudes or who use their own experiences as commentary on the South and how they came to terms with it, or failed to. That propensity — what Fred Hobson has so memorably termed "the southern rage to explain" — is what makes these studies of self so valuable to us now not only as windows into the region's history, but also as such bountiful sources through which to explore the complexities of race and ethnicity, of class, of kinship, of community, of education, of gender, and of politics. I hope I have captured and conveyed some of that bounty in the chapters that follow.

☆ ☆ ☆

There have been a host of friends and colleagues who have contributed to this effort over the years. It was during a visiting year at Rice in 1988–89 that I got to know John Boles and was inspired by a course he taught there on "Growing Up Southern." I designed my own version of that course soon after I returned to the University of Georgia and have been teaching it ever since. I'm grateful for that inspiration and for John's friendship and support on so many other fronts ever since. As for the course, I owe much to the several hundred students who have taken my course over the years. The papers they've written and discussions in which they've participated, both in class and in my office, have triggered many of the ideas, issues, and insights that have shaped my thinking about the myriad ways in which we can draw meaning from this rich and varied work.

Soon after I began teaching this course, Leah Rawls Atkins at Auburn University invited me to be part of a conference there that helped me realize the broad appeal this work could have well beyond academia. Two former colleagues and collaborators of sorts here at UGA were also early influences on this work: Robby Cohen, who partnered with me as part of an outreach initiative in the 1990s, first encouraged me to pitch this work to teachers and helped me realize the multiple pedagogical contexts and levels at which autobiography can prove so effective; and Tim Powell, with whom I explored the multicultural South with a number of honors students and graduate students in team-taught courses, and from whom I learned a great deal along the way. I also learned much from Eve Troutt Powell, who has shared with me some of her intriguing work on memoir, identity, and race in a very different setting — that of the Sudan and Egypt. The energy level here in Athens has not seemed quite as high since these three good friends have moved back north; they're all sorely missed.

Patricia Bell Scott has long been a muse of memoir and journal writing; that and her good work on Pauli Murray have much enhanced how I teach *Proud Shoes*, one of the richest of all southern memoirs from a historical perspective (though it was Joel Williamson at UNC years ago who first put me onto its many merits). Pat has visited my class several times to talk about memoir and journal writing, and I very much appreciate her support of and contribution to that course and my own work stemming from it. I'm especially grateful for a wonderful semester-long faculty forum on just these issues that she organized here at UGA in 2006, which allowed those of us working with memoir and memory to share new perspectives with colleagues in disciplines far beyond history. It's great to have so many colleagues and former colleagues here at UGA — in history and beyond — whose work intersects with some of my own and from whom I've learned a great deal that has found its way into this book in one form or another. For that, I thank Jim Cobb, Will Holmes, Bob Pratt, Ronald Butchart, Diane Morrow, Steve Berry, George Justice, Hugh Ruppersburg, Linda Bachman, Judith Ortiz Cofer, Barbara McCaskill, Mark Schultz, Melanie Pavich, Warren Rogers, and Glenn Eskew; many of them have worked with autobiographical material or other issues of identity and self in fresh and creative ways. Kathleen Clark has let me tap into her expertise on memory and race on a number of occasions and provided sharp critiques of several pieces of this book.

I am especially grateful to three good friends for pushing me to turn this course into a book. Most Athenians know that there is no one more fun to talk with about all things southern than Peggy Galis. She's been a wonderful friend to our family ever since we moved to Athens twenty-five years ago, and we've met a host of fascinating southerners through many parties and dinners she and her husband Denny have hosted over the years. Peggy has also introduced me to countless books, articles, and authors, many of which have made their way into my courses in some way or another, and a number of which show up here in this book. I spent a full year reading southern autobiographies with her book club and was thoroughly spoiled by their warm hospitality, great food, and lively discussions about books that often took far different turns from classroom discussions with undergraduates on the same works. That experience reinforced my conviction that these works have much to say to all of us, from middle school to middle age (sorry, girls), and that we can draw very different lessons, points of reference, and inspiration from them depending on our backgrounds and stage of life.

Jamil Zainaldin has been a great asset to Georgia in countless ways since he came here to head the Georgia Humanities Council in 1998, not the least of which has been his effort, along with Laura McCarty and a terrific staff, of defining the humanities so broadly and articulating how they can and why they should be infused into all levels of education in the state. In addition to being the driving force behind *The New Georgia Encyclopedia*, Jamil has been very supportive of other endeavors of mine, and his enthusiasm is infectious and much appreciated. It was a lecture on autobiography and race that he asked me to do several years ago (part of what's now chapter 1), and his suggestion — along with Nancy Grayson's — that it could be the core of a book, that started this ball rolling. I'm very grateful for his friendship and his leadership and for all he's done for me and for all of us as Georgians.

It's always a pleasure to work with Nancy Grayson, an old friend with whom I've worked in several capacities now. I'm grateful to her for seeing a book in that lecture early on and for pushing me to make it happen. She's a wonderful editor, and has made this a far more collaborative process than I'm used to with other single-authored projects. This final product is much stronger because of her input at every stage of its development. I'm also grateful for the expertise and support of other UGA Press staff members, including John Joerschke, Beth Snead, John McLeod, and Nicole Mitchell. They make a great team, and I always enjoy my dealings with them and many others not directly involved in this project. The manuscript is tighter, clearer, and more coherent thanks to the sharp eyes and editorial pen of copyeditor Douglas Clayton, who was also a real pleasure to work with.

Specific pieces of this work have benefited from a variety of opportunities I've had to present them, and the good feedback I've gotten from so many. I appreciate my friend Martin Crawford including me in a wonderful conference on "reading southern poverty" at the University of Keele in England, which led to an essay collection from UGA Press, and to chapter 3 here. Catherine Clinton, another good friend, and her colleagues Brian Ward and Anthony Stanonis were wonderful hosts at Queens University in Belfast in 2008, where I gave a lecture that became chapter 2. They, along with their graduate students, offered valuable feedback that has considerably improved that essay. Chapter 5 grew out of many long discussions with Tom Dyer on autobiographical accounts of college life, which we've been collecting in hopes of producing an anthology, and he offered a number of good, strong suggestions for improving that essay. Kate Black at the University of Kentucky, an old friend through Appalachian

Studies, asked me to take on a review essay on several Appalachian-based auto-biographies that I've expanded into chapter 6. Sandy Ballard and Pat Beaver at Appalachian State University have also put me onto several good memoirs by southern highlanders and have helped me sharpen my thinking about what we can make of them both individually and collectively.

I am very grateful to the two readers of this manuscript for the press and their perceptive criticisms and suggestions. One of those (the only one I know by name) is James Watkins at Berry College, who urged me to move "beyond the binary" and explore autobiographical work of southern "Others," which prompted me to write the final essay in the volume. He pointed me to a number of titles I did not know, as did Theda Perdue and two of my Latin Americanist colleagues here at the University of Georgia, Reinaldo Roman and Pamela Voekel.

I have benefited from knowing a number of people who have recently written or are writing their memoirs or family histories, and I appreciate now, more than ever, all that goes into that process and the great value in doing so. Janisse Ray, Connie Curry, Allen Speer, Joseph Gatins, Judith Cofer, Jim Minick, Jean Friedman, Michael Fellman, and Tom Dyer have all approached their own pasts and those of their families or colleagues in moving and creative ways, and it's been a pleasure listening to them discuss the hows and whys of their approaches. Janisse has visited my classes on several occasions and always enthralled us with candid revelations of the variety of personal and emotional challenges she faced in writing—and then publishing—*Ecology of a Cracker Childhood*. It's especially fun to talk with Tom Dyer (who enjoys informing his many admirers that he's up to volume 6 of his memoirs—"The High School Years") about the rich history of his family farm in Missouri, and the detective work at which he so excels in recapturing that history.

Finally, I thank those family members, past and present, who took the time to commit pieces of their life stories to print and left so rich a legacy for those of us, Inscoes, Cunninghams, and Hawkinses, who've come behind them. Several of my own generation have facilitated the production and dissemination of these works in one way or another, but none more so than my brother Joe, who has been the driving force behind much of the Inscoes' autobiographical output, and my brother-in-law Charles Hawkins IV, who has done the same for his father.

WRITING THE SOUTH THROUGH THE SELF

Introduction

I HAVE LONG BELIEVED that autobiographers are, or can be, among the most astute chroniclers of the South. Much of what makes their self-portraits so accessible — indeed, so memorable — is that they tend to privilege storytelling, dramatic turning points, and cathartic or revelatory moments, all of which are packed with meaning, insight, and feeling, sometimes well beyond anything intended by their authors. As Flannery O'Connor once noted, "The Southerner knows he can do more justice to reality by telling a story than he can by discussing problems or proposing abstractions. . . . It's actually his way of reasoning and dealing with experience."[1]

Autobiographers then, as both historians and storytellers, have much to tell us about what it has meant to be southern, whether black or white, male or female, rich or poor, at various times and from various locales, all of which allows us to see and understand the region and its people in ways that elude more conventional treatments drawn from more traditional sources. By allowing us to view the South through a multiplicity of contexts and voices and time periods, autobiography and memoir comprise what I believe are among the most moving and vividly expressed forms of historical documentation.[2]

Part of the power of southern autobiography, in particular, lies in the fact that southerners, far more consciously than most Americans, have long seen themselves and their world in terms of place — whether the South as a whole, or some specific part of it. Louis Rubin once asked, "Isn't it significant that the imagination of the Midwestern writer — I think of Dreiser, Hemingway, Fitzgerald — has so often been directed outward, while that of the southern writer has generally insisted upon finding its direction within the community?"[3] While Rubin was thinking primarily of novelists, his observation holds birth to age eighteen, who lived in one town — a town like every other southern town in that it shared a common history, an economic deprivation, an unending moral struggle, and memories of war and reconstruction, but unlike most towns in that it was inhabited by people with power who were unusually capable of compassion, apparently unpoisoned by uncontrolled defensiveness, and possessed of the gentle manners and good will that southerners have always boasted of and so rarely actually had.[9]

Smith was, in effect, revealing much about her view of the South through the very act of delineating the exceptional nature of Green's community and of his depiction of his experience within it.

Edwin Yoder expressed the same sentiment in noting the value of Willie Morris's *North Toward Home*. In an introduction to a recent edition of the book, Yoder labeled it a "vehicle of more than mere self-regard. It can be read as the memoir of an especially sentient American provincial, but also as the universal story of anyone who has known the same 'love for a small, inconsequential place.' That 'inconsequential' is irony, to be sure. No place, or places, that inspire a book of such humor and poignancy can be inconsequential."[10]

No one has made this point better than Rick Bragg. In *All Over but the Shoutin'*, one of the most moving, indeed masterful, portraits of southern poverty and its degenerative effects, he states at the outset: "This is not an important book. It is only the story of a strong woman, a tortured man and three sons who lived hemmed in by tin cotton and ragged history in northeastern Alabama, in a time when blacks and whites found reason to hate each other and a whole lot of people could not stand themselves." He dismisses the term "memoir" as too fancy a word for himself and his family, claiming instead that "it is only a story of a handful of lives, in which one tall, blond woman, her back forever bent by the pull of that [cotton] sack, comes off looking good and noble, and a dead man gets to answer for himself from deep in the ground. In these pages, I will make the dead dance again with the living, not to get at any great truth, just a few little ones. It is still a damn hard thing to do, when you think about it."[11]

It is indeed a hard thing to do, and yet, in the skillful hands of writers like Bragg, they make the particularities of their lives as vital as the universals we derive from them. Just as no place is too small to contribute to the bigger picture of region or of the historical forces that defined it, no individual life is too minor, nor "truths too little," to be equally enlightening.[12] One way of overcoming any hint of the "inconsequential" in the places, or indeed, in the lives, chronicled by those who lived them is to juxtapose multiple accounts and consider them in relation to each other in order to draw from them broader insights and more complex truths about the South and its past. This, in part, is what I attempt to do in my course, and what I attempt to do here.

Autobiographers themselves are often well aware of these tensions between the uniqueness and the typicality of their life stories, and they have often felt the need to justify to their readers why their stories matter. I've always liked the opening sentences of *Yonder*, a quirky and far too little-known memoir by East Texan Jim Corder, in which he states forthrightly: "If this is a memoir or an autobiography, I'll be surprised. Some historian, say, and my mother, were she still here, might testify that I have no occasion to write a memoir or autobiography; the historian, perhaps, because I am not notable and have not been where the momentous occurs, my mother, perhaps, because if I've called attention to myself, I ought to be ashamed and hush." Corder concludes: "I don't know how to respond to what my mother might have said, but the historian would be wrong: every one of us occasions a book — or a library — because each of us is unique, and because each of us is not unique."[13]

Bragg is even more explicit in linking his parents' sad saga to those of other marginalized southern whites in the 1960s and 1970s. Their story, he claims, was one that "anyone can tell . . . and that's the shame of it."

> A lot of women stood with babies on their hips in line for commodity cheese and peanut butter. A lot of men were damaged deep inside by the killing and dying of wars, then tried to heal themselves with a snake oil elixir of sour mash and self-loathing. A lot of families just came to pieces in that time and place and condition, like paper lace in a summer rain. You can walk the main street in any little town, in any big one, and you will hear this story being told behind cigarette-scarred bars, before altars, over fresh-dug ground in a thousand cemeteries.[14]

One reason this book resonates so with my students is that many of them recognize this world, even if they've only known it secondhand or observed it from the margins.

Other autobiographers are even more explicit in articulating their obligation to place themselves within some larger world in order to justify the self they've chosen to share with a broader reading public. In one of the most incisive meditations on the genre, *Where Memory Speaks*, Australian memoirist Jill Ker Conway noted: "Whether we are aware of it or not, our culture gives us an inner script by which we live our lives."[15] Southerners, perhaps more than most, have been acutely aware of their culture as a major source of their "inner scripts." Mississippian Eudora Welty made the same point in her *One Writer's Beginnings*: "The outside world is the vital component of my inner life," she insisted. "My imagination takes its strength and guides its direction from what I see and hear and learn and feel and remember of my living world."[16] I find this statement somewhat curious, in that Welty's is among the most insular and inward-focused of southern self-portraits. She has little to say about Jackson, about Mississippi, or about the southern society into which she fit — or didn't. I have never assigned her book to my classes, for, as charming as it is in its descriptions of herself and her family, and as eloquent a treatise on the writing process, her modest memoir offers little insight into southern history or the forces that have driven it.

Others expound upon those forces far more purposefully and effectively. Willie Morris, for example, wrote of a rather shocking incident when he was twelve years old. For no discernible reason, he attacked a much younger black child who walked in front of his house. The story, to be dealt with in more detail later in this book, serves not so much as a singular incident of childhood cruelty but as a reflection — even an indictment — of the nature of southern race relations in general. "My own alternating affections and cruelties were inexplicable to me," Morris wrote, "but the main thing is that they were largely assumed and rarely questioned. The broad reality was that the Negroes in town were *there*: they were ours, to do with as we wished." His awareness of this reality, he insisted, was "rooted so deeply in me by the whole moral atmosphere of the place that my own ambivalence . . . was secondary and of little account."[17] Even as a child, much of his behavior, he seems to be saying, was determined by the South.

No one worked more consciously or to fuller effect in fusing self with South than did Lillian Smith. She opens her semi-memoir *Killers of the Dream* with a startling statement. "Even its children knew that the South was in trouble," she declared. Smith was very guarded in terms of what she revealed about her adult life, and much of what she wrote of her childhood was told through oblique references to traumatic incidents resulting from her confusion over race. Alternating between first and third person, she insisted that her own feelings were those of most white children of her class. She concludes one story by admitting that it "was an incident that has rarely happened to other southern children," but only at one level. At another, it was "a private production of a little script that is written on the lives of most southern children before they know words. Though they may not have seen it staged this way, each southerner has had his own private showing." Ultimately, Smith acknowledged outright: "I realize this is a personal memoir, in one sense; in another sense, it is Every Southerner's memoir."[18]

Some writers questioned whether anything in their lives even justified their sharing it with a reading public. William Alexander Percy, among the most self-effacing of autobiographers, had serious doubts about whether he had anything worth saying in autobiographical form. Fellow Greenville, Mississippi, resident David Cohn in his own memoir writes of Percy, a close friend and mentor, "a modest man, he felt that he had done nothing distinguished that would warrant an account of his life" and that he had achieved nothing worthy of note. Cohn wrote that he told Percy that "the point was not whether he had acquired a special distinction. . . . It was, rather, this: His recorded life to some extent would reflect the lives of all men. It would offer a glimpse into the mystery of personality and partially illuminate man's life on earth. In this sense every man had the 'right' to set down an autobiography." Cohn quoted Montaigne to him: "Every man carries within himself the whole condition of humanity."[19]

Percy came around, of course, though whether or not Cohn was the impetus for his doing so is unclear. The great irony is that the result, the 1941 classic *Lanterns on the Levee*, which appeared just before his death, does indeed provide an invaluable perspective on the mindset of the early-twentieth-century planter class and the comfortable but slowly dying world it had made for itself and others. (As such it, along with Richard Wright's *Black Boy*, is the only book I consistently assign every time I teach my course.) At the same time, much of its appeal lies in the fact that Percy is utterly unlike any other autobiographer we read; he stands nearly alone as so self-deprecating and gentle a voice of the conservative elite.

Even Wright, among the most self-absorbed of autobiographers, sensed that in telling his life story he was articulating the plight of African Americans writ large — or that he should be. "I sensed that Negro life was a sprawling land of unconscious suffering," he wrote, "and there were but few Negroes who knew the meaning of their lives, who could tell their story."[20] The implication was, of course, that Wright could do so, and therefore should, and the searing account he left us of the traumas he endured in Jim Crow Mississippi does indeed reveal a reality endured by so many other southern African Americans as well.

Though nearly Wright's contemporary, it would be sixty years later that John Hope Franklin made a similar point in his autobiography, tellingly titled *Mirror to America* (2005). He opens the book by stating, "Living in a world restricted by laws defining race, as well as creating obstacles, disadvantages, and even superstitions regarding race, challenged my capacities to survive. For ninety years I have witnessed countless men and women likewise meet this challenge. Some bested it; some did not; many had to settle for any accommodation they could." But for Franklin, it was a career as scholar and activist that allowed him a chance to do what most of them could not: like Wright, he could tell their story through his own. "Along with much else," he wrote, "the habits of scholarship granted me something many of my striving contemporaries did not have. I knew, or should say know, what we are up against."[21]

On the other hand, many southerners — particularly African Americans — were very clear about not claiming any universality in their own lives and experiences, especially in terms of race. Very few of the fugitive slave narratives actually chronicled a typical slave experience, even as they sought to inspire and mobilize American readers in their opposition to the institution as a whole. Think of the exceptional circumstances in which Harriet Jacobs, Frederick Douglass, Solomon Northrup, or William and Ellen Craft experienced their bondage, and yet none of them had any problem in drawing from their very atypical lives powerful indictments of slavery and its abuses, both physical and psychological.

Zora Neale Hurston was perhaps the most blatant in not making the plight of southern blacks an integral part of her own story. She was unequivocal in stating at the beginning of *Dust Tracks on the Road*: "There could be something wrong with me because I see Negroes neither better nor worse than any other race. Race pride is a luxury I cannot afford." In a foreword to a new edition of the book, Maya Angelou called it "a puzzling book" and noted skeptically that Hurston "does not mention even one unpleasant racial incident in *Dust Tracks on a Road*. The southern air around her most assuredly crackled with the flames of Ku Klux Klan raids" during her early-twentieth-century childhood in north Florida, "but Ms. Hurston does not allude to any ugly incident."[22]

Henry Louis Gates Jr. was equally forthright in declaring in his memoir, *Colored People*, that "I am not Everynegro . . . nor can I claim to be 'a citizen of the world.' I am from and of a time and a place — Piedmont, West Virginia [in the 1950s and early 1960s] — and that's a world apart, a world of difference. So this is not a story of race, but a story of a village, a family, and its friends." Gates articulated more fully than anyone I know the ambivalences of racial identity. While he proudly acknowledged his African American roots and took pride in the achievements of prominent blacks, he also resented attempts to make that the sole reference point for defining who he is. "I rebel at the notion that I can't be part of other groups, that I can't construct identities through elective affinity, that race must be the most important thing about me. Is that what I want on my gravestone: Here lies an African American?"[23]

Even without such explicit pronouncements, readers of more than one of these works quickly realize that their appeal lies in their unique voices, and that we can learn as much from the atypical as from the typical. While common themes emerge in the essays to follow, it is equally important to recognize the sheer variety of experience, of circumstance, of personality, that is so integral to autobiographical work. It is not a genre from which we should seek consensus, or try to glean any norm, average, or even commonalities.

The individualities that come through so clearly and distinctively in all of this work — or certainly the best of it — make for valuable teaching tools both because of the particular circumstances and singular voices through which they are conveyed and because their stories contribute to our broader sense of the South's intricate and multifaceted realities. In one of the most astute approaches to southern autobiographical writings, Jennifer Wallach confirms the value of juxtaposing multiple voices, memories, and perspectives. "Each depiction of the South," she writes, "contains part of the social reality of Jim Crow and we should endeavor to understand all of these depictions. . . . The social and emotional reality of Jim Crow exists solely from the standpoint of the historical agents who created and sustained it, and an understanding of this reality is unattainable without recognizing their distinct individual perspectives."[24] I would argue that the same holds true for other aspects of the southern experience, from slavery and the Civil War to the civil rights movement, and to issues of class and gender as well as race.

★ ★ ★

For the most part, I take these writers' words and memories and interpretations at face value. My primary interest lies less in categorizing these works as either creative nonfiction or conventional history, and more in the many subtle and not-so-subtle realities they provide about the southern experience. Whether through faulty or selective memories, conscious or subconscious agendas, or overly imaginative enhancements, autobiography and memoir make up a genre that invites close scrutiny by those interested in either their construction or their credibility. Those interested in *how* autobiographers tell their stories or *why* they do so are driven by questions of subjectivity, selectivity, and authenticity, as well as theories of selfhood, ego, and memory, both conscious and subconscious. I have benefited greatly, as have my students, from these far more sophisticated theoretical approaches — psychological or historical or literary.[25] Yet my primary intent in this book, as in the classroom, is somewhat more elemental.

In introducing his memoir *Confessions of a White Racist*, Larry L. King was forthright in declaring: "I don't think many writers sit at the typewriter with lying in mind," he declared, "though perhaps by standard measurements we accomplish our share of it." Acknowledging that "pure unadulterated truth does not automatically leap from pen to page," he also insisted that "in no case have I altered the spirit, the basic circumstances, or the end result of my recollections."[26] Put another way, Judith Ortiz Cofer made clear that as she moved from poet and fiction-writer to memoirist, she had no intention of merely setting down facts, and she was quick to see the past, her past, as "mainly a creation of the imagination as well." She reasoned that "one could go to the sources and come up with a *Life* in several volumes that will make your mother proud and give the satisfaction of having 'preserved' something. I am not interested in merely 'canning' memories." She turned to Virginia Woolf to assure her that "the very act of reclaiming memories could provide a writer with confidence in the power of art to discover meaning and truth in ordinary events."[27]

In an idiosyncratic treatise on memoir, tellingly titled *Vanishing Point: Not a Memoir*, Ander Monson makes the point more bluntly: "The unreality, the misrememberings, the act of telling in starts and stops, the pockmarked surface of the 'I': that's where all the good stuff is, the fair and foul, that which is rent, that which is whole, that which engages the whole reader."[28]

The very title of Jennifer Wallach's recent study — *Closer to the Truth than Any Facts* — gets at that same reality: that the subjective nature of memoir not only fails to detract from its value as historical source material; it actually enhances it. I fully agree and have been very pleased to have Wallach's book to use and discuss with my classes. However, I tend to deal with these writers and their work in more straightforward terms and to use their words and stories to get at what it means to be southern, without worrying much about just how "real" those words and stories actually are. Like Larry L. King, I tend to overlook those blemishes, maybe even potholes, in terms of verifiable truth, at least as far as the lessons I seek to draw from these writings. I accept, even embrace, the spirit of the work and what inspired it. Thus I even incorporate autobiographical fiction — by Thomas Wolfe and William Styron, among others — into my course and utilize it here on occasion in the belief that it can complement or reinforce both basic and more subtle truths as fully as do more presumably factual accounts.

I fully realize that I am entering what has long been a very fertile field of study. Fred Hobson's work remains the Alpha and Omega of southern autobiography; his seminal *Tell about the South* established for the first time the great value in using what southerners have said about themselves and their region to more fully understand the South and its distinctiveness. Hobson's subsequent study, *But Now I See*, is a more focused but equally essential exploration of how and why certain southern whites underwent conversion experiences that led them to shed their racist assumptions, and how those conversions shaped their impulse to tell their stories in print.[29]

Bill Berry of the University of Central Arkansas added much to the corpus by bringing together historians, literary critics, and genuine autobiographers for conferences in the late 1980s. The subsequent essay collections — *Located Lives* and *Home Ground* — that evolved from those conferences have provided much fodder for my course, and I've often made selections from them assigned readings for my students.[30] John Boles has also produced two collections of autobiographical essays by some of the most prominent of southern historians, whose stories tell us much about the forces that drove them to make careers of pursuing the region's past so prolifically.[31]

Anthologized selections of southern autobiographical work have been equally useful in making readily accessible and easily comparable much of the best of these writings. Suzanne Jones's *Growing Up in the South* combines memoir and short fiction to focus on the myriad ways in which southern children have come of age. Even more on point for me has been James Watkins's *Southern Selves*, an especially strong collection of excerpts from most of the "classics" of autobiography; it's a book that I have used to good effect, I think, with middle- and high-school teachers over the years, as well as with my own students.[32]

More recently, historians have made effective use of autobiography to shed new light on the psychology, sensibilities, and social mores that defined the southern racial order for so much of its history. Jennifer Ritterhouse's masterful *Growing Up Jim Crow* demonstrates that autobiography and memoir can serve as means to other ends — in her case, demonstrating, as her subtitle so succinctly puts it, "how black and white southern children learned race." In her *Sites of Southern Memory*, Darlene O'Dell is equally inventive in utilizing a more limited set of autobiographical works to explore the Lost Cause. Through the eyes of three women very troubled by its more tangible manifestations — its monuments, rituals, and celebrations — we are made to see these phenomena from fresh perspectives. Most recently, Jennifer Wallach, whose book I've already cited, gives us new ways of engaging the psychological and emotional impact of Jim Crow through her fresh readings of six classics of southern autobiography — three by black authors, and three by white. All of these studies remind us that there is no more intrinsic historical source than autobiography and memoir for tapping into young people's perceptions, attitudes, and experiences at particular moments of time.[33]

★ ★ ★

What follows are seven self-contained essays that explore a range of themes that are basic to the southern experience — from miscegenation to racial oppression and harassment, both sanctioned and unsanctioned; from poverty to education; from the love of home to the impulse to escape. By filtering these struggles and challenges through the self-narratives of those who defined their lives or some part of them, often their early years, in relation to these formidable issues, we can view them from fresh, and often quite altered, perspectives.

The opening essay is a somewhat overstuffed version of a talk I have delivered over a number of years now — often to middle- and high-school teachers in Georgia and occasionally in North Carolina. It is an overview in which I attempt to stress the pedagogical value of autobiographical work as a means of dramatizing and humanizing some complex issues in southern history, especially that touchiest of subjects for teachers at those levels — race.

I was asked several years ago to bring an autobiographical perspective to a conference on southern poverty between the world wars, which led to what appears here as chapter 3. In that talk, I sought to explain how middle-class white children were exposed to the region's poor whites in the 1920s and 1930s, and how that experience shaped their consciousness of class differences that only later, and in only some cases, led to more open-minded inquiries as to the inequities of race.[34] Since, I have expanded the original essay to look at a significant shift in more recent times, in which poor whites have come to tell their own life stories, without the literary intermediaries that the middle class once provided, though the focus still remains most fully on those years between the first and second world wars.

Two essays were inspired primarily by student interests and explore topics that often show up in the questions and observations they raise in class, the discussions they generate, and the papers they write. One of these makes up chapter 2, a look at mixed-race identities and personal narratives that wrestle with how children and adolescents come to terms with their implications, a topic that is, of course, more timely than ever in the Obama era. (In fact, I write this during the week in which new revelations of the First Lady's white ancestry were announced — revelations that inspired a class discussion that centered on why neither Mrs. Obama nor her mother knew of these ancestors before now, and why it took a third party to initiate the research that brought her family heritage to light.)

Segregated rail travel is perhaps the most ubiquitous of experiences chronicled in over a century of African American autobiography, and along with my students I have long been struck by the range of emotional and even traumatic confrontations black authors have described as having occurred on trains. Convinced that it is the most universally experienced manifestation of Jim Crow, I suggest in chapter 4 that the sheer number of incidents related by black writers allows us to trace the full chronological arc of the practice's manifestations, both formally and informally, from Reconstruction until the dawn of the civil rights era.

Chapter 5 focuses on students coming of age on southern college campuses and stems from a project that Tom Dyer and I have been involved with for some time now — pulling together an anthology of autobiographical accounts of American college life over the past two centuries. We're finding a treasure trove of rich chronicles of all facets of that most formative and often formidable transition from adolescence to adulthood, an experience many have written passionately about. It is also a topic to which, for obvious reasons, our own undergraduates can readily relate. In this essay, I focus on white southerners and how their relationship with their native region was somehow transformed or clarified as a result of what they learned, felt, or did during their undergraduate years. This is a topic with multiple facets, and I could have pulled together an equally full essay on southern black experiences on college campuses, both predominantly black and predominantly white. I could also explore the experiences of southerners, black and white, who left the South in search of higher education in the North, and the often traumatic adjustments they faced in leaving their home region for the first time. But I have kept the focus here on white southerners on southern campuses.

In chapter 6 I return to the part of the South that has long been my comfort zone — Appalachia — to examine a series of recent autobiographical works by residents in and exiles from the highland South. In so doing, I am more convinced that Southern Appalachia is, as John Shelton Reed once termed it, "the South's South." By that he meant — or could have meant — that the mountain South offers a more intensely felt version of the love/hate, push/pull dichotomies that have characterized so many southerners' sense of place, home, and identity, but that among highlanders have been played out in far more pronounced, and often much rawer, forms. A broad sampling of recent work by Appalachian writers confirms the often ambivalent interplay between regional opportunity or oppression and its impact on one's sense of self, though in complex and contradictory ways.

I am fully aware that, except for the variables inherent in Appalachia, much of the framework on which these essays rest casts the South in the familiar binary of black and white. James Watkins, who read the manuscript for the press, suggested in his report that I acknowledge the presence of Native Americans and "other Others" as a more integral part of what we now recognize as a far more multiracial, multiethnic, and multicultural South. Rather than give mere lip service to this reality, I have concluded the volume with an overview of autobiographical work by Native Americans, Asians, and Latinos in the South. While merely a sampler, I hope that it serves as a reminder that there are other ways of being southern, and other issues and tensions that many in the South have faced and continue to face largely because of the fact that they are neither black nor white.[35]

As disparate as these topics might seem at first glance, I contend that they represent variations on a theme, or several themes. The power of place, the struggle for identity, and some sense of empowerment or vulnerability infuse most of the life stories discussed in these essays. Throughout all six chapters and the afterword, we see southerners, most often as young people, confronting at least one, and often multiple, aspects of the South that they found troublesome, perplexing, or challenging to their sense of who they were or what they could be. Only by recalling and recreating experiences of many years before were these authors able to infuse a greater meaning into their pasts, and in so doing provide valuable lessons for the rest of us as we seek to understand the South by better understanding what it has meant to so many southerners who came before us. (I should also note that the connective threads among these chapters means that I've had occasion to retain a few quotes and examples in more than one essay, and I beg the reader's indulgence in the occasional passages that may give a slight sense of déjà vu.)

In her extraordinary memoir, *The Woman Warrior*, Maxine Hong Kingston pondered the scope and limits of her Chinese-American identity: "When you try to understand what things in you are Chinese, how do you separate what is peculiar to childhood, to poverty, insanities, one family, your mother who marked your growing with stories, from what is Chinese?"[36] It's a question that often arises in my classes — what makes one's life a distinctly southern life, and what aspects of one's experience, behavior, angst, or identity can one attribute to his or her southernness rather than to more particular or universal human traits or behavior? Perhaps because southern authors so often make place, community, region, and the social order so integral to their sense of self and the men and women they grew into, it is easier to see those links than it would be with others. But I would suggest that not everything has to be, indeed can be, explained by geographic setting. It is those peculiarities — of personality, of family dynamics, of mental health — that also give these stories their universality, as Kingston found in trying to categorize the factors that make her who she is. Yet because these variables in these works all played out in southern settings, and because southerners often see themselves and their region in far more specific — if stereotypical — terms than do other Americans, it is natural that regional identity has long been a more integral part of southerners' self-definition than is often true elsewhere.

Finally, I hope the essays that follow reflect my firm belief that autobiography and memoir are history at its most humanistic. Lillian Smith once confided to a friend that she found the work of most historians far too cut-and-dried. She singled out Charles Beard as a particular culprit, stating that "he was so intent on selling his idea of the economic interpretation of history that he brushed off much that is psychological and human and 'racial.'" She concluded that "real history, in my opinion, has never been written and won't be until historians are willing to deal seriously with men's feelings as well as with events."[37] In response to critics who suggested that she was too passionate in her analysis of southern society, she wrote to her publisher regarding the revised edition of *Killers of the Dream* in 1961: "Too much feeling? Perhaps. I could snip off a little of the pain, rub out a few words. But no; let's leave it, for it may be the most real part of the book."[38]

There is indeed something very "real" about these narratives, in large part because most convey so fully what Richard Wright once labeled his "crossed-up feelings, his psychic pain." It is the emotional resonance, the psychological subtexts, and the intimate details integral to these life stories that allow for levels of empathy, sympathy, and ultimately understanding on the part of students in a way no textbook or conventional historical narrative can duplicate. I always hope that, after reading ten or twelve of these books and excerpts from many more, most of my students will come to see and appreciate the South and its past in more complex and compelling ways. It is what I hope readers will take from this book as well.

CHAPTER ONE

Lessons from Southern Lives

Teaching Race through Autobiography

ONE OF THE BIGGEST challenges we face as history teachers — whether work-ing with middle- or high-school students or college undergraduates — is mak-ing sense of the vast complexities and variables that have always characterized the interactions of white and black Americans. It is all too easy to oversimplify the subjects of race and racism in the classroom. Textbooks, the popular media, and even we teachers are often prone to broad generalizations in characterizing the ways in which whites have treated blacks. In his indictment a decade ago of high-school history texts, *Lies My Teacher Told Me*, James Loewen devoted a full chapter to "The Invisibility of Racism in American History Textbooks," and it seems to me as if little has changed since then.[1] As part of the second genera-tion born after the civil rights movement had run its course, our students all too often seem oblivious to past or even current struggles for racial justice, and they react with genuine surprise at the extent and intensity with which "the color line" long defined both southern and American society.

One of the most insightful and accessible sources for conveying both the hard realities and the more subtle nuances of race relations in the college class-room — and beyond — is autobiography. I have found this genre to be an effec-tive and immensely satisfying teaching tool for a number of reasons that I lay out below, and in ways that I hope inform these essays as well.

Autobiography, as William Dean Howells once noted, is "the most demo-cratic province in the republic of letters." This is because anyone and everyone "from presidents and generals to ex-slaves and convicts" can write his or her own story. As a result, the cumulative effect is that, as another critic has written, "they have been like a private history of the amazing crimes, achievements, banalities, and wonders of American life. Orthodox history is, by contrast, a bland soup."[2] Its appeal to me, as a teacher, is that it offers windows into the historical past at its most intimate, its most emotional, its most human. Autobiographers can bring that past alive in ways that more objective scholarly historians rarely do; as such, they engage us in ways that no history textbook can.

Yet another unique feature of autobiography that makes it such an effective teaching tool for both high-school and college students is that, unlike any other historical genre, it is one in which youthful experiences, from both childhood and adolescence, hold such sway. From the Salem witchcraft trials to the desegregation of Central High School in Little Rock, there have been occasional moments in American history in which teenagers have been catalysts in the unfolding of significant developments. Otherwise we must turn to autobiography, which offers a vast array of case studies of young people struggling with issues and circumstances of historical import — which in the South means slavery, Civil War, emancipation, Jim Crow, and civil rights. Is there any other form of historical documentation to which adolescents can relate so readily in terms of the perspectives and experiences of their peers? (Has any work enlightened more people about the traumas of the Holocaust, for example, than the diary of a teenage girl hiding in an Amsterdam attic?) It is no coincidence that that formative age and all it encompasses — the learning processes, discovery, experimentation, social development, the questioning, probing, and challenging of ideas and authorities — are among the most vital and richly expressed components of autobiography.[3] When applied to matters of race, authors' insights into their early observations, perceptions, and experiences can be profound.

These are stories infused with strong emotional content; they are also narratives in which moral values and ethical dilemmas are often at the forefront. As such, they can serve as vital resources in the character education of students today. Historian and Georgia Humanities Council president Jamil Zainaldin has spoken eloquently about how integral character education is to citizenship in the twenty-first century, and about the role, in turn, of the humanities in making character education happen. "The humanities," he says "are the heart and head working together. They are the food of citizenship; the conscience of communities." The humanities are also stories, Zainaldin reminds us. "They are stories read and told, and shared. Stories are the building blocks of the craft of citizenship"; their power as such comes through their "power to inspire."[4]

From a more sociological perspective, Diane Bjorklund includes a chapter on "Autobiography as Moral Performance," in her book *Interpreting the Self.* She notes there that among the primary functions autobiography serves, it is a "public explanation of how [authors] have led their lives," in effect as much a justification of one's life as a recounting of it. To achieve that, autobiographers must "negotiate their place in relation to cultural norms and values," which they do by "speak[ing] of their beliefs, actions, intentions, choices, and goals." Because they have shaped and pursued those attitudes and behaviors within "a social context where others may be harmed or helped, their actions and intentions become moral topics."[5]

Both of these approaches seem especially relevant to the stories of southerners coming of age, if only because so many of the norms and values of that society embodied repression, inequities, intolerance, and even cruelty. How these authors challenged, overcame, negotiated, or succumbed to those realities, sometimes on behalf of themselves and sometimes for others, is central to many of their narratives. In justifying their attitudes and behavior to us as readers, they also provide concrete — and again teachable — examples of courage, responsibility, kindness, integrity, tolerance, and other character-building traits.

This is what I hope to lay out here — examples of how voices telling stories, very personal and often painful, have the power both to inspire students and to make them think in new ways about the struggles other young people, fellow southerners, have endured and, for the most part, triumphed over. In so doing, these testimonials can also make students think about how they themselves would respond to the same or similar challenges in their own lives. As Bjorklund suggests, "Autobiographies can help us make sense of our lives and give voice to thoughts and feelings that we also may have had. We may be reassured to learn what we share with others, while also getting a glimpse of the compass of human experience yet unknown to us."[6] This can be especially true for young readers in their formative years, and at the same time provide an effective means of making history relevant and understandable to them.

It was as children that southerners black and white were first introduced to the harsh and often perplexing realities of racism in their worlds. Coretta Scott King notes in her autobiography that "despite efforts by African American parents to protect their children from the dreadful hurt of segregation and discrimination, sooner or later, all African American children lose their racial innocence. Some incident suddenly makes them realize that they are regarded as inferior."[7] Lillian Smith suggests that this process was more gradual and insidious. In her 1949 memoir, *Killers of the Dream*, one of the most devastating critiques of the segregated South ever to come from a white southerner, Smith wrote:

> From the time little southern children take their first step they learn their ritual, for Southern Tradition leads them through its intricate movements. And some, if their faces are dark, learn to bend, hat in hand; and others, if their faces are white, learn to hold their heads high. Some step off the sidewalk while others pass by in arrogance. Bending, shoving, genuflecting, ignoring, stepping off, demanding, giving in, avoiding. . . . So we learned the dance that cripples the human spirit, step by step by step, we who were white and we who were colored, day by day, hour by hour, year by year until the movements were reflexes and made for the rest of our life without thinking.[8]

As subtly and perhaps gradually as these behaviors and attitudes were learned over the course of southern childhoods, autobiographers tend to focus more on the "single incidents" to which Mrs. King referred in explaining how they learned that "crippling dance," or on their discoveries of those racial mores that would shape their own lives and become in their own minds and memories crucial turning points in defining their relationship to the world around them. Those incidents and discoveries often make for the most memorable and teachable moments, and it is around them that this essay is built.

Among the most dramatic expressions of such struggles are the quests for learning and the traumas of achieving it. Both Frederick Douglass and Richard Wright, for example, provide striking accounts of how they were made aware of what empowerment literacy represented to black teenagers more than a century apart. For Douglass, a slave, it came when he overheard a dispute between his beloved Baltimore mistress and her husband, when the husband discovered that she had been teaching her black charge the alphabet. "Learning would spoil the best nigger in the world," his master scolded his wife. "If you teach him how to read, there would be no keeping him. It would forever unfit him to be a slave." Those words, Douglass wrote, "sank deep into my heart, stirred up sentiments within that lay slumbering, and called into existence an entirely new train of thought. It was a new and special revelation, explaining dark and mysterious things. . . . I now understood the white man's power to enslave the black man." "I was gladdened by the invaluable instruction," he added, "which by the merest accident I had gained from my master. . . . The argument against which he so warmly urged, my learning to read, only served to inspire me with a desire and determination to learn. In learning to read, I owe almost as much to the bitter opposition of my master as I do to the kindly aid of my mistress."[9]

Toward the end of *Black Boy*, Richard Wright describes a discovery of similar import. A mere sixteen years old and well aware that his formal education had ended with his eighth-grade graduation, Wright had left his native Mississippi and was living on his own in Memphis when he came across a denunciation of H. L. Mencken in the local newspaper. Curious as to "what on earth this Mencken had done to call down upon him the scorn of the South," Wright managed to trick a librarian into allowing him to check out one of his books. In his small rented room that night, Wright described his reaction to what he read: "I was jarred and shocked by the style, the clear, clean, sweeping sentences. Why did he write like that? How did one write like that?" I pictured the man as a raging demon, slashing with his pen, consumed with hate, denouncing everything American . . . laughing at the weaknesses of people, mocking God, authority. Yes this man was fighting, fighting with words. He was using words as a weapon, using them as one would use a club. . . . I was amazed not by what he said, but how on earth anybody had the courage to say it." "I concluded the book," Wright wrote, "with the conviction that I had somehow overlooked something terribly important in life. I had once tried to write, had once reveled in feeling, had let my crude imagination roam, but the impulse to dream had been slowly beaten out of me by experience. Now it surged up again and I hungered for books, new ways of looking and seeing."[10] From that experience, Wright became an avid reader, and the intellectual revelations that sixteen-year-old boy gained remained central to his determination to leave the South and ultimately to become a writer himself.

Could there be any sharper contrast than the description by fellow Mississippian William Alexander Percy of his educational opportunities and what he did with them? In *Lanterns on the Levee*, his often melancholy memoir of his privileged life as a planter's son in the Mississippi Delta, Percy wrote wistfully of the vast amount of schooling to which he had been subjected. After attending the University of the South at Sewanee and Harvard Law School, both due more to his father's connections and initiatives than his own, Percy noted with rather disarming self-deprecation that neither had provided him with much sense of purpose or direction in life. "For eight years — in fact for twenty-three," he wrote, "a great number of people have been pouring out money, skill, time, devotion and prayers to create something out of me that wouldn't look as if the Lord slapped it together absent-mindedly. Not Alexander the Great nor Catherine II had been tended by a more noble corps of teachers." And yet, there was little in all that training that had inspired a career-choice. "Obviously," Percy mused, "I was cast to justify the ways of man to God, as it were. But how? What does one do with a life, or at any rate, intend to do?"[11] Ultimately, for lack of a better option, he returned home to Greenville, Mississippi, and opened a law practice. Far more of the undergraduates we teach today are likely to identify with Percy's dilemma than with those of Douglass or Wright, but perhaps in reading of these vastly different degrees of educational yearning, they won't take their own opportunities quite so much for granted.

The fact that it was men of Percy's station in life who often proved to be the most formidable barriers to the opportunities or aspirations of black children often added to the frustration of black writers looking back on their school experiences. In *I Know Why the Caged Bird Sings*, Maya Angelou provided an impassioned account of her high-school graduation in Stamps, Arkansas, in 1940. The upbeat mood of the school's African American students and faculty was dampened considerably by the condescending address by a white official who extolled the achievements of former white graduates of the county school system, and only as an afterthought made reference to a football tackle at the state's A&M college and a basketball player at Fisk in whom his black audience could take pride.

Angelou seethed in her seat, and on paper years later. "The white kids," she wrote, "were going to have the chance to become Galileos and Madame Curies and Edisons and Gauguins, and our boys (the girls weren't even in on it) would try to be Jesse Owenses and Joe Louises." While she acknowledged that they were indeed "the great heroes of our world," she went on to ask, "What school official in the white-goddom of Little Rock had the right to decide that those two men should be our only heroes; . . . which concrete angel glued to what county seat had decided that if my brother wanted to become a lawyer he first had to pay penance for his skin by picking cotton and hoeing corn and studying correspondence books at night for twenty years?" She recalled the moment with vehemence:

> The man's dead words fell like bricks around the auditorium, and too many [of those bricks] settled in my belly; . . . to my left and right the proud graduating class of 1940 had dropped their heads. . . . Graduation, the hush-hush magic time

of frills and gifts and congratulations and diplomas, was finished for me before my name was called. The accomplishment was nothing. We were maids and farmers, handymen and washerwomen, and anything higher that we aspired to was farcical and presumptuous. . . . It was awful to be a Negro and have no control over my life. It was brutal to be young and already trained to sit quietly and listen to charges brought against my color with no chance of defense. We should all be dead.[12]

And that's only the beginning of a rant that continues for another couple of pages. These are strong words, and they still have the power to move and even shock students reading them today. Where else does one find such anger, such frustration, such pain, and such defiance in historical documentation, particularly on the part of adolescents?

More public events often brought home for southern young people, black and white, the subtleties and emotional depth of racial identity on both sides of the color line. Few events seem to have been remembered more often in print or portrayed in more dramatic prose than were boxer Joe Louis's victories over white opponents in the 1930s — over Primo Carnera in 1935, and Max Schmeling in 1938. Again, Maya Angelou offers one of most notable of those memories. She vividly sets the scene in her grandmother's store in Stamps, Arkansas, into which the entire black community was wedged, all staring intently at the radio. Angelou captures how momentous this occasion was not only for those gathered in anticipation, but for black America at large. She wondered at one point if the announcer "gave any thought to the fact that he was addressing as 'ladies and gentlemen' all the Negroes around the world who sat sweating and praying, glued to their 'master's voice.'"

Angelou described the reaction as Louis was pounded by Carnera early in the first round: "My race groaned. It was our people falling. It was another lynching, yet another Black man hanging on a tree. . . . This might be the end of the world. If Joe lost we were back in slavery and beyond help. It would all be true, the accusations that we were lower types of human beings. Only a little higher than the apes. . . . We didn't breathe. We didn't hope. We waited." When things quickly turned around and Louis knocked Carnera out, Angelou gushed:

Champion of the world. A Black boy, Some Black mother's son. He was the strongest man in the world. People drank Coca-Colas like ambrosia and ate candy bars like Christmas. Some of the men went behind the store and poured white lightning in their soft-drink bottles. . . . It would take an hour more before the people would leave the store and head for home. Those who lived too far had made arrangements to stay in town. It wouldn't do for a Black man and his family to be caught on a lonely country road on a night when Joe Louis had proved that we were the strongest people in the world.[13]

A far more measured account comes from Jimmy Carter, who in his childhood memoir, *An Hour before Daylight*, remembered the Louis-Schmeling fight of 1938 as it played out for his family and their black tenants on their southwest Georgia farm. "For our community," he explained, "this fight had heavy racial overtones, with almost unanimous support at our all-white school for the European over the American." Despite such sentiments, a delegation of black employees and neighbors approached Carter's father to ask if they could listen to the broadcast, and he put his radio in the window so that the crowd gathered in the yard could hear it. The fight ended abruptly in the first round, with Louis almost killing Schmeling. Carter describes the reaction: "There was no sound from outside — or inside — the house. We heard a quiet 'Thank you, Mr. Earl.'" The visitors then walked silently away, crossing the road to gather again in a tenant's house. Once they were all in, and the door closed, "all hell broke loose, and their celebration lasted all night." Carter concludes: "Daddy was tight-lipped, but all the mores of our segregated society had been honored."[14]

A year younger than Carter, thirteen-year-old Russell Baker listened to the same broadcast from an apartment in Baltimore. In his Pulitzer Prize–winning *Growing Up* (1982), Baker provides almost a mirror image of Angelou's perspective, agreeing only that the implications of Louis's win were momentous for both races. From the vantage point of an apartment window in a white, working-class neighborhood in the southwest part of the city, Baker declared that the year 1938, when Hitler invaded Czechoslovakia and Neville Chamberlain conceded his right to do so, "was the year the dignity of the white race hung in the balance." While uptown Baltimore debated "war and the future of civilization," his own neighbors sat on their stoops and "pondered a cruel theological mystery . . . why had God allowed Joe Louis to become the heavy-weight champion of the world? . . . How could faith in the universal order be justified so long as Louis, a black man, was allowed to pound white men senseless with so little exertion?"

Baker's excessive eloquence nearly matched Angelou's as he described the response of the African American residents on a back alley called Lemmon Street to the 1938 broadcast. Given their minority status in a predominantly white neighborhood, the blacks on Lemmon Street had never made much of a fuss after Louis's earlier victories, thinking that "too much celebration would be indiscreet." But in 1938 he discovered that "their spirit was not completely lifeless." With the sudden knockout of Schmeling, they began pouring out of their houses and marching onto Lombard Street, as others joined them from other neighborhood alleys. They were not loud or raucous, and yet, for all their restraint, the very space they occupied spoke volumes to Baker. "Joe Louis had given them the courage to assert their right to use a public thoroughfare, and there wasn't a white person down there to dispute it. It was the first civil rights demonstration I ever saw, and it was completely spontaneous, ignited by the finality with which Joe Louis had destroyed the theory of white superiority."[15]

Even given the hyperbole apparent in two of these three accounts (Carter remains among the most understated of autobiographers), together they provide a vivid sense of what this fight and fighter meant to blacks and whites in three very different parts of the South: a farm in south Georgia, a general store in Arkansas, and a mixed-race neighborhood in Baltimore. Blacks' response to that fight had much to do with their surroundings: the comfort in numbers that Baltimore blacks enjoyed in moving onto white territory, yet controlled enough to keep the noise level low as they did so; the much more exuberant celebration that broke out within the confines of an all-black store, yet one sobered by the dangers that lurked once they moved beyond the security of its bounds on a night that clearly upset their white neighbors; and the shared experience of listening to the fight on almost, but not quite, shared space — whites inside the house, blacks outside — and the awareness of the latter that their celebration could not begin until they had moved back onto their own turf nearby. At this rare moment of black triumph in the Jim Crow South, the deeply engrained inhibitions and mores of southern society were only slightly, and only fleetingly, challenged. In each case how that triumph was expressed — or repressed — had everything to do with where and with whom the moment was experienced, all of which makes for a very teachable moment in time.

The brutal lynching of Emmett Till in the summer of 1955 evoked far different but equally powerful responses from a number of southerners seared by its implications. The death of this fourteen-year-old black boy from Chicago, murdered by Mississippi whites for making a suggestive, but merely playful, remark to a white woman, sent shock waves through much of the nation. The narratives of three Mississippi natives, one black and two white — two adolescent and one a young adult — illustrate the varying impacts of this most horrific of race crimes. No one offered as chilling a commentary as did Anne Moody. In her classic *Coming of Age in Mississippi*, she provided one of the few windows into what that incident meant to other black adolescents in the state, and the new fears it raised for them all. Also fourteen at the time it occurred, Moody gave this memorable — and often cited — description of her reaction to the news:

> Before Emmett Till's death, I had known the fear of hunger, hell, and the Devil. But now there was a new fear known to me — the fear of being killed just because I was black. This was the worst of my fears. I knew once I got food, the fear of starving to death would leave. I also was told that if I was a good girl, I wouldn't have to fear the Devil or hell. But I didn't know what one had to do or not do as a Negro not to be killed. Probably just being a Negro period was enough, I thought.[16]

Two white writers, both novelists, saw the crime from somewhat different perspectives, and they were troubled as much by the responses of fellow whites as by the incident itself. In her beautiful and far too little known memoir, *Landscapes of the Heart*, novelist Elizabeth Spencer recounts having just returned home to Mississippi after two years traveling abroad when the Till murder took place. She was appalled by the crime, of course, but also shocked and deeply troubled by her parents' reaction to it. Spencer described her father, a wealthy businessman with extensive landholdings in the Delta, as "difficult and autocratic and many times lacking in any understanding of my feelings," and yet "he had at least been forward-looking about racial matters." He was, she thought with assurance, as fair-minded in his treatment of blacks as anyone she knew and a great supporter of Hodding Carter and his liberal newspaper, the *Delta Democrat-Times* in Greenville.

This was the man with whom she thought she could talk about Emmett Till, but she found that "he reacted to the crime the way a stone wall might if hit by a BB gun." He refused to discuss it or to listen to anyone else discussing it. He dismissed his daughter and her concerns by stating simply, "we had to keep things in hand." Even Spencer's mother, who acknowledged once in a fit of anxiety that "something ought to be done to those men," quickly retreated to a response that was far more acceptable to Delta whites, declaring that "that boy may have been just fourteen but he was grown, he was a *man*, and he shouldn't have been looking at any white woman." Deeply disappointed in her parents and seeing a side of them she had not expected, Spencer ultimately concluded that she could no longer live with them. "It took a while for me to come around to verbalizing the extent of what had happened," she wrote. "I knew it in my bones, in the sick empty feeling there inside long before I could say to myself what I had been given to understand: *You don't belong down here anymore.*[17]

Lewis Nordan, who wrote a well-received novel based on the Till murder titled *Wolf Whistle* (1993), recounted his actual memory of the incident seven years later in a memoir of his youth in Itta Bena, Mississippi, *Boy with Loaded Gun.* Nordan was seventeen years old and in his high-school football locker room when he heard teammates discussing the black boy whose body had been found in the Tallahatchie River with a cotton gin fan barbwired to his neck. "Despite the horror of the content of the conversation," he recalled, "the tone . . . was one of general approval, even hilarity," with general agreement that this "Chicago kid who had wolf-whistled a white woman" had gotten what he deserved. They even joked that he had stolen the gin fan and drowned when he tried to swim across the river with it. "I wish I could report honestly that I was higher-minded and exempt from complicity in the general sense of approval and jocularity, but I cannot," he admitted. Instead, "I was jealous that I had no details to add and no social standing that would have allowed my participation in the first place." (He was merely the waterboy for the team.)[18]

But the most memorable part of this incident for Nordan was still to come. For one boy did speak up, and said simply, "I'm for the nigger." That statement drew silence from the group, and everyone stared at the speaker. "It ain't right," he stated. "Kill a boy for that. I don't care what color he is." Nordan reflected on his teammate's courage:

> This was not the captain of the team, or the quarterback, who I suppose could have exhibited such outrageous individualism without fear of reprisal or ostracizing; and it was not the team geek, or waterboy, or manager, myself I mean — who had no status to lose anyway and thus . . . impervious to ridicule. This was simply a boy on the team, a quiet country boy who had everything to lose and nothing except a lifetime of self-respect to gain, and he said, "I'm for the nigger. It ain't right." For forty years I have wished I had been the boy who spoke those outrageous words.[19]

Emmett Till was not the only youthful victim of racial violence, nor was his lynching the only crime that opened other eyes to the tragic implications of racial hatred in the South. The bombing of Birmingham's Sixteenth Street Baptist Church in September 1963 and the deaths of four young girls in their Sunday school class takes on new meaning when one reads Morris Dees's account of how white Alabamians responded to it. In his 1991 autobiography, *A Season for Justice*, Dees, who would later go on to found the Southern Poverty Law Center and Klanwatch, recounts what happened in his own white congregation in Montgomery the following Sunday. A lifelong member of the church, he rose and asked the congregation, friends and acquaintances all, to pray for "another Baptist church that needs our help." These "good hearted, charitable people," as Dees calls them, nodded in approval until he mentioned what church it was. "The blood drained from my friends' faces, the nodding stopped." They were all either angry at his suggestion or too shocked to be angry, and the only verbal response came from an old woman who stood up and said, "This ain't none of our business, Morris Jr." Even his attempt to lead them in a silent prayer was met with a quickly emptied sanctuary. "More than a quarter of a century after the fact," Dees wrote,

> it seems such a small gesture. Asking for a contribution, praying for the souls of little girls, hardly seems extraordinary, certainly not worthy of self-congratulation. I hadn't gone to Washington, DC for Dr. King's march; I've never marched period. I hadn't stood up to Bull Connor in Birmingham. Just a silent prayer, an act consistent with Christian teachings, praying for the souls of other Christians. *Children.* And yet my good friends and neighbors could not free themselves from the slavery of southern tradition and, forgetting about color, do the Christian thing.[20]

Equally moving are accounts of early integration efforts a generation later. Melba Pattillo Beals, one of the nine black students to integrate Little Rock's Central High School in 1957, suggests the trauma and the drama of her story in a single diary entry she reprinted in her memoir, *Warriors Don't Cry*. "Everything in my life is so new," she wrote after her first day of class. In what seems almost a prayer, she continued, "Could I please do some of the old things that I know how to do again. I don't know how to go to school with soldiers. Please show me . . . P. S. Please help the soldiers to keep the mobs away from me."[21]

Or Mae Bertha Carter, a Mississippi Delta sharecropper who in 1965 decided with her husband to make seven of their children the first blacks to desegregate the white schools of Sunflower County. While not technically an autobiography, author Constance Curry tells much of their story in their own words in her account of their experience, titled *Silver Rights*. Thrown into a situation in which the Carter children, ages seven to seventeen, faced up to four years of "spitballs, name-calling, ostracism, and unceasing harassment," Mrs. Carter described her feelings during the first days of their ordeal: "When the bus pulled off, I went in and fell down cross the bed and prayed. I stayed on that bed and didn't do no work that day. I stayed on that bed until I heard the bus coming back in the afternoon. When they came off one by one, then I was released until the next morning. But the next morning I felt the same way, depressed, nervous, praying to God. I wasn't saying a whole lot of words; just saying 'take care of my kids.' After about a month I started easing up a little bit. I had prayed to God so much! I had been going to church and talking about trusting in Jesus, but I never trusted Jesus until my children went to that all-white school. That school sure brought me to God!"[22]

Five years later, when integration became mandatory in Mississippi, a very different scenario unfolded elsewhere in the state. In the last chapter of his memoir, *The Last Days*, Charles Marsh describes the integration of his junior high school in Laurel in 1970. As the culmination of a decade of racial violence (Laurel was the headquarters of the state Ku Klux Klan and the home of its imperial wizard, Sam Bowers), the opening day of school in September was fraught with tension and uncertainty.

Marsh, a white seventh grader, wore a thick winter coat on that hot September morning, thinking that the extra padding might come in handy if he were attacked. (He explained that he was thinking of the comment of a sixth-grade neighbor safely ensconced in a segregationist academy, who had told him he "was crazy to go to school with niggers" and could likely "expect a knife in the gut.") Marsh was quick to notice that the black students seemed just as apprehensive as he was, not having forgotten the "not-so-long-ago days of Klan violence and mayhem." He hung up his coat in an assigned locker between those of two black students with the same last name as his — a girl named Angela, who wore a shiny blue dress, and Deon, who reached out and shook his hand, at which point he states, "The next day, I left my winter coat at home."

"With a wretched decade behind us at last," Marsh marveled, "we were finally all together in Gardiner seventh grade: sons and daughters of Klansmen and civil rights activists, of circuit clerks and deputy sheriffs, of black militants and Citizen Councilors, of society matrons and union organizers." Isaac Buckley, the son of a local Klansman, a "pathetic child" who had been harassed for years by his white classmates, made a surprising discovery — he liked his new black classmates better. "They didn't meet his idiosyncrasies with cruelty. His new friends were Unkgang Harrison and Flip Freeman, muscle-ridden boys who thought nothing of Isaac's oversized clothes, his scarred face and body odor, or his Klan father."[23]

most disconcerting thing kept happening. I forgot that they were black." He admitted that the first time it happened, he thought he was having a nervous breakdown, but that "pesky thing" started happening more and more often, as he forgot about their race, and they his. ("They didn't treat me like a 'white man.' Of course they didn't need to, here in Europe.") James told his son: "It finally got to bothering me so much I just determined to make it light on myself and forget about color while I was here and just go back to the old way when I got home. But, you know, things never were the same after living with my friends and not thinking about what color we were. It certainly ruined me as a Klansman, that's for sure."[30]

When he returned home to Alabama, James Zellner was prepared to "come out from under the hood," and yet he did so only gradually. Bob wrote that whenever he asked his father why their family had different attitudes than most white southerners, he always came back to that experience in Russia when he'd "been struck blind to color." As a Christian, Zellner reasoned, his father was forced to wrestle with religious beliefs instilled since childhood. "In the final analysis," he states, "he could not reconcile his belief in white supremacy with the high ideals of his country, the teachings of his church and Bible, his innate intelligence, and now, his experience in Europe." Bob's mother, he claims, was only a "lukewarm racist," and "when Dad finally broke with his Klan brothers in the mid-1940s, she happily cut up his Klan robes and made white shirts for us boys to wear to Sunday school."[31]

Two Birmingham women recounted the role of their own relatives in Klan activity in masterful but far different types of autobiography. In her Pulitzer Prize–winning combination of memoir and deeply researched history, *Carry Me Home*, Diane McWhorter recalled how she grew up "on the wrong side of the revolution" underway in her hometown in the early 1960s. "What were 'civil rights'?" she asked. All she knew was that "they were bad and that my father was fighting against them." This is why he was rarely home at night, with her mother offering as explanation only that he was "at one of his civil rights meetings." McWhorter grew increasingly suspicious of his attitudes and behavior, and "soon those sensations of anxiety and shame would crystallize into a concrete fear: that my father was a member of the Ku Klux Klan."[32]

Those fears were suddenly heightened after the bombing of the Sixteenth Street Baptist Church that killed four young black girls in September 1963, fears she continued to live with for nearly two decades; she mulled over why this product of Birmingham's elite somehow could have fallen so far. "Way in the future," she wrote, "I would often review that Saturday night. . . . I would wonder if, one night when I had fallen asleep with nothing more on my mind than what I was wearing to church the next day, my father might have found some marvelous opportunity to identify with fate: to out-tough his father, yet also be true to the bigoted principles of his community, and once and for all prove that a boy from Mountain Brook could keep up with the real men of Birmingham."[33]

Yet it was only when she began researching her book in the early 1980s that she finally confronted her father about what he had done and whether her worst nightmare would be confirmed: that he had been involved in the bombing and shared responsibility for the four deaths that resulted from it. Her exchange with him makes for fascinating reading, as he wavered between claiming a central role in the Klan and close association with its leaders and a contrary effort to distance himself from that level of activism. ("Well, you had Klan plus and you had Klan minus," he explained. "We were Klan minus.") At one point, he claimed that he had been an informant for the FBI, the CIA, the John Birch Society, and the Klan. Finally, after constant probing from his daughter, he offered a bottom line that she was more than willing to accept. "I didn't get involved in any rough stuff," he told her, almost apologetically. "If I got involved any deeper, I would have had to kill people, but primarily because of my religious background, I don't believe in taking another man's life, unless it's absolutely necessary. Going around bombing people wasn't my cup of tea. I might stick a needle in 'em, but I wouldn't bomb 'em."

At last, Diane concluded, "one of my childhood fears had been laid to rest. My father had not killed anyone." But at the same time she was baffled by "the grandiosity that would make someone falsely claim intimate knowledge of the most horrible crime of his time," as he had done for so long. Just what he had done all those nights he was out working on "civil rights," she'd never know. But she felt that that insoluble mystery served to reveal a much greater truth. "I did not understand my father, but because of that I learned to see the world in a new way. For in order to define him, I had to invoke the history of a race, of two races, and of a place."[34] Hence her drive to become both historian and autobiographer.

Elizabeth Cobbs, on the other hand, had no doubt as to her uncle's central role in the local and statewide Klan activity, including that infamous church bombing. In a book that my students probably find as unsettling as anything we read, she chronicles the unease that came from growing up in the 1940s and 1950s with her uncle, Robert Chambliss, the mastermind behind the bombing.

He had joined the Klan at age twenty in 1924, most likely inspired by seeing *The Birth of a Nation* during one of its several rereleases to southern theaters in the decade after its 1915 premiere. (Cobbs notes that it continued to serve as "the epic of self-definition" and that her uncle saw to it that the film continued to be used to rally new recruits into the 1960s and 1970s.) While primarily a fraternal organization that slowly declined during the Depression years, its resurgence after World War II took a very different form, and Chambliss welcomed the opportunity to revive the waning local group, the Robert E. Lee Klavern, and he quickly became a very forceful leader. In reports to his niece, Chambliss told of "fires and dynamite, usually styled as 'punishment' for people who 'got out of line.'"[35]

Cobbs was shielded from little of this expanding enterprise, in which her uncle took much pride. At nine years old, in 1949, she attended a Klan rally with him and other family members. She recalled that as a teen in 1956 she sewed Klan robes and hoods with her mother and aunts, and she took pride that she was entrusted with applying the handmade emblems (a cross with a single red dot, representing a drop of blood) onto the left breast of each robe. In 1961, she and her young son accompanied Chambliss on a tour of the Klan's secret meeting places: a "bomb factory" just north of Birmingham and an even more remote antebellum plantation house where Chambliss pointed out the blood stains on a basement wall where "niggers had been shackled and 'disciplined'"; he then showed them a burial ground out back that had begun as a slave cemetery but was full of new additions as a result of the activity that took place in the basement.[36] As with McWhorter's account, the 1963 bombing forms the centerpiece of Cobbs's memoir. Fully aware that her uncle was behind the deaths of the four girls on that fateful September morning, she came forward only in 1977, when she testified against him in court with crucial testimony that helped convict him to a life in prison. She describes in riveting detail that moment of facing her uncle in court, separated only by the judge's bench. "I knew from that point on," she wrote, "that this was a life and death struggle. Either he got life imprisonment, or I got death."[37]

These four episodes could hardly vary more. While some of those differences can be attributed to different times and circumstances — childhood recreations of the heroic Klan in turn-of-the-century Georgia, an interracial encounter in the 1930s Soviet Union, and the contrasting traumas of a daughter and a niece who found themselves only a step removed from the Birmingham bombing of 1963 — all of these accounts demonstrate the means by which autobiographers can humanize the victims, the families, and even, on occasion, the Klansmen themselves. At the same time, these writers reveal much about the strengths and weaknesses, motives and mindsets, of everyone they write about, and they do so at levels not nearly so apparent in other, more conventional, accounts.

Other firsthand commentaries on the civil rights movement defy assumptions or traditional treatments, the most surprising coming from black authors. Who would expect Henry Louis Gates Jr., for example, to state that there were certain advantages to segregation and things that he and other blacks missed once it was dismantled? In his incisive portrait of the African American community in Piedmont, West Virginia, titled simply *Colored People*, Gates writes of how much his family missed the Jim Crow railroad cars on which they had to travel to visit relatives elsewhere in the state. "So what if we didn't feel comfortable eating in the dining car? Our food was better. Fried chicken, baked beans, and potato salad . . . a book and two decks of cards . . . and I didn't care if the train ever got there." Gates also admitted how much he missed *Amos and Andy*, once it was deemed too politically incorrect and racially stereotyped and was no longer shown on television. Everyone loved it, he insisted. "I don't care what people say today. For the colored people, the day they took *Amos and Andy* off the air was one of the saddest days in Piedmont."[38]

Or how shocked students are to read Anne Moody's skeptical reaction to the March on Washington in 1963, which she attended and where she heard Martin Luther King's "I Have a Dream" speech. Far from inspired, Moody wrote that she sat on the grass in front of the Lincoln Memorial and "listened to the speakers, to discover we had 'dreamers' instead of leaders leading us. King went on and on talking about his dream. I sat there thinking that in Canton [her Mississippi hometown] we never had time to sleep, much less dream."[39] Such passages tell us much about the human dimensions to the movement that allowed for such mixed emotions and reservations on the part not only of Gates and Moody, but probably many other southern blacks as well.

Young white southerners could exhibit equally perplexing behavior, which often reflected the confusion stirred by the ambivalent signals sent them as children. Another child of the Lost Cause, Virginia Durr, declared of her coming of age years in Birmingham in the 1910s: "You can't imagine the contradictions in my life, the total contradictions." She had been surrounded by African American men as a child, "sweet, lovely old men whose laps I sat on as a child, and the mailman, the yardman, the furnaceman. Not one of them had ever been anything but kind and decent to me." Yet at the same time, Durr "thought of the Klan as something noble and grand and patriotic that had saved the white women of the South. I remember seeing *Birth of a Nation*, and oh, I thought it was the most thrilling, dramatic, and marvelous thing in the world when the Klan rode in there and rescued the poor white girl from the black soldier."[40]

It probably shouldn't surprise us that some white children were less "innocent" of supremacist sensibilities than were others, though some acted upon those prejudices in unexpected or atypical ways. In *North toward Home*, Willie Morris, like Virginia Durr, expressed both the absurdity and the ambivalence of white racism. Growing up in the 1940s in Yazoo City, Mississippi, Morris recounted a chilling incident when, as a twelve-year-old with no provocation or malice aforethought, he pounced upon a three-year-old black boy passing in front of his house, beating and kicking him until his victim's older sister halted the attack by shouting, "What'd he *do* to you?" Morris wrote that he went back into his deserted house, where "for a while, I was happy with this act, and my head was strangely light and giddy. Then later, the more I thought about it coldly, I could hardly bear my secret shame."

With the hindsight of adulthood, Morris sought to explain his action. It reminded him of an earlier episode in which he had captured and then pin-pricked a small sparrow before releasing him. "My hurting the Negro child, like my torturing the bird," he wrote, "was a gratuitous act of childhood cruelty — but I knew later that it was something else, infinitely more subtle and contorted." He went on to admit that throughout his youth, his conduct toward blacks was a "relationship of great contrasts. On the one hand there was a kind of unconscious affection, touched with a sense of excitement and sometimes pity. On the other hand there were sudden emotional eruptions — of disdain and utter cruelty."

Such are the self-revelations of southern autobiography that one can extrapolate from Morris's account — or for that matter from Durr's: not only their own behavior and attitudes but those of the white South in general for much of the region's history. Morris almost hints at that greater truth himself when he concludes: "The broader reality was that the Negroes in the town were *there*; they were ours, to do with as we wished. I grew up with this consciousness of some tangible possession, it was rooted so deeply in me by the whole moral atmosphere of the place that my own ambivalence . . . was secondary and of little account."[41]

Occasionally it is acts of kindness that resonate as fully as the cruelty and oppression that characterizes so much of this literature. Lillian Smith, in her lesser-known follow-up to *Killers of the Dream*, another semi-memoir called *The Journey* (1954), told a story that I have only recently discovered but find as fascinating as any in her more familiar writings. Traveling through south Georgia in 1952 in search of her family's roots, Smith stopped overnight at a motor court near Waycross, Georgia, where she was befriended by the middle-aged white couple who served as her hosts. In the midst of a long, late-night conversation, Tim and Ellen told her of an incident that occurred several weeks before. Late one stormy evening, a car had pulled up in front of the motor court, where it sat with the headlights on but from which no one emerged. Eventually, Timothy went out to the car and found two African American women sitting there, "well dressed and terribly scared." They nervously told him that they knew of no place to go in the storm and asked if he could suggest a black family who might take them in for the night. "I got sick at my stomach," Smith quotes Tim as saying:

> Here was a place supposed to be open to strangers. And this was America; my country; theirs, too; and I loved it and was proud of it and had good cause to be. . . . Yet, *this* question could be asked.
>
> I said — and God help me, do you know I was more scared than when I got the shrapnel in my hip at Argonne! — I said, If you would care to stay here, there is a vacant room and I believe you would be comfortable. One stared at me as if I had accosted her. The other never looked up. I don't know what they were thinking — a white man had — I just don't know what came into their minds. But there was no trust in their faces. So I called my wife. Ellen came out in the rain and invited them in. We put them in room seven. We both went with them and got them settled. They paid the fee and filled out a card. And I heard Ellen say as quietly as her mother would have spoken, "If you ladies would like breakfast, we begin to serve at seven o'clock." I almost yelled *Ellen, what in the name of God are you saying! This is Geor . . . .*
>
> And then, inside me suddenly, I knelt down. Yeah, I asked Him to forgive me for my sin. I saw it as plain as Saul of Tarsus saw on the road to Damascus. I had done what was right to do but with only half of me. And Ellen had done what was right with her whole heart.[42]

The story doesn't end there. For Ellen spoke up at that point and said simply: "Because of Henry's letter, Tim." They told Lillian that the women had politely declined their offer of breakfast, saying that they needed to be on the road by six. Later that evening though, Ellen told her husband, "Tim, there comes a time in a life when if you don't go the second mile, you'll never take another step. You'll sit there the rest of your days justifying why you didn't move. That time has come for me." Tim replied, "OK, Ellen. My muscles feel like a little hike might be the very thing to take the kinks out of them, too." And at five-thirty the next morning they took a breakfast tray to room seven. "There was nowhere, and we knew it, for them to get a cup of coffee."

Only at that point in the story do they explain the letter Ellen received from Henry. He was their younger son, fighting in Korea, and he had written several weeks earlier about an incident in which he was wounded in his leg and was left behind by his company as nightfall approached. Grappling in the dark, he stumbled onto something hard, heard an American voice speaking softly, and then felt a hand pull him down to the ground. He blacked out and only later, when he came to, did he realize this man had bandaged his leg. They couldn't see one another, and given the proximity to North Korean troops, they lay side by side, eventually overcoming the stillness by whispering to each other, finding out that they were from Georgia and Alabama. They fell asleep, and Henry awoke at dawn and noticed a black arm resting across his chest. "And I lay, Mother, and looked at it. And you know all I was thinking for you and Dad have thought it too." This black man from Alabama named Bud had risked his life to save that of a white Georgian. "And I knew something," Henry concluded. "I knew when I went home, I was going to have Bud come visit me. And if I haven't got the guts to do it — because I know you and Dad have — then I hope a bullet will get me. I'd deserve a communist prison but I'd settle for a little less." Smith concluded the story with a simple quote from Tim as to why he and Ellen had done what they did for their black guests. "We were sort of getting ready for Bud's visit," he chuckled.[43]

Smith was at her best in recounting such stories, and in seeing in them omens or portents of the goodness that she — at least at times — felt were inherent in most southern whites. The cause and effect here seems at once so simple and so convoluted: an act of kindness by a black man toward a white soldier in Korea led his parents in Georgia to defy southern tradition and respond in kind by crossing the "color line" in a way that surprised them as much as it did the ben-eficiaries of their kindness.

A generation later, a white Alabamian, one of far different socioeconomic means, was himself the beneficiary of another kindness across the "color line" — and learned a similar lesson. In *All Over but the Shoutin'*, his best-selling memoir of growing up dirt poor in tenant shacks, trailer parks, and worse in the 1960s and 1970s, Rick Bragg wrote of an incident involving black neighbors: "In the middle of hating and fear, was a simple kindness from the most unexpected place, from people who had no reason, beyond their own common decency, to reach across that fence of hate that so many people had worked so hard to build."

In 1965 Rick was six years old. His mother, pregnant and too sick to lift herself from her bed and abandoned by her alcoholic husband, was unable to do anything for Rick and his little brother. They had hit "rock bottom," with almost no food and resources. One day there came a knock at the door from a small black boy, whose family lived just down the road. "He said his momma had some corn left over and please, ma'am, would we like it." Bragg said of their benefactors: "They must have seen us, walking that road. They must have heard how our daddy ran off. They knew. They were poor, very poor, living in unpainted houses that leaned like a drunk on a Saturday night, but for a window in time they had more than us." Bragg reflected:

> It may seem like a little bitty thing, by 1990s reasoning. But this was a time when beatings were common, when it was routine, out of pure meanness, to take a young black man for a ride and leave him cut, broken or worse on the side of some pulpwood road. For sport, for fun. . . . It was a time of horrors, in Birmingham, in Montgomery, in the backwoods of Mississippi. This was a time when the whole damn world seemed on fire. That was why it mattered so.

He wrote that they had only seen these neighbors from a distance; in the few contacts they had with them as children, Rick and his brother had thrown rocks at them. He ends this episode on a sobering note: "I would like to say that we came together after the little boy brought us that food, that we learned about and from each other, but that would be a lie. It was rural Alabama in 1965, two separate, distinct states. But at least, we didn't throw no more rocks."[44]

Two of the most poignant examples of lessons white boys learned from elderly black acquaintances come from William Styron and Melton McLaurin, who related encounters with elderly African Americans that were, at least in hindsight, cathartic. In 1935 a ten-year-old William Styron watched a ninety-nine-year-old black man named Shadrach wander into his small Tidewater Virginia town — "a black apparition of unbelievable antiquity, palsied and feeble, blue-gummed and grinning, a caricature of a caricature." In the most memorable of the recollections in his fictionalized memoir, *A Tidewater Morning*, Styron relates the story of Shadrach, who as a slave boy in 1850 had been sold from Virginia to Alabama and then, nearly a century later, walked all the way back in order to die and be buried on the plantation grounds of his first master. Though little looked familiar to the former slave, his craggy face seemed to respond only to a millpond and local children swimming in it. Bewildered at first by this strange nostalgia for a place in which he had been enslaved and sold away, the young Styron slowly came to understand the reason for Shadrach's return. As he gazed at the millpond, Styron wrote,

> his face was suffused with an immeasurable calm and sweetness, and I sensed that he had recaptured perhaps the one pure, untroubled moment in his life. . . . I had no way of knowing that if his long and solitary journey from the Deep South had been a quest to find this millpond and for a recaptured glimpse of childhood, it might just as readily have been a final turning of his back on a life of suffering. Even now, I cannot say for certain, but I have always had to assume that the still young Shadrach who was emancipated in Alabama those many years ago was set loose, like most of his brothers and sisters, into another slavery perhaps more excruciating than the actual bondage. . . . His return to Virginia, I can now see, was out of no longing for the former bondage, but to find an earlier innocence.[45]

A generation later, historian Melton McLaurin described an equally revelatory moment that he experienced when he was only a few years older than Styron had been in 1935. In Wade, a small crossroads in rural eastern North Carolina, McLaurin worked in his grandfather's general store in the late 1950s and, in that capacity, came to know local African Americans who did business there in a way that few white teenagers did in that era. "My appreciation of Wade's blacks as individuals," he wrote in *Separate Pasts: Growing Up White in the Segregated South*, "presented me at an early age with the complex intellectual and emotional dilemmas of segregation."[46]

McLaurin's book consists of character sketches of these individuals, his relationships with each, and how in a variety of ways each forced him to make some difficult moral judgments about the injustices of racism, including the poverty to which it sentenced many accomplished African Americans, who by any other measure would have enjoyed the comforts of middle-class life. The most striking of these was Carrie McLean, "the only black woman I ever heard whites address as Miss, the universal term of respect for all mature white women, married or not." Miss Carrie was a retired school teacher and "looked and acted every inch a school marm." When she came into his grandfather's store, McLaurin recalled, "she ordered me about as if I were a student, her voice filled with humor and kindness but sharp enough to command my full attention." While he knew Miss

Carrie and her husband Jerry better than any other black residents of Wade, McLaurin knew them only on his own terms, seeing them outside their homes, in the store, or around the community. Black homes, he wrote, "remained private — they formed a world of which I knew little. When delivering groceries to black families I was never asked to carry packages into their homes."[47]

"Since I didn't enter black homes," McLaurin continued, "I assumed they were somewhat like mine and those of my friends. I knew that some poor blacks probably didn't have the furnishings that we did, that their houses were smaller, but if I thought about it at all, I thought that their homes were simply scaled-down versions of my own. Not until I was seventeen did Miss Carrie invite me into her home. I will never forget that visit or the impact it had on me." Entering her sparsely furnished kitchen, he saw a rustic room, with wood-planked walls covered by old newsprint. A newspaper photograph of FDR hung on one wall, a picture of Jesus on another, and a cardboard, hand-lettered sign "God Bless Our Home" on the other. "Nothing about my relationship with Jerry or Miss Carrie had prepared me for this moment," McLaurin wrote.

> The emotional impact of her kitchen produced the physical responses one feels as a roller coaster begins its downward plunge: the tightening of the stomach; the quick gasp for breath; the queasy sinking feeling inside. Stunned by the appearance of the room, I searched for words while bursts of understanding exploded through my brain. . . . Appalled by what I saw, by the realization that these people whom I admired had so little, I wanted to somehow disappear from the scene, to sink through a crack in the floor and avoid this confrontation with reality. I felt as if I had invaded their privacy and discovered some long-kept secret, which I had.

McLaurin concludes this story by stating that his relationship with Jerry and Miss Carrie remained unchanged, and yet "the visit to their home had confirmed my growing suspicions that I could not become a part of what had been, that I could never completely accept the racial etiquette that had been an essential reality in the world of my father and grandfather. It thus made inevitable my final rejection of the segregated South."[48]

Such vignettes speak volumes about the traumas of the southern black experience, and while perhaps neither a ten-year-old nor a sixteen-year-old would have articulated his reactions so eloquently at the time, these revelations, cast by skilled writers reconstructing the emotional realizations of their more innocent youths, resonate ways no textbook analysis can duplicate, and make these stories among those I most enjoy introducing to students.

It is not always simple matters of right and wrong that are conveyed through these life stories. In describing the ups and downs of her own life story, Pauli Murray noted, "Great art is not a matter of presenting one side or another, but presenting a picture so full of the contradictions, tragedies, and insights of the period that the impact is at once disturbing and satisfying."[49] It is not merely the contradictions, but often the quirks, the flukes, the unexpected or perplexing incidents or observations that remind us that racial interactions throughout southern history have been subject to as many foibles as has human nature itself.

Sisters Sadie and Bessie Delany were both over one hundred years old when they recorded their memories of growing up black in turn-of-the-century North Carolina — the daughters of a slave who rose to become an Episcopalian priest and college administrator in Raleigh — in a 1993 best-seller, *Having Our Say*. Their father provided a powerful role model to both girls for his diplomatic mastery of survival tactics in an increasingly oppressive turn-of-the-century racial climate. Like Booker T. Washington, he stressed economic advancement and mutual support as vital weapons in battling discrimination. "So," recalled Bessie, "Papa would drag us all the way to Mr. Jones' store to buy groceries, since Mr. Jones was a Negro. It not only was inconvenient to shop there; it was more expensive. We used to complain about it, because we passed the A&P on the way . . . but Papa would say 'Mr. Jones needs our money to live on, the A&P does not. We are buying our economic freedom.' So Papa put his money where his mouth was." But, his daughters added, "lest you think Papa was some kind of saint, well, he did have a weakness. He did slip into the A&P now and then and buy that Eight O'Clock Coffee, which he was very partial to. So you see, he wasn't perfect, but Lord, he did try!"[50]

For other southerners, it was as young adults in the work place that they first faced ethical dilemmas growing out of the racial order about which they had been so complacent. For a manicurist, a journalist, and a high-school teacher, the revelations and moral confusions that each experienced in their first jobs make for especially teachable moments and fodder for student discussion. Zora Neale Hurston worked as a manicurist while attending Howard University, and she described an incident she observed in the black-owned barbershop in Washington that employed her. One of several such shops that served an exclusively white clientele, the black manager had no qualms in turning away a black man who came into the shop one day, took a chair, and asked for a haircut and a shave. When the man refused to leave and demanded his constitutional right to be served, all of the barbers joined forces to throw him out onto the street.

Hurston wrote that she did not participate in the melee, "but I wanted him thrown out too." Only in analyzing the situation in bed that night did she realize "that I was giving sanction to Jim Crow, which theoretically, I was supposed to resist." But she wrote, "here were ten Negro barbers, three porters, and two manicurists all stirred up at the threat of losing our living through loss of patronage." While it would have been a "beautiful thing" for them to have banded together in an act of defiance and racial solidarity and cut the black customer's hair, she also resented the fact that he felt that he was justified in jeopardizing the jobs of fifteen fellow blacks. "So I don't know what was the ultimate right in this case," she concluded. "I do know how I felt at the time. There is always something fiendish and loathsome about a person who threatens to deprive you of your way of making a living." At the same time she acknowledged, with a bit more ambiguity, "That was the first time it was called to my attention that self-interest rides over all sorts of lives."[51]

Anne Braden began her career as a newspaper reporter in her native Anniston, Alabama, before moving on to Birmingham in the mid-1940s. It was there that earlier qualms about segregation blossomed as full-scale opposition, and she credits one seemingly minor slip of the tongue as one of those transformative moments. In covering the courthouse for the Birmingham paper, she became all too aware of the fact that there were two kinds of justice practiced there, one for whites and one for blacks. The realization that one cannot remain neutral about that fact came to her one morning in a local cafeteria. Her practice was to check the county coroner's office first thing each day and call in any newsworthy cadavers to the paper before partaking of a leisurely breakfast nearby. On this occasion, she met a colleague there, and he casually asked, "Anything doing?" to which Braden responded, "No. Everything quiet. Nothing but a colored murder." She explained in her memoir, *The Wall Between*, that as a news story, the killing of one black by another was not big news — and that like many reporters she had "learned to think in terms of news values rather than human values," and that she meant that she didn't have to rush off to write it up for the first edition but could take her time with breakfast.

Braden wrote that she might never have given that comment a second thought except for the fact that a young black waitress was pouring coffee for them at the moment she said it. Suddenly, she became aware of what she had said. "I forced myself to look up at her. Her body was stiff; and her hand on the coffee pot jerked. But her face was a stony mark, her eyes cast down." Braden's first impulse was to rush over to her and explain the context of her remark, to say that "I don't feel that way; it's a newspaper; they say what the news is — I don't. I am not a part of this thing that says a Negro life does not matter. It isn't me."[52]

But then that moment of revelation hit. "All of a sudden," she wrote, "like a shaft of morning sunlight over that breakfast table — the truth dawned on me. I *had* meant what I said; . . . if it had not been buried in my mind, I would not have said it." She expounded on this disturbing realization in rhetoric worthy of Lillian Smith:

> I could not shift the blame to my newspaper; I was a part of this white world that considered a Negro life not worth bothering about. If I did not oppose it, I was a part of it — and I was responsible for its sins. There was no middle ground. Unless a person did something to change it, he was strengthening it — and the first thing he knew, its octopus arms were closing about his own soul, twisting it out of shape, hardening it, making it callous.

Suddenly, Braden realized that she herself felt strangled. "I wanted air. I wanted freedom," she insisted. Soon thereafter, she left Alabama to go work for the *Louisville Times*, and it was there that her long career as a civil rights agitator and activist flourished.[53]

And how, other than through autobiography, could we be taken inside a South Carolina high school on the day of Martin Luther King Jr.'s assassination in April 1968, or hear a white teacher describe the reactions of his black students to that tragedy? Pat Conroy claimed that he loved teaching high school. It was there, he wrote, that "I dwelt amidst the fascists and flag-wavers in relative obscurity, and I liked the students." In the spring of his first year as a teacher at Beaufort High School, he described a dramatic encounter with black students that altered his views not only of race but of human nature. Some of the white students — those Conroy labeled "the village rednecks" — cheered at the news of King's assassination and referred to Mrs. King as "the black widow." The few black students in the predominantly white school walked the halls in silence, Conroy wrote in *The Water Is Wide*, with "tears of frustration rolling down their cheeks and unspoken bitterness written on their faces in their inability to communicate their feelings to their white teachers." They asked that the flag in front of the school be lowered to half mast, but the principal declined to do so, fearful of community reaction to such a statement.[54]

On the day of King's funeral, Conroy talked quietly with a group of black boys he had established some rapport with over the course of the year, but he was soon approached by a far more militant set of black students — all female. "On this momentous, hysteric day," he wrote, "the girls came for me." Swarming around him, the largest and most outspoken of the group, Lily, shouted at him: "What are you doing here, white man? You sent here by the white man to make sure we don't do anything de-structive?" A companion took up the cry, yelling in his face: "Why don't you get back with the rest of those honkies and let us cry in peace? We don't need you to tell us how sorry you are or how much it disturbed you to see us upset. Just get your white ass back into that school and leave us alone." Conroy continued: "I tried to say something, something redemptive or purgative, but no sound came from my throat. A sea of voices surrounded me, washed over me, and sucked me into a great whirlpool of sound and confusion." This set off even more hostile cries from both the boys and the girls that ranged from abusive epithets at their teacher to threats of destruction and chaos that would make whites regret what they had done to King. One girl drove her fingernails deep into Conroy's arm, drawing blood, and another scratched his neck and attempted to strangle him. "The entire mob," he said, "was convulsed with raw, demonstrative sorrow. 'Martin's dead, Martin's dead, Martin's dead,' they chanted. 'The whites eat shit,' said a boy. 'Fuck you, Conroy,' said a girl. And the bell mercifully rang."[55]

He concluded this story by noting that several months later, he heard black students laughing and snickering when Lurleen Wallace, the Alabama governor and wife of the South's most prominent segregationist, died of cancer. Conroy questioned whether such a response was any more appropriate than that of the white crackers when King had died. "But she was a racist," the students responded in unison. "The mortar of cynicism was hardening," Conroy concluded. "I was convinced that the world was a colorful, variegated grab bag full of bastards." He went on to appease his "white guilt" by establishing, in this majority white high school, a course in black history, which was "about as common in those days as a course in necrophilia."[56] But he left the school soon thereafter and moved on to the opportunity that is the focus of his book and that inspired his writing career — his year teaching the black children on Yamacraw Island.

It is these passages and dozens of others like them that make autobiography such a powerful medium for historians and such rich fodder for teachers and their students. Yet none of these authors or experiences I've cited can be considered typical or representative of most southerners, black or white. One does not read autobiography for the "typicality" of the lives they reveal. It is the particularities of their stories, their situations, their viewpoints, and their voices that make them so revealing, so compelling, so engaging. Yet more universal truths emerge from these individual voices. Ralph Ellison once observed that autobiographical works both emerge from history and allow us access to it. "One of the reasons we exchange experiences," he wrote, "is in order to discover the repetitions and coincidences which amount to a common group experience."[57]

In *South to a Very Old Place*, a highly original and provocative account of growing up black in early twentieth-century Alabama, novelist Albert Murray notes: "The ironic thing about these two great hyphenate minorities, the Southern-Americans and the Negro-Americans, confronting each other on their native soil for three and a half centuries, is the degree to which they have shaped each other's destiny, determined each other's isolation, shared and molded a common culture. It is in fact impossible to imagine the one without the other and quite futile."[58]

It is indeed, and the interaction and interdependency of the two races is a theme that pervades the autobiographical work of southerners. Yet equally prevalent — and certainly evident in the works discussed here — is the tremendous gulf that separated black and white worlds for so much of our southern past. In the late 1950s, a twenty-two-year-old Willie Morris found himself in Paris. Knowing that Richard Wright had grown up not far from Yazoo City and had long been a Parisian exile, Morris looked him up. He called him, told him that he was a "white Yazoo boy," and Wright told him to come on over. "We went out to an Arab bar and got a little drunk together, and talked about the place we both had known." Morris asked Wright if he would ever come back to America, and Wright replied: "No, I want my children to grow up as human beings." Morris concluded that anecdote by saying: "After a time a silence fell between us, like an immense pain — or maybe it was just my imagining."[59] These two men, far removed from the Jim Crow world that had so defined their youth, could not leave it behind them in Paris, and they never sought out each other's company again.

It is not then simply our "common group experiences" that we extract from this rich array of self-revelation. Even if they shared the same race, gender, class, and moment of time in which they came of age, no two of these authors, black or white, experienced slavery, Jim Crow, or the civil rights movement in the same way. The sheer variety of what they witnessed, felt, responded to, and were ultimately shaped by leaves us with a far greater sense of the complexity and diversity in their own and their region's past. It was the vagaries of human nature that determined how these individuals behaved, felt, thought, and chose to remember and share their stories on the printed page.

For many students, especially at high-school or middle-school levels, exposure to this vast range of topics and viewpoints may prove perplexing and unsettling. But the issues raised by these very intimate and human stories serve to broaden the ways in which character education can infuse the study of history, of literature, of life. Jamil Zanaildin has noted: "The humanities promote empathy. What better way to know about the other than to walk in her shoes, see the world through the eyes of another, to find common connections in tragedy, pain, and joy."[60] And how better to understand our own identities as southerners and Americans than to read about how others have wrestled with and come to terms with theirs?

To give Lillian Smith the last word, she once noted of southern mores that "there is a structural, bony sameness throughout the region we call 'the South'; but it is fleshed out in ten thousand different ways — ways often strikingly inconsistent with the 'beliefs' that seem inherent in that structure." It is those inconsistencies, variables, and deviations from norms that make the autobiographical work of southerners, black and white, endlessly intriguing and instructive. In an introduction to one such work, Smith characterized it in a way that made it more applicable to all. "Perhaps one reason this book is so fascinating," she wrote, "is that we feel nuances we have been unaware of; we guess at actions we had not dared think southerners were capable of; we learn that differences between each of us are terribly important to cherish even though we value more and more our common humanity. And we learn this in a subliminal fashion as we listen to this soft voice telling a tale that sends shivers down the spine."[61] And so it is for all the other writers, who in soft and not so soft voices, in subliminal and not so subliminal ways, reveal through their stories both our differences and our common humanity.

CHAPTER TWO

"I Learn What I Am"

Adolescent Struggles with Mixed-Race Identities

OF THE MANY eyewitness accounts we have of the Atlanta race riot of 1906, none is more chilling than that describing a thirteen-year-old black boy's confrontation with an angry white mob on the steps of his home. That young man was Walter White, who grew up to become the executive secretary of the NAACP and an influential civil rights activist. He began his 1948 autobiography, *A Man Called White*, with this incident in a chapter titled "I Learn What I Am."

White provided his own racial identification in the first sentences of his book: "I am a Negro. My skin is white, my eyes are blue, my hair is blond. The traits of my race are nowhere visible upon me." He elaborated, in explaining why he ultimately made the choice he did to remain black. "I am not white," he wrote. "There is nothing within my mind and heart which tempts me to think that I am. Yet I realize acutely that the only characteristic that matters to either the white or the colored race — the appearance of whiteness — is mine. There is magic in a white skin; there is tragedy, loneliness, exile, in a black skin. Why then do I insist that I am a Negro, when nothing compels me to do so but myself?"[1]

White credits a single incident as the answer to that question, so often posed to him by others, either directly or indirectly. "I know the night when, in terror and bitterness of soul, I discovered that I was set apart by the pigmentation of my skin . . . and the moment at which I decided that I would infinitely rather be what I was than, through taking advantage of the way of escape that was open to me, be one of the race which had forced the decision upon me." That night was Sunday, September 13, the second night of the Atlanta race riot. A day earlier, the young White was caught downtown with his father, a postman, who was making his rounds when the riot broke out on that fateful Saturday afternoon. From their wagon they witnessed the savagery of the white mob as they pursued defenseless black victims through the streets and beat them to death "to the accompaniment of savage shouting and cursing," and then moved on after "new prey." Because of their light skin color, father and son made it safely home, but they learned the next day that the white hooligans were regrouping and planned to move into their neighborhood to "clean out the niggers." White provided a harrowing account of his family's preparations for the onslaught to come. He and his father, armed with guns, waited on the front porch of their home, which they had been warned was to be the torch-carrying mob's first target, while his mother and sisters hid in the back of the house. His father instructed him: "Son, don't shoot until the first man puts his foot on the lawn and then — don't you miss!"[2]

The mob surged toward the house but was quickly dispersed by a volley of shots from neighbors before the Whites had to fire themselves. It was at that moment, Walter later wrote, that his epiphany came. As he put his gun aside, he found himself "gripped by the knowledge of my identity, and in the depths of my soul I was vaguely aware that I was glad of it. . . . I knew then who I was. I was a Negro, a human being with an invisible pigmentation which marked me as a person to be hunted, hanged, abused, discriminated against, kept in poverty and ignorance, in order that those whose skin was white would have readily at hand a proof of their superiority."[3]

White continued this extraordinary diatribe against the white race and all it had inflicted on other races: "I was sick with loathing for the hatred which had flared before me that night and come so close to making me a killer; but I was glad I was not one of those who hated; I was glad I was not one of those whose story is in the history of the world, a record of bloodshed, rapine, and pillage. I was glad my mind and spirit were part of the races that had not fully awakened, and who therefore had still before them the opportunity to write a record of virtue as a memorandum to Armaggedon." He concluded his first chapter from the hindsight of the late 1940s, when he wrote his autobiography: "It was all just a feeling then, inarticulate and melancholy, yet reassuring in the way that death and sleep are reassuring, and I have clung to it now for nearly half a century."[4]

Few life stories open as dramatically as White's, and few black autobiographers ever came to terms with their racial identities as suddenly or as surely as

White claimed to have done in 1906.[5] But he was by no means alone in confronting the realities of race and what it meant to discover and cope with that troublesome reality as black southerners coming of age during the Jim Crow era. As has been noted before, one of the unique features of autobiography is that it offers a vast array of case studies of young people struggling with a wide variety of issues, including — and often foremost — that of coming to terms with who they are and where they fit into the society to which they and their families belong, especially in the South, where race was so dominant and defining a part of one's status and identity. Expressions of these issues can be among the most vital and richly expressed components of autobiography, and their authors' observations, perceptions, and memories can be profound. This is particularly true when their own racial identities and those of the people around them become sources of confusion, frustration, resolve, and sometimes despair. It is this aspect of these writings that is the focus of this chapter. At the same time, these personal testimonials add a much-needed human dimension to the ever-growing scholarship on America's mixed and multiracial heritage, the vast majority of which writings have been legal, policy, or theoretical approaches to the issues involved. Rarely are the feelings of individuals integral to these studies, nor are the emotional and psychological implications of mixed-race identity ever seriously considered as part of historical inquiries into miscegenation or amalgamation.[6] More than any other genre, autobiography serves to internalize what is often viewed in far more detached ways. It is primarily through autobiography as well that the focus shifts to the offspring of these liaisons, with the writers exploring their own racial makeup and the genealogy behind it, which may extend back two, three, or more generations.

As mentioned earlier, Lillian Smith once stated that all southern children — both black and white — had to be initiated into the "intricate movements" of southern tradition, and had to learn how to negotiate, accept, and move through "the labyrinth made by grownups' greed and guilt and fear."[7] Those children and adolescents spotlighted here are among those to whom these lessons did not come easily; those African American boys and girls who, in addition to the trauma faced by all black children, had to face the confusion created by their own genetic makeup — the realization that they were of mixed-race descent and the reasons, familial and biological, that accounted for it. How these writers came to grips with the harsh realities of the segregated South had much to do with how they came to terms with their identities as what Joel Williamson has called "new people."[8]

Walter White made that theme central in introducing himself to readers: how children, defined as black, dealt with the discovery and meaning of miscegenation and its implications on their own mixed-race identities; how they in effect "learned what they were," and how that knowledge shaped their sense of self and direction in life. While one's blackness and/or whiteness was at one level a sliding scale determined by the unions of one's parents, grandparents, or other ancestors, the "one drop" rule of racial definition tolerated far less fluidity or flexibility in one's status under the South's segregated regime. It was these contradictions that became the source of much of the perplexity and frustration for those so defined.[9]

This is a more common theme in African American autobiography than one might expect, from the earliest slave narratives to the present. Frederick Douglass — who on occasion referred to "blended people" and counted himself among them — stated the problem forthrightly in his 1845 *Narrative*: "It is plain that a very different-looking class of people are springing up at the south, and are now held in slavery, from those originally brought to the country from Africa. . . . Thousands are ushered into the world, annually, who, like myself, owe their existence to white fathers, and those fathers most frequently, their own masters."[10] His quest to identify his own father provided an important subtext for all three of his life stories.

Other slave narratives dealt just as forthrightly with the issue. Harriet Jacobs wrote of both voluntary and involuntary assignations she had with white men and the children produced from one of those unions; and William and Ellen Craft's remarkable escape story from Georgia was predicated on Ellen's very light skin — the product of her master's paternity — which, along with her slight build, allowed her to disguise herself as both white and as a man and travel "a thousand miles to freedom" under the guise of being her own husband's master. As prelude to their own story and as a means of putting his wife's racial makeup in context, William Craft reminded his readers that "slavery in America is not at all confined to any particular complexion; there are a very large number of slaves as white as any one," and he followed by documenting a number of other cases like his own and his wife's, built on the confusions and ambiguities of racial identity in the slave South.[11]

It is a theme that has long resonated in American literature, film, and popular culture. More recently, it has taken on renewed urgency in American life: from the new assertiveness with which celebrities, such as Tiger Woods, Mariah Carey, and Halle Berry, have defined themselves as multiracial (though most others see them as black), to the newly established options for categorizing one's racial and ethnic identity in the 2000 census, to the controversy surrounding the Thomas Jefferson-Sally Hemings liaison and their descendants, black and white, the American public has been exposed to these issues in a variety of ways over the past two decades. Literary manifestations have been far more rampant as well—from Alice Randall's controversial *The Wind Done Gone*, narrated by Scarlett O'Hara's half-black half-sister, to Philip Roth's *The Human Stain*, whose protagonist passes as white until forced to expose his identity when accused of using a racial epithet, and on to *Finn*, Jon Cinch's 2007 novel focused on Huckleberry's father, "Pap," and the astonishing revelation that his famous offspring's mother was African American.[12] Ultimately, of course, the election in 2008 of an American president whose mother was a white Kansan and father was a black Kenyan brought into the public arena more fully than ever before the pervasiveness of mixed-race identities and how integral they have long been and continue to be to the American experience.

Thus these examinations of how young people of earlier generations wrestled with these issues in far less permissive or enlightened times offer a timely perspective on the challenges Williamson's so-called "new people" have faced throughout America's history.[13] It is a prevalent theme in African American autobiographies, which grant us uncommon entrée into a range of psychological and emotional responses to their own and others' mixed-race identities, and it occasionally appears in white life stories as well. In fact, one of the most compelling testimonials of childhood racial confusion comes from a white southerner.

In one of the most often cited passages from *Killers of the Dream*, Lillian Smith described a strange incident in which her parents, living in a small north Florida town, took in what a local social worker assumed was a white girl who had been found in the "colored section" of town, living in a broken-down shack with a black family who had just moved there. The assumption was that she had been kidnapped. Janie, as she was known, was to be brought up in the Smith household. She shared a room with Lillian and was generally made a part of the family. She was, Smith wrote, "dazed by her new comforts and by the interesting activities of my big lively family; and I was as happily dazed, for her adoration of me was a new thing; and as time passed a quick, childish, and deeply felt bond grew up between us."

Then one day, a phone call from a black orphanage led to nervous meetings, much whispering, and finally an announcement made by Lillian's mother that

Janie would be returning to the black family from which she had been taken. The only explanation offered was that Janie was found to be "colored." In response to repeated queries from Lillian in all her innocence and confusion as to why Janie had to leave, how she could be colored, and why she couldn't continue to play with or ever see her roommate and companion again, her mother finally said, "You're too young to understand. And don't ask me again, ever again, about this!" Mother's voice was sharp but her face was sad and there was no certainty left there, Lillian wrote. "I knew that something was wrong. I knew my father and mother whom I passionately admired had betrayed something which they held dear. And they could not help doing it. And I was shamed by their failure and frightened, for I felt they were no longer as powerful as I had thought."[14]

While Smith clearly meant this incident to serve as a key event in her road to racial redemption (it is actually one of the few tangible clues she provided as to the source of the enlightenment that became her calling and her passion), one must also consider the far more devastating and yet unexplored dimension of this story: how it affected Janie herself.[15] For Lillian, this was the loss of a playmate, a companion, a friend. As traumatized and confused as she was by what had happened and why, the effects must have been far more devastating to Janie, whose voice is lost, as is any means to recover the alternative path her life ultimately took. Only for a couple of weeks was she exposed to the comfortable, middle-class lifestyle of a southern white family and treated as a white child herself. The memories of that fleeting experience must have reminded her throughout her life of all that would never be offered her again in the Jim Crow South.

Other black children faced similar traumas and grew up to write about them. For some, it was not their own skin color but that of other family members that served as a source of bafflement and confusion. In *Black Boy*, his wrenching narrative of growing up in the 1910s and 1920s in Mississippi, Richard Wright articulated that youthful naiveté about the discrepancies between racial identity and the appearance of one's skin. He wrote that as a child, "though I had long known that there were people called 'white' people, it had never meant anything to me emotionally. I had seen white men and women upon the streets a thousand times, but they had never looked particularly 'white'. To me they were merely people like other people, yet somehow strangely different because I had never come in close touch with any of them."[16]

Part of the reason that neither their presence nor any significance based on skin color occurred to Wright earlier, he explained, was "that many of my relatives were 'white'-looking people. My grandmother, who was white as any 'white' person, never looked 'white' to me." It was on a train trip with his mother to visit his grandmother in Arkansas that Wright was first made fully aware of segregation. He was full of questions as to why "we Negroes were in one part of the train and that the whites were in another. Naively I wanted to go and see how the whites looked while sitting in their part of the train."

As was so often the case with Wright's constant curiosity, his mother sought to squelch his many questions: "I wanted to understand these two sets of people who lived side by side and never touched, it seemed, except in violence." And then, there was his grandmother: "Was she white? Just how white was she? What did the whites think of her whiteness?" Finally, after a series of evasive answers to the young boy's queries, his mother slapped him and he cried. Only later did she grudgingly explain that "Granny came of Irish, Scotch, and French stock in which Negro blood had somewhere and somehow been infused." Further probing revealed that his father, who had abandoned the family earlier and whom Wright barely knew, had "some white and some red and some black" blood in him. "Then what am I?" Richard asked. "They'll call you a colored man when you grow up," his mother replied. "Then she turned to me and smiled mockingly and asked: 'Do you mind, Mr. Wright?'" Wright wrote that her response angered him, and he did not reply. "I did not object to being called colored, but I knew that there was something my mother was holding back." In a passage strikingly like that of other black writers frustrated by the reluctance of their elders to clear up their confusion, Wright said of his mother: "She was not concealing facts, but feelings, attitudes, convictions which she did not want me to know; and she became angry when I prodded her."[17]

Wright concluded this crucial episode with that fragile mix of confusion, defiance, and resignation that he conveys so vividly throughout his book:

> All right, I would find out someday. Just wait. All right, I was colored. It was fine.
> I did not know enough to be afraid or to anticipate in a concrete manner. True, I
> had heard that colored people were killed or beaten, but so far it all had seemed
> remote. There was, of course, a vague uneasiness about it all, but I would be able
> to handle that when I came to it. It would be simple. If anyone tried to kill me,
> then I would kill them first.[18]

A far different childhood led to very different sources of confusion for another southern black boy nearly a generation older than Wright, and in a far dif-

ferent part of the South. One of the most self-conscious narratives documenting childhood confusion over one's racial identity and sense of place within
the Jim Crow regime is Ely Green's autobiography, titled *Ely: Too Black, Too
White*. In an opening paragraph similar to Walter White's in its direct confrontation with his own racial makeup, Green stated: "I was born in a small town
in Tennessee — the name Sewanee, so called The University of the South. It was
in 1893. My father was a white man. My mother a so-called Negress. So I was
looked on as a half white bastard and so called that by almost everyone that
knew me."[19]

Green grew up in the rarified atmosphere of the Episcopal college town
perched atop a mountain. Ely was light enough to "pass" for white, but everyone in town knew of his parentage — his mother, a seventeen-year-old black
maid; his father, one of three white sons of the wealthy widow for whom she
worked. Ely and his mother were taken in by the family next door to her employer, and they and other affluent families for whom she worked coddled the
young child as his mother's health deteriorated with consumption and she eventually died. They treated him with a degree of affection that led him to observe,
"All white people down South seems to love colored children." That sense of
love, of belonging was only surface deep. As Lillian Smith put it in an unusually
pointed foreword to his book, "Eli's childhood was spread with a meringue of
love — white people's love, white people's generosity, white people's superficial
concern: a fluffy, sweet meringue which covered a pie made of ashes and dung
and broken metallic bits of 'history.' The slave's history."[20]

So comfortable and secure did Ely feel in this idealized paternalistic environment that it was in the black community — where he had to attend school
and was shunned as "clabber" by schoolmates — that he felt out of place and
unwanted. "I was the only real light-complected one in the school," he wrote.
"The rumor soon was out that I was a bastard and that my white uncle was a
nitwit. . . . All the children poked fun at me." But that experience proved tem-
porary (he only attended the school for two weeks) and had little effect on
the far happier circumstances of his days spent among Sewanee's white elite,
his mother's employers. He roamed the university campus freely with the white
boys that were his closest companions, admiring the local military academy's
cadets as they paraded, and fantasized along with his white playmates about
growing up to become part of that grand uniformed corps.[21]

An incident at the age of nine suddenly shattered Ely's complacency and first
raised confusion as to the implication of his black ancestry and how it would

affect his future within a community far more race-conscious than he had yet had reason to realize. In a soda shop that he had often visited, he and two white playmates ordered three malted milks (or eggflips, as they called them). The dispenser — a new employee — made two drinks and handed them to his companions. When one of them asked where Ely's drink was, the dispenser said, "I don't make drinks for no nigger. He's a nigger." This, Ely said, "was the first time I ever felt hurt, except when my mother died."[22]

His bewilderment at the term "nigger," which he had never heard before and about which his trusted white guardians became very uncomfortable and evasive when he asked them to define it, becomes a theme that spans much of the rest of Green's memoir. Only gradually and partially did he come to realize just what the implications of being a "nigger" were, and how negative a turn this represented in both his own self-image and in how others saw him. Father Eastern, an Episcopal priest who had befriended Ely, finally explained the term to him but offered reassurance by urging him to leave the white enclave in which he had lived and to begin to develop friendships with "colored children" like himself. "This will help you in many ways," the priest assured him. "You will see they are very happy and lovable people. There is nothing bad about being a Negro." But in answering Ely's next question, he destroyed any such assurance in Ely's mind. "Father, will I go to the military academy when I grow up?" the nine-year-old asked. The priest replied: "No, Ely, colored people don't go to school with white people in the South," Green wrote. "This to me was about the hardest blow that I could experience. This was the greatest dream of all the boys I had known. . . . It just seemed that everything of hope had just floated out of me, and I was just a shell."[23]

Because so much of Green's appreciation of white life came through his close observation of activity on the University of the South campus and the vicarious pleasure he had taken in witnessing it, his ultimate realization that he could never do more than that proved a source of pain and frustration. During Commencement Week every year, numerous entertainments were held on campus, and "the colored people went to see the styles that the ladies from other colleges wore and the different dances," he wrote. "It was something to see." He accompanied his sister Ann to one such dance, where they stood outside and peered in the windows of the gymnasium. A gentlemen, seeing them out in the cold, told them to go to the stage entrance of the building and to sit on the stage, where they could look down on the dance floor. While Ely found this "a beautiful sight," and his sister commented admiringly of the many white ladies she recognized at the ball, it proved another revelatory moment for him. "This was the first time I realized something about me that was not fair," he wrote. "White people just let a Negro go so far and no farther, though we were a part of them and they were a part of us. Why were we at a handicap? No answer. I had worn out the patience of everybody asking questions."[24]

The source of Green's confusion was based in large part on the unusual degree of good will and paternalistic care with which Sewanee's white elite embraced the young boy — a side of white people never seen by Richard Wright. On the other hand, both Green and Wright were shielded from full engagement with local black communities in their early years — well after the point at which such interactions served to initiate and define black children's sense of identity and the parameters of the color line. One critic has noted that "if *Black Boy* is the story of the Negro folk system of education, it is the story of its failure. Richard Wright could not learn his role."[25] That failure also proved to be Wright's salvation, for whatever spirit he brought to his quest to break out of those bounds and define himself and his abilities on his own terms stemmed at least in part from the mixed signals about his own and others' racial identities that stalled his capitulation to the full demands of Jim Crow and southern tradition while at a younger, more malleable stage of development. For Green, his late exposure to all that he had been sheltered from proved far more traumatic, damaging a psyche that emerged even more troubled and alienated than Wright's.

Yet, a mixed racial identity did not always result in frustration and confusion for young people seeking to find themselves and their place in the racially repressive South. A number of black writers, like Walter White, were never shielded from the sources of their mixed blood — children who were told quite frankly about, and even knew personally, their white ancestry, and who absorbed such revelations with pride, satisfaction, and a much more stable sense of self.

Sadie and Bessie Delany, the inimitable African American sisters who at over a hundred years of age in 1993 saw their recorded life stories become a best-selling book, *Having Our Say*, were unusually well grounded from an early age about who they were and the interracial unions that had produced them. Their father was born a slave and, through the educational opportunities offered him during Reconstruction, rose to become an Episcopalian bishop who headed Saint Augustine College, a black school in Raleigh, North Carolina, on the grounds of which the Delany girls and their eight siblings were raised.

Their mother (who could pass for white herself and often did so until Jim Crow laws brought new rigidity to the color line) was the product of an unusual union: a fifty-year monogamous relationship in Virginia between a white man, James Miliam, and his free black "lady love," Nancy Logan, who was herself the offspring of a slave man and his white mistress. Nancy was one of four daughters, "all only one-quarter black, but in the eyes of the world they were colored." They were apparently told all of this at an early age and took it in stride. The Delany sisters visited their white grandfather and mulatto grandmother every summer; the only aspect of their relationship that struck them as unusual was that they had to call him Mr. Miliam. "Grandma was the boss," the Delanys recalled. "And they say folks found it amusing to see this colored woman just bossing around the fiercest-looking white man in Pittsylvania County."[26]

Much of the success — and popular appeal — of the Delanys' memoir lay in their remarkable candor about their own achievements and American race relations as they observed and experienced them over the course of a century. They were particularly astute on matters of miscegenation and the implications of skin color, beginning with their own multitoned family. "People would look at us Delany children and wonder where in the world this bunch came from," Sadie stated in her typically disarming way. "We were every different shade from nearly white to brown-sugar. I was one of the lighter children, and Bessie was darker. As children we were aware we were colored but we never gave it a second thought. Papa was dark and Mama was light and so what?"[27]

While they noted throughout the book the ways in which the two of them were treated differently because Sadie was lighter than Bessie, they demonstrated none of the inhibitions apparent in other black autobiographers in addressing the issue head-on. "You see, a lot of this Jim Crow mess was about sex, about keeping the races separate, so they wouldn't interbreed," the sisters said. "Ironically, there were very few white people in those days, especially in the South, who did not have some nigger blood. All these white folks who thought they were above Negroes, well, many of them were not pure white! Some of them knew it, some didn't. But colored people could always pick them out. Papa used to joke that Negro blood must be superior, it must be strong stuff, 'cause it always showed up! You would see these beautiful white-skinned women with kinky hair, and honey, they got it from *somewhere*!"[28]

Combining a sense of historical perspective with their personal experience, the Delanys noted that some race mixing was "left over from slavery days, because white men would often molest their slave women." "But," they were quick to follow up, "a lot of this race mixing, especially after slavery days, was just attraction between people, plain and simple, just like happened in our family, on Mama's side. You know when people live in close proximity, they can't help but get attracted to each other."[29] One might argue that it was the chronological distance of the 1990s and the wisdom of old age that allowed these remarkable women to express such comfort with their racial identities and such a straight-forward sense of their mixed-race heritage. But one senses that both this comfort level and understanding of who they were and where they had come from were instilled in them by parents who felt equally secure in their identities and made sure that their children did as well.

Georgia writer Raymond Andrews also dealt with his mixed-race ancestry in objective, almost detached terms that suggest that he, like the Delanys, was never troubled or confused by it. Early in his 1990 memoir of growing up in the 1940s in rural and small-town Morgan County in north central Georgia, *The Last Radio Baby*, Andrews's description of his paternal grandparents suggests that he knew about their complex pasts from a fairly young age. His grandmother, Jessie, born in 1872, was the daughter of a half-black woman and a half-white, half-Cherokee father. She was the lightest of seven children fathered by at least three different men. Andrews wrote of his maternal ancestry: "The colored community . . . was indeed colorful, consisting of tar, brown, yellow, pink, red, and even white-skinned people with nappy, curly, and straight hair. They were all black."[30] Though never married, Jessie maintained a longtime monogamous relationship with "Mister Jim," one of the most powerful white men in the community.

If the implications of all this on his own identity never seem to have bothered Raymond, the same cannot be said of his father, the son of Jessie and Mister Jim, who demonstrated considerable discomfort in his skin. "Daddy was overly conscious of his skin color, which was light, as in white, and his blond hair," Andrews wrote. He stated that his father never wanted anyone to think that because of his appearance he considered himself better than any other black man. "A colored person of that time," he explained, "accused of thinking himself or herself 'better' than another colored person was committing one of the deadliest sins in the colored community."[31]

He was equally determined that whites not get the idea that his light coloring privileged him in any way. "Around whites he could 'out-Tom' the original Uncle," his son wrote. He refused any favors offered him, which whites often did, "perhaps because he looked so much like them." He found this an embarrassment and shunned their attentions. His sensitivity carried over to his treatment of his own children. Raymond wrote that of his father's ten offspring, "Daddy favored Harvey, the oldest, and years later, Veronica, number eight down the birth line, because of their darker complexions. He wanted the public to see that in spite of his own light skin and blond hair, he was colored enough to produce 'natural' colored children."[32] It is curious that Raymond, one of the lighter and thus less favored of those children, never seemed to resent his father's attitude or to resort to any introspection or intimate revelations about his own feelings. Perhaps again, by waiting so long to tell his story — it was nearly a half-century after the events he describes that he wrote about them — he had insulated himself from any but a nostalgic and mostly factual account of his rich if tangled racial heritage.

Like Andrews, another Georgian autobiographer traces her more gradual discovery of her mixed-race ancestry. Charlayne Hunter-Gault, the prominent journalist and news correspondent, was one of the first two African Americans to attend the University of Georgia, and she wrote a moving memoir of that experience and her earlier life, titled *In My Place*, drawing on both literal and figurative meanings of that phrase. Growing up in nearby Covington, she noted that it was a place where her mother's family had roots and that "finding my own place among the many branches of these roots was sometimes difficult, and occasionally mysterious." Yet, she has no trouble in getting her mother to explain those multicolored roots; she did so "with neither pride nor embarrassment, but rather matter-of-factly," an approach that applies equally to Hunter-Gault's own assessment of her racial identity.[33]

The Hunters lived on Brown Street, which Charlayne learned was named for her mother's white grandfather — rarely talked about in the family because he never married her grandmother, who was herself a mix of Cherokee Indian and white. Two of their three children, Charlayne's great-uncle and great-aunt, moved away from Georgia and passed for white. The third sibling, her grandfather, remained in Georgia working as a barber in a shop with a white clientele and all black employees. He was so fair that he claimed many of the leading citizens and civic leaders as his customers. "He felt as important as any of them, and they treated him as one of them," Charlayne's mother told her. His fall was quick, though. Although his father promised to set her grandfather up in business for himself, he died of a heart attack just before doing so. The white side of the family summoned him to come and shave and trim the hair of the man whom they knew to be but didn't acknowledge as his own father. "It was the hardest thing he ever had to do in life," his daughter said. He charged the family ten dollars for his services, because "he knew that that was the last he'd ever get from the Browns, now that his father was dead, and he decided to get all he could."[34]

Hunter's grandmother's roots were just as "tangled" as her grandfather's — also with white and Cherokee blood — the result being that Charlayne's mother looked nearly white. Though delivered by a black doctor in 1918, her birth certificate lists her as "white." Charlayne's father was somewhat darker, and after an impromptu wedding in Atlanta four months after they met, his new father-in-law roared his disapproval. When Charlayne asked her mother later if his disapproval stemmed from his new son-in-law's dark skin, "she said no, quite emphatically. As light as they all were, they always identified themselves proudly as Black, even when they easily could have passed for white in some other location."[35]

In 1949, Hunter-Gault, then only seven years old, saw the movie *Pinky* with her mother at the "colored theater" on the edge of town in Covington. Elia Kazan's first film was groundbreaking in that it focused on the dilemma of a light-skinned black woman, played by white actress Jeanne Crain, who has passed for white while in nursing school in the North, but who returns home to her grandmother (there's no reference made to her parentage) and must wrestle with whether or not she can reenter the Jim Crow world from which she had temporarily escaped. Hunter-Gault doesn't make much of the incident — at age seven she was probably too young to ponder the full implications of what she was seeing — but she did recall turning to her mother while watching the movie and calling her "my Pinky." At that moment, she wrote, "she did look just like Jeanne Crain."[36]

For other African Americans, knowledge of their white ancestry was based more on their own genealogical and historical research than on firsthand exposure to their nonblack relatives. Thus it was often later in life that they came to terms with those issues of identity and bloodlines. Journalist and historian Roger Wilkins wrote only briefly about his ancestry in his moving meditation on the slaveholding founding fathers and the short- and long-term impact of their ambivalence about race and slavery. Relying on a combination of documents, family lore, and a photograph, he traced his maternal ancestry only as far back as his great-grandfather, "a distinguished-looking, light-skinned man" named Charles Wood, born in Virginia in 1832. This educated free black married a Cherokee woman named Percidia, and they became the parents of thirteen children, including Roger's maternal grandmother. "I have always wondered how this black man got his freedom and his light skin," Wilkins writes. His only clue is that Wood enjoyed the patronage of a nameless white woman, but beyond that he could only speculate, which he freely did. Family freedom may have originated in those few documented free blacks from mid-seventeenth century Jamestown, he supposed, but more likely it came later — from fighting in the Revolution, perhaps? "Or was Charles Wood light and free because he was the child of a slave and a white person — was his lightness the result of an owner forcing himself on a slave woman?" he asks. "Was the white woman who took an interest in him a relative, or simply a kind slave-owning woman who saw promise in the half-black child and so educated and freed him? Could she have been his mother?" Ultimately, Wilkins acknowledges that the most he can claim with any certainty is that "there surely had been a long journey of genes and circumstances from some door of no return to the light and educated man born thirty-three years before Lee surrendered at Appomattox."[37]

Pauli Murray also uncovered much of her multiracial roots through proactive research, and she makes her search as much a part of her narrative as its often disturbing findings. No one wrote as fully and forthrightly about her mixed-race ancestry, but unlike Andrews or the Delanys or Hunter-Gault or Wilkins, she revealed far more emotional engagement with that past and her struggles in coming to terms with it. The very title of Murray's 1956 memoir, *Proud Shoes*, suggests her stance toward her multiracial and multiethnic heritage. It is first and foremost a dual biography of her maternal grandparents, in whose household she was raised in Durham, North Carolina, in the 1910s and 1920s. Murray's grandfather, with whom she lived, was the son of a white woman of Swedish and French descent, Sarah Ann Burton, and of Thomas Fitzgerald, a "half-Irish mulatto," who had met and married in antebellum Pennsylvania. "We prized our Irish ancestry and free status long before the Civil War; both were distinctive in a small southern town dominated by names like Smith, Jones and Brown and haunted by grim ghosts of the slavery past," Murray wrote. The Fitzgeralds moved south during Reconstruction, and Pauli took great pride in her great-grandfather's courage and determination in establishing schools for freedmen first in Virginia, and then in Orange County, North Carolina, amid formidable local opposition and intimidation. But it was who they were even more than what they did that generated the greatest satisfaction for Murray. "Colored people grasped at any distinction to put distance between themselves and slavery. If one couldn't fall back on the amount of white blood he had in him, as Grandmother did, he'd rely on a free parent or free grandparent. And I could talk of free *great-grandparents*, something truly to be proud of in these times."[38]

Murray's lineage was not devoid of slavery, however, which is why she found her grandmother's parentage far more troubling and difficult to write about. She was the product of the multiple rapes of a young slave girl (of more Indian than African blood, according to Murray's grandmother) by Sidney Smith, the son of her owner, near Chapel Hill.[39] The baby — and her younger half-sisters, fathered by Sidney's brother — were raised by their spinster sister, Mary Ruffin Smith, who instilled in her mulatto nieces a great pride in the Smith lineage of which they were a part, a heritage Murray's grandmother fully embraced: "Child, you listen to your grandmother," she told the young Pauli. "Hold your head high and don't take a back seat to nobody. You got good blood in you — folks that counted for something — doctors, lawyers, judges, legislators. Aristocrats, that's what they were, going back seven generations right in this state."[40] Thus even the brutal circumstances that produced her — reflecting the worst abuses of the peculiar institution — allowed for "proud shoes" in Murray's Smith ancestry; yet she was all too aware of the painful irony that the source of that pride lay in identifying fully with the family of the man who had raped her great-grandmother.

It is clear from Murray's later reflections on how and why she came to write *Proud Shoes* that her full appreciation of the meaning and significance of her multicultural and multicolored ancestry developed only as she matured as a young adult. It is revealing, however, that she was made aware of this darker side of her heritage at an early age by her aunts and her grandmother, just as she was discovering the more uplifting story of her Fitzgerald ancestry. Yet even equipped with much greater awareness of the sources of her identity than was true of most of the other black youth discussed here, she was not shielded from confusion about what that meant in terms of where she fit within the context of her own community.

It is also telling that this perplexity seemed to play only a minor part in Murray's reaction to what she learned. Only once did she indicate any of the confusion that was so commonplace among the other writers dealt with here. Toward the end of her memoir, as she discussed her early childhood exposure to Jim Crow, Murray finally vented her personal frustrations with these sorts of categorization. "The tide of color beat upon me ceaselessly, relentlessly," she wrote.

"Always the same tune, played like a broken record, robbing one of personal identity. Always the shifting sands of color so that there was no solid ground under one's feet. . . . Two shades lighter! Two shades darker! Dead white! Coal black! High yaller! Mariney! Good hair! Bad hair! Stringy hair! Nappy hair!" Her diatribe continued as she vented about the value system that so confused and disgusted her:

> To hear people talk, color, features and hair were the most important things to know about a person, a yardstick by which everyone measured everybody else. From the looks of my family I could never tell where whites folks left off and colored folks began, but it made little difference as far as I was concerned. In a world of black-white opposites, I had no place. Being neither very dark nor very fair, I was a nobody without an identity. I was too dark at home and too light at school.[41]

While noting the presence of "White" and "Colored" signs throughout Durham and recognizing that segregation was rigidly enforced, Pauli nevertheless found the combination of white and black identities "very natural." "Before I was old enough to understand the full meaning of segregation," she wrote, "I knew there was something woefully wrong about those signs, since there could not possibly be anything wrong with my Fitzgerald grandparents." She admitted that she knew little of her African ancestry, most of which was "shrouded in shame," and she acknowledged how much more useful her Irish heritage proved to her sense of self. "It strengthened the growing shell [a term also used by Green and Wright] of pride used to protect the soft underbelly and wobbly legs of a creature learning slowly to navigate in a cruelly segregated world," Murray explained. "But more than anything else then, it kept me from acceptance of my lot. I would always be trying to break out of the rigid mold into which I was being forced."[42] Few African American writers who came of age during the Jim Crow era, not even the Delany sisters, were more shielded from the abuses and restrictions of segregation than was Pauli Murray, and it is obvious that it was the pride instilled in her by her extraordinary grandparents that insulated her — at least in her memories — from those realities.

Perhaps the only other writer besides Murray to articulate as effectively the personal struggle of coming to terms with mixed-race parentage is Essie Mae Washington-Williams. While wrestling with similar issues of identity and place in a later generation, her story is rendered all the more compelling by the secrecy, confusion, and ambivalence that defined her relationship with her father, Strom Thurmond, for more than half a century. In the opening sentence of her 2005 memoir, ironically titled *Dear Senator*, Washington-Williams states simply, "I always thought I had a fairly normal childhood, until I found out my parents weren't who I thought they were."[43]

She writes with great candor about the strange circumstances by which she discovered, in 1938 at the age of thirteen, who her real mother was; she had always thought that her mother's sister, who had raised her in Pennsylvania, was her mother, and she was shocked and confused when introduced to her real mother, who told her she had given birth to Essie at age sixteen in South Carolina. No mention was made as to who her real father was. That revelation — which came three years later — proved to be far more dramatic and life-changing for Essie. She traveled with her mother to Edgefield, South Carolina — her first time in the South — to be introduced to the maternal branch of her family. While there, her mother took her downtown to a law office, where with no preparation she was introduced to a middle-aged judge, Strom Thurmond, and told that he was her father. Only then did she also learn that her father was white.[44]

At both an emotional and intellectual level, Washington-Williams struggled to come to terms with this revelation and its implications for her life. Complicating this struggle was the ideological stance not only of Thurmond, whom she came to admire, even love, through the occasional, always covert, meetings she had with him over the next fifty years, but also the fact that her grandfather, Will Thurmond, was the chief advisor of the even more rabid racist, Ben Tillman. "How," she asked her mother, "could the son of this architect of white supremacy fall in love with my mother, a black woman?" Her mother merely shrugged, suggesting that love is colorblind and that "all that hate talk is just politics." Much of what makes Washington-Williams's story so effective is that she so carefully articulates the range of feelings brought on by the new identity so suddenly imposed upon her:

> Once something like the facts of your birth get into your head, you never can be the same again. In my darkest hours I began to look at all black people as victims and white people as oppressors, and everything in America struck me as grossly unfair. In my brightest hours, I began to look at myself as someone very special, an amalgam of all that was great about America. I had a brilliant white father and

a beautiful black mother; was I not a golden child? Alas, the real Essie Mae fell somewhere between these two poles. I was too humble to be conceited, too meek to be a firebrand. My mantra was "accept," and accept I did, at least outwardly. Yet inside me was pure turbulence.[45]

As Strom Thurmond became increasingly prominent in state and then national politics as a stalwart of white supremacy, culminating in his presidential bid as a Dixiecrat in 1948, his daughter became more perplexed and frustrated with the contradictions of her own relationship with him and her mother. On more than one occasion, Essie Mae echoed the sentiments of Walter White and the conscious decision he claimed in rejecting his white heritage as he became exposed to its hate-filled racism. She expressed relief that he "had disappeared from my life as quickly as he had entered it. For a moment, I had begun to think of myself as white or at least partly white. If the Tillman-Thurmond axis was the source of my whiteness, I didn't want a drop of it."[46]

An incident in 1950 summed up the burden all parts of her identity imposed on her. She had moved with her husband to Savannah, where she complained about what she saw as the complacency of the city's black community, which occasionally provoked her to break out of character and take action. "I was usually very self-effacing," she wrote.

> First I was a woman, who wanted to be a lady, and ladies weren't loud, or that hated word used by whites, "uppity." Second, I was black, or at least assigned to that category, so I felt second class and hence not entitled to speak my piece. Third, I was illegitimate and harbored a shame over my birth that stifled me, despite the fact that I knew it wasn't my fault. Finally, I had had a big secret to keep, as the illegitimate daughter of a famous white supremacist. I was under a lifetime gag order.

All this was prelude to a Rosa Parks-like gesture she made on a Savannah bus that year. Though no whites were on the bus, the back section, behind the "color line," was full, and rather than stand she "plopped down" on the last row of the white section. When confronted by the driver, who insisted she either move back or get off the bus, shouting repeatedly the words "White Only" to her, she was tempted to divulge her secret: "I wanted to tell him my father ran for president on the "whites only" ticket." But instead she sought to muster his sympathy by merely stating that she was pregnant. It didn't work, and even though he continued to press her to leave the bus, she wore him down. "He finally spat,

'You damn . . . woman,' and skulked back to his seat. I stayed in mine. The other blacks looked at me as if I were Mahatma Gandhi."[47]

Perhaps what makes Washington-Williams's story most remarkable is how she ultimately came to terms with both halves of her multiracial heritage and all that that implies. In her late seventies, after her father's death in 2003 at age one hundred and the Thurmond family's much belated public acknowledgment of her existence a year later, she at long last makes peace with her tangled roots. She wrote, "In a way, my life began when I was seventy-eight; at least my life as who I really was. . . . I had lived my life as an African-American. Now things had changed. Not that I wanted to live the rest of my life as a white person. I wanted to live out my life as an American, with all the delicious complexity that term has come to imply." She applied for membership in both the DAR and the UDC, and insisted that she had as much to offer them as they had to offer her. Almost defiantly, she ends her memoir with a frank assessment of the contradictions inherent in her genealogical makeup:

> I was a slave and I was a master; I was black and I was white; I was a Roosevelt
> progressive and I was a Dixiecrat; I was for Kennedy and I was for Nixon; I was
> a glorious president of the South and I was a lowly maid in Edgefield. Above all,
> I transcended all these internal contradictions to become a real person, my own
> person, a simple person who loves America as the wonderful place that has al-
> lowed me to discover, and to be, exactly who I am.[48]

Of course, this declaration stands in great contrast to the stance of any of the other authors considered here (except maybe Pauli Murray). It is the only memoir that extends not only well past the civil rights movement, but well into the twenty-first century, and even for a woman now in her eighties, it speaks to a confidence in both herself and the America in which she now lives that is not apparent in the revelations and aspirations of those autobiographers who preceded her.

Historian Barbara Fields has warned us as historians against according race "a transhistorical, almost metaphysical status that removes it from all possibility of analysis and understanding." "Ideas about color," she insists, "like ideas about anything else, derive their importance, indeed their very definition, from their context."[49] Nothing demonstrates as fully as these personal testimonials the extent to which that context was first established within the bounds of family and household. It was there that children and adolescents first faced the often perplexing evidence of racial variables, ambiguities, and contradictions. How secure parents or grandparents were with their own racial identities and ancestries had much to do with how willing and able they were to enlighten their children as to the mysteries of race and of their place within the hierarchical and prejudiced southern society in which they would come of age. Sooner or later, all of these writers would come to see themselves, at least in part, in terms articulated by Pauli Murray: "the product of a slowly evolving process of biological and cultural integration . . . a New World experiment, fragile yet tenacious, a possible hint of a stronger and freer America of the future, no longer stunted in its growth by an insidious ethnocentrism."[50]

In his book, *Forbidden Love*, Gary Nash describes "a past in which powerful Americans passed laws, spun scientific theories, judged court cases, wrote tracts . . . and preached the belief that every person has one and only one race and that walls must be built to prevent intimacy, love and marriage between people who supposedly belong to different races." While that book, subtitled *The Secret History of Mixed-Race America*, celebrates what he calls "a long line of rebels and idealists who have defied the racial code devised to keep people apart" — those he calls "insistent boundary patrollers and daring boundary crossers" — neither Nash nor most modern scholars of the subject deal with the product of their courage and determination: the children and grandchildren of interracial unions who had to pay a different sort of price, psychologically and socially, for the convergent gene pools that defined them.[51]

The stories of these offspring are fully as varied and complicated as the stories of their boundary-crossing elders; but they are stories told in different ways and for different purposes. More often than not they were told in the first person — from the mature perspectives and memories of adulthood looking back on childhood and adolescent experiences that shaped their sense of self and of the South. The very process of recreating these childhood experiences and feelings in writing can be seen as the ultimate resolution of these many writers' quest to "learn who and what they were"; in some cases the effects of providing poignant accounts of those quests proved liberating. Again to make Pauli Murray a spokesperson for them all, she said that it took her a lifetime "to discover that true emancipation lies in the acceptance of the whole past, in deriving strength from all my roots, in facing up to the degradation as well as the dignity of my ancestors." Like her, each of these men and women as boys and girls "had to embrace *all* the tangled roots from which [they] had sprung, to accept without evasion their own heritages, with all their ambivalences and paradoxes."[52]

Yet most did so in writing only. An equally significant facet of their stories is that, for most, the reality of being half black and half white had relatively little impact on the course of their lives or the ways in which they lived them. If Pauli Murray's and Essie Mae Washington-Williams's quests to come to terms with their multiracial genealogies provided them with a much-sought and ultimately achieved inner peace, and if they could celebrate — through their writings at least — the dual heritages to which they laid claim, they continued to live their lives as part of black families and black communities, and neither ever suggests that she could have done otherwise.

Only a few of the writers considered here seem to have utilized or tangibly benefited from their mixed-race identities — or more precisely, their white blood — in any substantive, or life-altering, ways. Ellen Craft was able to escape from Georgia by train and steamship because she could disguise herself as a white man. Walter White, as executive secretary of the NAACP, infiltrated local Ku Klux Klan chapters on a number of occasions to investigate lynchings and other instances of racial violence perpetrated in the 1930s and 1940s. And Pauli Murray, in her campaign for admission to the graduate program in sociology at the University of North Carolina in the late 1930s, used her Smith ancestry — the fact that her great-great-grandfather had served on its board of trustees a century earlier — in making her case (though to no avail).[53]

More prevalent among these autobiographers and their families, and perhaps more striking, are those who consciously downplayed their lightness for fear of alienation from the black community within which their identities and status more firmly rested. Several were quite explicit about the fact that they fully embraced African American identities, in the process giving up privileges or conveniences that they might have enjoyed by embracing their white halves as fully as they did their black. Joel Williamson found this quite a striking phenomenon, and one unique to America's racial culture. Only here, he noted, "do we still live with the paradox that white is black. Occasionally people who are visibly white declare themselves black, and millions of Americans who are more European than African in their heritage insist, sometimes defiantly, upon their blackness."[54]

So it was for Raymond Andrews, who wrote that his father was embarrassed by his light skin and seemed to favor his darker skinned children as a demonstration that he saw no advantage or superiority in skin tone. The Delanys too insisted that they always took pride in their black identities. (They never cared for the term "African American.") Bessie Delany acknowledged that "among some Negroes . . . to be lighter-skinned was more desirable. We saw in our own family that people treated the lighter-skinned children better." But, she insisted, "it was not something that was even *discussed* in our household. We were different shades, and it didn't make a bit of difference to us. It didn't matter if you were white, black, grizzly, or gray, you were *you*."[55]

On the other hand, some blacks much resented the fact that lighter-skinned blacks saw themselves as superior to those with darker skins. Ruby Goodwin, who wrote of growing up African American in the Midwest in the 1920s, recounted her father's resentment of blacks' own proclivities in terms of skin color. "I look at some of our folks," he told his daughter. "They want to be white so bad they can taste it. They think 'cause they're light brown or yellow, they're better than dark people. They ain't. They ain't as good. We're the only people I know who are proud of being black."[56] And Anne Moody resented her treatment by her father's second wife and her family, who looked down on her mother for "no reason other than the fact that she was a couple of shades darker than the other members of their family. Yet they were Negroes and we were also Negroes. I just didn't see Negroes hating each other so much."[57]

No one addresses those tensions more frankly than Pauli Murray. In one of several extended discussions of racial identity in *Proud Shoes*, she declared that "the sliding scale of color bedeviled everyone, irrespective of where one stood on the color chart." This was especially true within the bonds of family. When people had the same parents and the proportion of white blood was not a factor," she insisted, "gradation of color and features determined prestige within the family. Of these complexion had the greatest single value. Seldom was there a greater struggle for supremacy than among sisters and brothers who knew all the subtleties of caste. The wider the variation among them the more bitter the struggle." She claimed that many black families split over these differences, and she concluded that "a white skin has been a cruel weapon in the world at large but infinitely more cruel in the intimacy of family relationships."[58]

Never have such issues proved as timely or as relevant perhaps as the United States has reached an even more liberating turning point — the election of a president whose mother was white and whose father was Kenyan (and whose own memoir, incidentally, Charlayne Hunter-Gault has called "one of the most powerful books of self-discovery I've ever read"). There is nothing southern in Barak Obama's roots — his mother was a Kansan, and he was raised in Indonesia and Hawaii, certainly the most multiracial and multiethnic of American states, and yet there's much in his search for identity that echoes those of southerners in this earlier era. In *Dreams of My Father*, Obama wrote of the term miscegenation: "The word is humpbacked, ugly, portending a monstrous outcome: like *antebellum* and *octoroon*, it evokes images of another era, a distant world of horsewhips and flames, dead magnolias and crumbling porticos." It was only in 1967, he notes, when he was six years old, that Virginia's statute against interracial marriage was struck down by the Supreme Court. When his parents were married in 1960, "*miscegenation* was still described as a felony in over half the states of the Union."[59]

Yet as with most autobiographical works, it is not the straight history lessons but rather his personal testimonial that heightens our awareness of these realities. More than anyone else has done, indeed could do, President Obama has raised to new levels of sophistication and nuance the many ways and means through which he came to terms with not only his mixed-race identity, but also the multiple nations and cultures that shaped — and often confused and confounded — his sense of himself and of those who made him. In what must be one of the most remarkable speeches ever made during a presidential campaign — indeed, one of most open and personal speeches ever made by a politician anytime or anywhere — Obama addressed the issue head-on in the televised address he gave on race from Philadelphia in March 2008. After explaining his own parentage, he moved on to the racial heritage of his family, stating: "I am married to a black American who carries within her the blood of slaves and slaveowners — an inheritance we pass on to our two precious daughters. I have brothers, sisters, nieces, nephews, uncles and cousins, of every race and every hue, scattered across three continents, and for as long as I live, I will never forget that in no other country on Earth is my story even possible."[60]

In one of the more striking, and most discussed, passages in the speech, Obama illustrated the contradictions and conundrums that we have seen so often in southern experiences within mixed-race families. In dealing with his relationship with the controversial Rev. Wright, he stated that "I can no more disown him than I can my white grandmother — a woman who helped raise me, a woman who sacrificed again and again for me, a woman who loves me as much as she loves anything in this world, but a woman who once confessed her fear of black men who passed by her on the street, and who on more than one occasion has uttered racial or ethnic stereotypes that made me cringe."[61]

Colbert King was one of numerous journalists and commentators who, as part of the extensive media coverage of Strom Thurmond's black daughter when that story was revealed in 2003, noted that "as riveting as [it] may be to those hearing it for the first time, it is by no means unique. There are in America today thousands of stories just like hers."[62] If Americans didn't buy that in 2003, they certainly had to do so five years later, with a prime time speech by a man telling his own multiracial story as part of his bid to become the next president.

In a much earlier version of this essay, I wrote that "these stories are not as distant or remote as we — and certainly our students — seem to think." In the Obama era, we have of course been made even more aware of the relevance of these issues and should appreciate all the more the social context and historical legacy that makes our president's story far from unique by examining the life stories of so many others who either endured or celebrated their mixed racial heritage. As Joel Williamson has reminded us in *New People*, "the mixing of peoples of different colors and features that occurred in America was, of course, but a continuum of a process that is practically as old as human history," and that when we speak of it in America, "we are in actuality speaking relatively."[63]

If most of these autobiographers ultimately came to terms with their racial identities — and may even have used their life narratives as their means of so doing — the range of feelings and expressions of confusion they convey, often quite eloquently, tell us much about the times in which they came of age. Their stories speak to both the rigidity and the flexibility of the "color line" before, during, and well after the Jim Crow era. While we live in a very different era, we are all the richer for these testimonials and intimate revelations of how these individuals coped with — and, most would probably say, triumphed over — the many legal, social, and psychological challenges associated with their mixed-race parentage.

CHAPTER THREE

"All Manner of Defeated, Shiftless, Shifty, Pathetic and Interesting Good People"

Autobiographical Encounters with Southern White Poverty

IN *A TIDEWATER MORNING: Three Tales from Youth*, his fictionalized memoir of growing up in eastern Virginia in the 1930s, William Styron wrote of his boyhood fascination with the Dabneys, a poor family who lived nearby and with whom he spent a great deal of time as a ten-year-old. They lived in a "rambling weatherworn house that lacked a lawn. . . . On the grassless, graceless terrain of the front yard was a random litter of eviscerated Frigidaires, electric generators, stoves, and the remains of two or three ancient automobiles, whose scavenged carcasses lay abandoned beneath sycamores like huge rusted insects."[1]

The young Styron had found a ready playmate in the youngest of the Dabney children, a boy named Little Mole, who "had never been known to use Lifebuoy soap, or any other cleansing agent." But Styron's real fascination lay in the patriarch of the Dabney clan. While Vernon Dabney dealt in junk and auto parts, his true calling was producing bootleg whiskey. The Dabneys had not always been poor. Theirs was once a name associated with such FFVs (First Families of Virginia) as the Randolphs, Tuckers, Peytons, and Lees, but due to the unfortunate marriage of his father to a "half-breed Mattaponi or Pamunkey Indian girl from the York River," the family had "long ago slid down the social ladder" and the Dabney name "had lost almost all of its luster."[2]

Styron provides a portrait of the Dabneys that is at once both comic and poignant, as is the story in which they figure so prominently. It centers on the predicament they faced with the arrival, in 1935, of an ancient black man named Shadrach, who walked from Alabama back to Virginia because he considered himself a Dabney who wanted to die and be buried on the Dabney ground from which he had been sold away in 1850. Despite the hardships — financial and otherwise — that Shadrach's interment imposed on the Dabneys, their dynastic sense of *noblesse oblige* somehow rose to the surface and they made it their mission to "oversee his swiftly approaching departure, laying him to rest in the earth of their mutual ancestors." Vernon Dabney was not, Styron insisted, "an ill-spirited or ungenerous man (despite his runaway temper)." But he was a "soul beset by many woes in the dingy threadbare year 1935, being hard pressed not merely for dollars but for dimes and quarters, crushed beneath an elephantine and inebriate wife, along with three generally shiftless sons and two knocked-up daughters, plus two more likely to be so." Yet with Shadrach's appearance in Mr. Dabney's yard, Styron writes, "I saw him gaze down at the leathery old dying black face with an expression that mingled compassion and bewilderment and stopped up rage and desperation, and then whisper to himself: 'He wants to die on Dabney ground. Well, kiss my ass, just kiss my ass!'"[3]

What makes Styron's depiction of southern poverty so distinctive is how appealing a lifestyle it represented to the young boy. "Oh, how I loved the Dabneys!" he writes in the voice of youthful innocence:

I actually wanted to *be* a Dabney — wanted to change my name from Paul Whitehurst to Paul Dabney. I visited the Dabney homestead as often as I could, basking in its casual squalor. . . . The mother, named Trixie, was a huge sweaty generous sugarloaf of a woman, often drunk. It was she, I am sure, who propagated the domestic sloppiness. But I loved her passionately, just as I loved and envied the whole Dabney tribe and that total absence in them of the bourgeois aspirations and gentility which were my own inheritance. I envied the sheer teeming multitude of the Dabneys — there were seven of them — which made my status as an only child seem so effete, spoiled, and lonesome. Only illicit whiskey kept the family from complete destitution, and I envied their near poverty.

Much of the appeal of being a Dabney lay in the perfectly normal sensibilities of a ten-year-old boy. "They were Baptists," he wrote. "As a Presbyterian, I envied that. To be totally immersed — how wet and natural! They lived in a house devoid of books or any reading matter except funny papers — more envy.

I envied their abandoned slovenliness, their sour unmade beds, their roaches, the cracked linoleum on the floor, the homely cur dogs leprous with mange that foraged at will through house and yard." Styron concluded: "My perverse longings were — to turn around a phrase unknown at the time — downwardly mobile. Afflicted at the age of ten by *nostalgia de la boue*, I felt deprived of a certain depravity."[4]

In recreating a ten-year-old's perspective, Styron's youthful persona takes the Dabney's slovenly lifestyle in stride; there's no epiphany, no shock, no guilt or shame apparent in his matter-of-fact description of their squalor. As we've seen, it's quite the opposite — he revels in it. In some respects, the Dabneys serve as comic counterpoints to the real emotional and moral heart of the story: the experience of this hundred-year-old former slave and the meaning of his return home to die.

★ ★ ★

Styron's youthful exposure to poverty was not unique. A number of middle-class southern whites who came of age in the first half of the twentieth century also wrote vividly and poignantly about the circumstances in which they discovered the socioeconomic differences in their own comfortable lives and those of less fortunate neighbors. Some, like Styron, were intrigued by this class of people from whom they had either physically or intellectually been insulated until adolescence. But unlike Styron, few others found either the comic dimensions or the personal appeal in the circumstances that accompanied such material deprivation; certainly no others yearned for their own "downward mobility" in order to enjoy such desolation firsthand. Yet like Styron, for whom the Dabneys provide a mere framework for the more significant story of Shadrach, other writers did tie their awareness of and sympathy for poor whites to similar discoveries relating to race.

Among the unique features of autobiographical work as a historical genre is that it is one of the few in which childhood and adolescent experience holds so much sway, and its fascination for us often lies in how young people discover the world around them and begin to assess not only their place in it, but also the value system reflected by societal structure and tradition. For obvious reasons race is the most pervasive of those issues which southerners — white as well as black — had to confront and come to terms with.[5] In his second major book on southern autobiography, *But Now I See*, Fred Hobson narrows his focus to what he calls "racial conversion narratives," those works by southern whites who at some point in their lives — often during their adolescence — change their minds about what it meant to be white and what it meant to be black in the South.[6] They were compelled to explain such revelations in part to repent of past racist sins — their own or their families'. In so doing, the very telling of their stories became acts of contrition and moral indictments of the society in which those personal and communal sins were grounded.

For a few of these writers, especially those who came of age in the first part of the twentieth century, their "racial conversions" were preceded or accompanied by the discovery that race was not the only factor that divided their society. Through a variety of circumstances, these young southerners were exposed for the first time to poor whites. The impact that discovery had on them — either at the time or later in their lives — was considerable, and along with their new perspectives on the plight of African Americans in their midst, discovering the poor of their own race made them see themselves and their region in very different terms.

★ ★ ★

Because most other writers were more advanced in their adolescence than the ten-year-old Styron, their contacts with fellow southerners of a lower class were imbued with far more social consciousness. Katharine Du Pre Lumpkin's *The Making of a Southerner*, published in 1946, was among the first and most definitive of these racial conversion narratives; it is also perhaps the best example of how the discovery of poor whites served as the beginning of the transformative experience that would lead to racial enlightenment. Though not as drastically as the Dabneys, the Lumpkins too had once been among the planter elite who experienced considerable "downward mobility" — in their case, as a result of the Civil War and its ruinous economic aftereffects. Katharine grew up in Macon, Georgia, but was immersed in the rural, plantation heritage of her antebellum lineage — her grandparents' plantation, their slaves, and her father's wartime experience in the Confederate army. Referring to herself as "a child of the Lost Cause," Lumpkin never had any reason to question the natural order of the hierarchical social structure of which her family formed the apex until hard times forced her father to leave Macon and purchase a modest farm in rural South Carolina, soon after which he died.

In a chapter titled "Sojourn in the Sand Hills," Lumpkin explained that their farm did not actually lie in "the real Sand Hills," but was "very close to this desolate area, so much so that one could almost believe that the winds of heaven had drifted some of the sand across the border line into our woods and fields — and some of the inhabitants too . . . with their pasty faces, scrawny necks, angular ill-nourished frames, straw-like hair."[7] Most of the farmers around them were, Lumpkin noted, white and landowners — but owners "in name only; the heavy mortgages they carried were ever a threat to their tenure. Most had few acres and very poor little dwellings. A few more were renters, and some were croppers who had nothing, not even a mule or plow."[8] She recounted her sobering impressions of the field hands — more black than white — who were hired to work her family's two hundred acres of cotton, and she noted these "somber strangers coming and going . . . who seemed like people carrying some kind of burden with which they were preoccupied."[9]

But it was in a classroom that Lumpkin most closely observed this new class of southern whites and came to realize just how different their lives and experiences were from her own. As a fifteen-year-old student at the local school, she became painfully aware of the variety of ways in which her classmates' lower socioeconomic circumstances contrasted with her own. "There was everything," she wrote, "to keep us separate and hardly anything to bridge the gap save our common childhood." She described in detail their clothing, their lunches, their manners (characterized by reticence and lethargy), their limited knowledge, and even their language. "I was a city child and talked like one," Lumpkin explained. She bemoaned the fact that she couldn't adopt their speech patterns and vocabulary, if only because of how "hard they would stare at me when I talked, as though I were some kind of foreigner, as indeed they regarded me; and worse, as though I were 'putting on airs.'"[10]

Katharine was not alone in the advantages she held over most of her classmates. The daughters of the one other relatively affluent landowner in the area were also in the class, and it disturbed Katharine that they seemed to flaunt their superior knowledge and smugly answer questions that their classmates couldn't. Such "airs" by her social peers only added to her self-consciousness. "It was as though I had a pre-arranged advantage in a race which made me always win," she wrote. "I longed to hide what I knew if thereby I might escape from always having the better of them. I felt unfair and that they would think me so."[11]

These observations of her superior background, material circumstances, and breeding were to Lumpkin "new sensations." "As a city-bred child little of destitution had passed before my protected eyes, or at least it had not impressed me. Seeing any poverty, I no doubt accepted our spiritual lesson to explain it: 'The poor ye always have with you.' This would account for the poor whites among us. Negro poverty I would have taken even more for granted."[12]

If it was this experience through which Lumpkin discovered and came to sympathize with the plight of white victims of rural poverty, it would take a return to Georgia as a college student to introduce her to the effects of Jim Crow and its victimization of southern blacks. That process proved to be a more gradual and ultimately far more significant one in terms of her future activism and writings. Yet as she herself acknowledged at the end of her memoir, the white destitution and deprivation of the South Carolina sand hills was a crucial prerequisite to her conversion experience.

☆ ☆ ☆

No southerner chronicled southern poverty to greater effect than did Erskine Caldwell. The publication of *Tobacco Road* and *God's Little Acre* in the early 1930s, along with their subsequent stage and screen adaptations, conveyed to a vast American public the plight of rural white Georgians as deprived and depraved victims of both an agricultural system that had run its course and the exploitative trap of the cotton mills that provided yet another form of economic victimization for those who saw it as their only viable recourse. Among the most prolific of southern writers, Caldwell's massive body of work includes two autobiographies: one in 1951 (*Call It Experience*), the other in 1987 (*With All My Might*). In both, he revealed his own initial exposure to the poor in whose midst he lived.

The son of a Presbyterian minister, Caldwell moved several times with his family across Georgia and the Southeast. In 1918, when Erskine was fifteen years old, the family moved from western Tennessee to Wrens, a small town in eastern Georgia a few miles southwest of Augusta (and only a couple of counties away from the ancestral homeland in Oglethorpe County that Katharine Lumpkin described so fully in her autobiography). It was there that he first observed the rural poor around whom he would later construct his most famous novels. Although Wrens was situated amid what was still fertile cotton-growing farmland, Caldwell noted that it was not far from "the barren sand hills and depleted soil of the tobacco lands between Wrens and Augusta." He saw its unfortunate inhabitants both in Wrens and in traveling through the surrounding countryside and described them in his second autobiography: "The impoverished people from the sand hills and tobacco roads, hungry and ragged, were frequently in town begging from house to house for handouts of food and clothing and a little money with which to buy cure-all medicine. There always seemed to be one or more feebly crying, sickly looking babes in arms among the begging families."[13] In his 1951 memoir, he wrote of traveling through the country, first with his father as he made his ministerial visitations, and later with both a local doctor and the county tax assessor. There he saw many of the same people — tenants and sharecroppers — in their own homes and on the very land that victimized them. "Most of the landowners lived in comparative comfort in the nearby towns of Waynesboro, Louisville, and Wrens, while in the country itself there was poverty on all sides, the only apparent variation being in the degree of it."[14]

Caldwell's teenage consciousness of the plight of these poor farmers seems primarily based on his parents' contrasting reactions to them. "The most persistent mendicants," he wrote, "had perfected the technique of sitting on the doorsteps of a house and, for hours at a time, alternating knocking loudly and moaning in a distressed voice to gain the sympathy of a householder." The Caldwell manse was among those on whose steps these so-called "Weepers" planted themselves, and their presence soon became so constant that Erskine's mother quickly lost any sympathy for them. Her son recalled that she "became so provoked that she jabbed the tufted end of a broom at a small group of Weepers who had remained on our porch and continued their pathetic moaning long after my father had given them a large sack of sweet potatoes and several cans of pork and beans." Concerned with their own marginal financial status, Mrs. Caldwell insisted that she felt sorry for the Weepers, but that "there's got to be a limit to how kindhearted we can be at this house." [15]

His father extended his outreach to the needy well beyond his front porch. In his earlier memoir, Caldwell stated, "I do not remember a single occasion when my father was not asked for food during our trips into the country. He made it a habit, even when my mother said that there was none too much for the three of us, always to carry a sack of potatoes or flour and a bag of grits or black-eyed peas in the car with him wherever he went." Erskine's portrayal of his mother's beneficence was somewhat softer than it would be later. He ended this memory by noting that she "more often than not added a small bag of candy for the old people and children."[16]

There is little sense of revelation, inspiration, or even compassion in these descriptions; Caldwell wrote nonjudgmentally of his mother and father's differing responses to the poor around them (and in two different books). He made little effort to link these early impressions with the vivid personal portraits and bleak lifestyle he would create in his fiction. It was only in returning to the region years later that he found the inspiration to portray what he observed in his writing. After stints at writing short stories and screenplays while living in Maine and California, he wrote in his 1951 memoir, "I felt that I would never be able to write successfully about other people in other places until first I had written the story of the landless and poverty-stricken families living on East Georgia sand hills and tobacco roads." He returned to his parents' home in Wrens in 1930 and began retraveling the country roads he had ridden over so often as a teen. "It was not a pleasant sight," he stated, "more dispiriting to look upon now than it had been several years before."[17]

At last, Caldwell conveyed some real feeling as to what he saw and how it inspired him. "Day after day I went into the country," he wrote, "becoming more and more depressed by what I saw as I traveled farther and farther from settlements and highways. I could not become accustomed to the sight of children's stomachs bloated from hunger and seeing the ill and aged too weak to walk to the fields to search for something to eat." Back home in the evenings, he made notes on what he had seen, but he remained frustrated. "Nothing I had put down on paper succeeded in conveying the full meaning of poverty and hopelessness and degradation as I had observed it. The more I traveled through [these] counties, the less satisfied I became with what I wrote."[18]

Just as it had taken a return to Georgia to fully conceptualize the depths of poverty among those who would become his literary subjects, Caldwell decided that only with distance from them could he do them justice. So he moved to New York, where he began work on his greatest successes — *Tobacco Road* in 1932 and *God's Little Acre* a year later. The physical distance he put between himself and his Georgia characters seemed to restore the emotional detachment of his adolescent years.[19] The unsympathetic and even grotesquely comedic portraits of Jeeter Lester and Ty Ty Walden and their families fully captured the futile, hand-to-mouth existences Caldwell had observed firsthand, but strikingly absent from either novel is any sense of the compassion or sympathy with which he had claimed to view their real-life counterparts just before he began fictionalizing them.

☆ ☆ ☆

Lillian Smith emerged as the white South's most outspoken racial conscience during the 1940s and 1950s, but despite several autobiographical works — most notably, *Killers of the Dream*, first published in 1949 — she was far more evasive about the childhood or adolescent roots of the remarkably strong convictions that drove her diatribes, both fictional and nonfictional, on southern racism and class exploitation. She provided only a few tantalizing anecdotes of early experiences that shaped her sensibilities regarding her region's racism and poverty. More in private correspondence than in her autobiographical writings, Smith recalled her unusual powers of observation and empathy toward those around her. "I could walk into a room (at age 9 or 10)," she later confided in a letter, "and feel almost instantly how each person in that room was feeling." She claimed to have been "almost overcome, sometimes, by my vicarious 'suffering.'"[20]

As with Katharine Lumpkin, a move by her family prompted Smith's raised consciousness of southern poverty. In 1915, the year in which she graduated from high school, the Smiths hit hard times when her father lost his business. They moved from Jasper, a small mill town in northern Florida, to Clayton, in the Blue Ridge Mountains of northeast Georgia, where Calvin Smith opened a hotel and, soon thereafter, a summer camp for girls. There Lillian discovered the desolation of rural mountain life and was shocked by the hand-to-mouth existence, ignorance, and lack of initiative or spirit among the highlanders she observed. In moving to Baltimore to study music at the Peabody Conservatory two years later, she was exposed to the urban poor as well, and learned much about "slums, poverty, factories — much I had known nothing about."[21] Curiously, neither mountain whites nor urban industrial workers ever became central to the indignation Smith mustered in her later condemnations of the South's social and economic inequities.

It was an incident soon after the Smiths' move to Clayton, having nothing to do with poor mountaineers, that serves as the most revealing example of Lillian Smith's awakening to the outcasts in southern society. In one of her few flights of nostalgia, she reminisced in a *Life* magazine essay in December 1961 about early Christmases and described a remarkable act of generosity by her father that made one such holiday memorable. As he and his family struggled to make ends meet in what she called "our year of austerity," Calvin Smith invited a chain gang to have Christmas dinner with the family. Disturbed after having encountered the convicts in the shabby railroad cars in which they lived while assigned to state road work in the area, he came home and declared to his wife that "there's more misery in the world than even I know; and a lot of it unnecessary." He then proposed the Christmas visit, and Mrs. Smith reluctantly agreed.[22]

At noon on Christmas Day, the Smiths watched forty-eight men in stripes, both white and black, along with their guards, heading toward their house. According to his admiring daughter, Calvin "moved among them with grace and ease" and broke the early awkward moments with a warm welcome. The "wonderful absurdity" of the situation soon had them "all laughing and muttering Merry Christmas, half deriding, half meaning it." Three of the guests — a killer, a rapist, and a bank robber — pitched in to put the meal on the table, Lillian notes wryly. "My sister and I served the plates. The murderer and his two friends passed them to the men. Afterward, the rapist and two bank robbers and the arsonist said they'd be real pleased to wash up the dishes."[23]

While this story comes across as more of an amusing anecdote than is typical of Smith's writing, it is a tale with a moral. When the chain gang left after a satisfying visit for all concerned, Calvin gathered his family around him as "the old look of having something to say to his children settled across his face." He began his lecture: "We've been through some pretty hard times, lately, and I've been proud of my family. Some folks can take prosperity and can't take poverty; some can take being poor and lose their heads when money comes. I want my children to accept it all: the good and the bad, for that is what life is." He went on to talk about their recent guests, reminding his children that they were merely men who had made mistakes, as they all would at some point in their lives. "Never look down on a man," he told them. "Never. If you can't look him straight in the eye, then what's wrong is with you?"[24]

Despite this sermon with which Smith closes her story, it is obvious that she has told it more as a tribute to her father than as a transformative moment in her own views. Like Erskine Caldwell's father, Calvin Smith was key to Lillian's sensitivity toward poor whites. But despite the fact that the chain gang he invited into his home included both black and white men, she indicated elsewhere that there were limits to his humanitarianism. In *Killers of the Dream*, she wrote in far more critical terms of her parents' hypocrisy when it came to race. "The father who rebuked me for an air of superiority toward schoolmates from the mill and rounded out his rebuke by gravely reminding me that 'all men are brothers,' trained me in the steel-rigid decorums I must demand of every colored male." As with so much of Smith's commentary, this was an indictment not only of her parents but of southern society in general. "They who taught me to split my body from my mind and both from my 'soul,'" she concluded, "also taught me to split my conscience from my acts and Christianity from southern tradition."[25]

The plight of poor whites never inspired the sympathy or the rage in Smith's adult social conscience to the extent that racism did. This was true of others as well — though it is curious that Smith never chronicled nearly so definitive a turning point in the creation of her racial consciousness as she did with this minor, nostalgic holiday anecdote on a lesson taught about the poor.[26]

★ ★ ★

Jimmy Carter came of age on a peanut and cotton farm in southwest Georgia in the 1930s, and he wrote a meticulously detailed account of those years in his 2001 memoir, *An Hour before Daylight* (the title is a reference to when the work day began for almost everyone involved in farm labor — men, women, and children, farm owners as well as their tenants and sharecroppers). Carter's memoir is very much centered on race relations, if only because so many of his earliest acquaintances were African Americans, including a playmate his own age, with whom he spent far more time — and had far fonder memories — than he did with his siblings or white comrades.

If only indirectly, Carter's memoir serves as an explanation for his politics; his human rights agenda and sense of social justice have obvious roots in the experiences of his childhood and the people — black and white, family and friends — who shaped those values. He concludes the book by stating that "my own life was shaped by a degree of personal intimacy between black and white people that is now almost completely unknown and largely forgotten." He then lists five adults other than his parents who he says most deeply affected his early life; three of those five were African American.[27]

Carter only devotes a few pages to his awareness of poor whites; he does so both as an illustration of the most tangible manifestations of the Great Depression for a young southern farm boy, and as a tribute to the generosity of his remarkable mother, Lillian Carter, a nurse who would much later in life, at the age of seventy, become a Peace Corps volunteer in India. In a chapter titled "Hard Times and Politics," Carter writes that the most common visitors to their Sumter farm during the worst years of the Depression were "tramps." Whether coming off boxcars on passing trains or moving on foot toward either Savannah or Columbus, these men traveled alone or in small groups, or occasionally with wives and children. "When Mama was home we never turned away anyone who came to our back door asking for food or a drink of water," Carter recalled. "They were invariably polite. . . . We enjoyed talking to them, and learned that many were relatively well educated and searching for jobs of any kind." They offered to do yard work or other odd jobs in return for something to eat, and Mrs. Carter always obliged them.[28]

Once when his mother mentioned to a neighboring farm wife how many tramps she had fed one week, the latter responded, "Well, I'm thankful that they never come in *my* yard." This led Mrs. Carter to ask the next vagrants who came to the Carters' door why they chose to stop at their house rather than that of their neighbors. One of them reluctantly revealed that "we have a set of symbols that we use, to show the attitude of each family along the road." Reminiscent of the underground railroad, these transients marked mail boxes for fellow travelers, and they had obviously made it apparent on the Carter's box that this was a household where they would be treated well. After these visitors had moved on, Carter states, "we went out and found some unobtrusive scratches; Mama told us not to change them."[29]

While these visitors obviously made a strong impression on young Jimmy, he admitted that, at the time, he was even more intrigued by the chain gangs that worked on roads near his farm. "We boys were fascinated with criminals and their punishment, and would observe the chained men from a distance, imagining them to be mysterious gangsters who were discussing Pretty Boy Floyd, Baby Face Nelson, Al Capone or John Dillinger." Carter pulls back from his boyhood mindset to explain the nature of the South's convict lease system, from the reasons gangs consisted of far more white than black men to the actual mechanics of their shackles and the security system that held them in place. Only at the end of that extended analysis does Carter draw again on his own memory, with a concluding anecdote in which, as with Lillian Smith, a parent brought him into more intimate contact with these prisoners. He remembered a day when his mother stopped her car near one of the road gangs. After a brief consultation with the guard on duty, she returned home and summoned Jimmy and a playmate to come to the kitchen and take a bucketful of lemonade to the men in chains. "It was quite an adventure being this close to them," Carter wrote. "We were somewhat disappointed to find that they resembled the older boys and young men who went to church with our families." Their crimes, it seemed, were thefts resulting from "abject poverty."

Like the vagrants he had come to know through his mother's beneficence, the young Carter realized that these convicts were also victims of economic forces far beyond their control. For both groups, close contact erased any sense of otherness and made him almost as empathetic as sympathetic with the plight of these transients and prisoners who were merely victims of circumstance.

Curiously, Carter sensed that his feelings for the latter group were more widely shared by others in the community. "Most folks in Archery," he concluded, "felt some sympathy for them as they swung their axes, bush hooks, mattocks, or scythes, not singing a lyrical song, as in the movies, but keeping time to a fundamental rhythm that they hummed or chanted in unison."[30]

★ ★ ★

As editor of the *Atlanta Constitution* during the civil rights movement, Ralph McGill emerged as one of the white South's most influential voices of liberalism — or at least moderation — during those critical, tension-filled years. In the midst of that era, in 1963, he published his autobiography, *The South and the Southerner*, in order to explain himself and his perspective on the region as he had known it through a lifetime of experience and observation. Like Lumpkin and Smith, McGill's exposure as a teenager to the white underclass of southern society served as a prelude to his later sensitivity to the plight of their African American counterparts.

Growing up in a suburb of Chattanooga, Tennessee, in the 1910s, McGill wrote of two summer jobs that exposed him to very different types of poor people in the vicinity. He spent one summer working as a flagman for a surveying team. Though the project on which he worked involved running a line up Signal Mountain (now itself a suburb of Chattanooga), McGill was entranced by the contrast it presented to the comfortable, suburban world he had known. He considered the job "a frontier adventure" and marveled at the "wild beauty of the wilderness through which he surveyed." In the course of that adventure, he discovered Appalachian residents as well. Moving deep into one of the creek valleys where "we felt like pioneers in the new world," the team came across what he described as "an ancient log cabin in a clearing of small fields." An old man on the porch and his daughter-in-law welcomed the crew and served them coffee. McGill was obviously fascinated by these people, and was quick to apply to them all the stereotypical assumptions he knew about "hillbillies." When told that the woman's husband was "away on a job," he said, "we imagined a still or perhaps a prison term for moonshining." Even more intriguing was the family's ancestry: "The old man told us his name was Hesse." He explained that he'd always "heared" that his great-great-grandfather had been a Hessian soldier captured by the British in the American Revolution. When the war ended, "he had made his way down to Tennessee and taken up land. The old fellow had no papers," McGill concluded. "His name was just a story handed down."[31]

For McGill, these mountain people intrigued him less for their poverty than for their primitiveness — the "otherness" of their existence; to him they represented what others have called "yesterday's people," a reference to the timelessness of their simple, premodern lifestyle. In some respects, the encounter only reaffirmed for this teenager the wilderness adventure — the sense of having suddenly discovered a frontier environment complete with frontier inhabitants — and all within easy access to the comfortable, complacent, and modern suburban world of which he was a product.

Equally fascinating but more disturbing for McGill was his discovery of the urban poor. Not only were these encounters somewhat more significant in their impact as the future journalist found himself coming to terms with the South in all its facets; it is nearly unique in terms of southern autobiography. (Only Lillian Smith and her experience in Baltimore, which she never discussed in her published work, comes to mind as another white writer who encountered poverty within a southern urban environment.) The summer before his mountain surveying adventure, at a mere fourteen-and-a-half years of age, McGill took a job collecting overdue bills for a local drug store, or as one co-worker characterized it: collecting "small, mean bills, some of them damned old and mean." In that job, McGill "learned all the mean streets and slum neighborhoods." Though he described the characters he encountered, both "weird and wonderful," he noted that "the poverty and squalor about some of the mills and ironworks were a shock. I had seen coal-miners' poverty in Soddy, Tennessee, but this was worse."[32]

It was not merely the degradation of their surroundings that bothered McGill: he was equally struck by the degeneracy of their lives. "From one of my old accounts," he wrote, "I learned a new word — incest." In listening to a group of men gathered in the store, McGill heard them "damning some man who lived in the neighborhood who had had a child by his daughter. Someone knew the word incest. He said he had once served on a jury which heard a like case. The story and the word depressed me all that summer." Yet his overall impression of Chattanooga's less fortunate residents was more mixed. He summed up the summer as "hot, sweaty, and lonely," and stated, "I met all manner of defeated, shiftless, shifty, pathetic and interesting good people."[33]

McGill seemed dismissive of the impact of his exposure to these people at the time, for he followed that summary of his summer as a bill collector by stating that the company was pleased with his collection results and that all the walking involved in the job built his legs up enough that he made the all-city football team that fall. Only with the Depression's impact over a decade later did McGill fully realize the lessons of his adolescent summer jobs. Like Caldwell, it took adult sensibilities to fully appreciate the implications of what he had earlier observed far more innocently. As part of a fact-finding team of academics and journalists, McGill traveled through Georgia in the 1930s, visiting sharecroppers and tenants. "Their wretched cabins and the pitiful meagerness of their possessions and existence were eloquent evidence of the inequities of an agricultural social and economic system which had ground to a halt," he wrote. "I recall thinking, with a surge of pity, on seeing them on the roads, sometimes whole families of them ragged, now and then barefooted, I had never seen despair."[34] Not only did McGill convey their plight with far more feeling than he did that of the mountaineers and slum residents he encountered as a teenager; he was by then also ready to examine the causes of their poverty, which he did with great insight in a chapter of his memoir titled "What the Depression Taught Us."

★ ★ ★

Willie Morris came of age later than the rest of these writers. Born in 1934 in Yazoo City, Mississippi, Morris would have more casual encounters with poor whites; like Lumpkin's, they were built into the most leveling of local institutions — public schools — which he referred to as "a democracy, a seething, turbulent cross-section of rural and small-town humanity," where each day "the daintiest daughters of prosperous plantation owners and the meanest last sons of the most downtrodden sharecroppers came in together." While Morris himself fell between these two socioeconomic extremes — his father was a low-level municipal worker and his mother gave piano lessons — he fully identified with the town residents, and thus with the elite in the student body's social hierarchy.

In grammar school in the early 1940s, Willie came to recognize class distinctions in the not-so-subtle favoritism exhibited by his teachers, who seemed to invest themselves a bit more fully in the education of the children of the town's middle class than in that of the majority of what he called "the slower children of the families from 'out in the country.'" These privileged few "probably sensed we would make it through all right," Morris admitted, "and someday in the far-distant future be sturdy citizens of the place — planters or store owners or druggists or lawyers." They knew that they were the teachers' favorites and played their parts — as did their parents — in a mutual game of flattery, favors, and respect. As a result, he noted, "the red stars on the bulletin board were always next to our names, we got the A's and the 1's on our conduct reports . . . and we knew that the stirring challenges they laid down were secretly meant only for us."[35]

At some point, Morris began to take more interest — though in a rather detached way — in the "redneck" boys in his class, who were referred to merely by the part of the county from which they came: "the boys from Graball Hill." Morris described them "as distinct a group as any in the school," in their dress — "faded khakis or rough blue denim"; their appearance — bad teeth and uncombed hair; and their demeanor — often surly and belligerent, not only fighting each other, but thrashing out at blacks as well, especially small children unfortunate enough to have to pass by them. They would call them "coon" or "nigger baby" and follow them "with a barrage of rocks and dirt clods." Morris wryly added that much later, as an adult watching local law officials and mobs pummeling civil rights demonstrators on television, "I needed no one to tell me that they had been doing the same thing since the age of eight."[36]

Morris's assessment of the boys from Graball remains matter-of-fact and nonjudgmental, even as he ties their behavior and appearance to their poverty. He noticed that they kept to themselves at lunch time, often gathering at the Confederate monument in the town square across the street from the school. Some would buy a nickel Moon Pie or Baby Ruth; others ate nothing. He stated that they suffered from "strange maladies, like sleeping sickness and diarrhea," that often kept them out of school longer than the fall cotton-picking season, which in itself kept them away for weeks at a time. When Morris himself became a target of their rough-housing, he soon learned that he could easily run circles around them, in that they tired quickly and "began panting like hounddogs on a long hunt." He acknowledged that he came to treat them with "diffident respect," if only because they were bigger and older, often a grade level behind due to their extended absences. Yet the only hint of any sympathy or empathy lies in Morris's statement that he particularly liked the "gentlest one from Graball," a boy named Bo. He was the slowest reader in the class and wore the same clothes every day. To complete his character sketch, Morris simply noted that, "Once, after Christmas, when our teacher polled every child in class about what he got for Christmas, [Bo] said: 'I didn' get nothin'. I ain't studyin' toys.'"[37]

By high school in the early 1950s, the same demographic mix remained in place: "the children of the town's middle class mingled casually with the sons of tenant farmers, bankers' daughters dated boys from the other side of the Yazoo River, and the athletic teams were composed equally of the town and the country." Violence still served to distinguish the latter, though Morris noted that sports usually managed to soften "that pent-up destructiveness that would sometimes erupt in fist-fights for no reason, or a frenzied and indiscriminate shoving, stomping, and kicking." Curiously, Morris found this behavior more appealing than he had earlier, and being a "good old boy" became as much a priority as anything else not only for him, but for other boys he "ran around with." This feigned persona — casualness verging on cynicism — was as much a matter of style and demeanor as it was a mindset.

> So you would banter about grades as if they were of no account, curse the teachers, and develop a pose of indifference to ambition in all its forms. And you would speak the grammar of dirt-farmers and Negroes, using *ain't* and reckless verb forms with such a natural instinct that the right ones would have sounded high-blown and phony, and pushing the country talk to such limits that making it as flamboyant as possible became an end in itself.[38]

In effect, Morris became like the young William Styron, who "longed to be a Dabney." The appeal of the Graball boys to Morris and his friends was very similar to what drew Styron to the Dabney household, where he "basked in their casual squalor" and "envied their near poverty."[39] Yet Morris was then old enough to maintain that allure without sacrificing the advantages of his social standing and what that meant for his future. The "good old boy" persona never replaced the more deeply engrained code of behavior and "standard of success" imposed by and fully expected of parents and teachers. ("Among our elders, the thing that mattered was 'form.'") Thus, he explained, "we would laugh off the violence, engaging in it occasionally ourselves, while conducting ourselves according to the code as courteous and only slight syrupy gentlemen, always ready with the proper word or the hospitable gesture." This duality, Morris realized, was one that characterized the South itself, or his home state at least. "That curious apposition — of courtliness and extraordinary kindness on the one hand, and sudden violence on the other — was a phenomenon which never occurred to me." It was a schizophrenia that he and his comrades had absorbed with little thought or effort, and they wore it with "mindless contentment."[40]

Morris never cast such incidents in terms of any epiphany or enlightenment. In a very real sense, his memoir is not centered on either class or racial awakenings, as are most of the works discussed here. He never became a journalist, a politician, a reformer, or a social activist in the way that the other authors did, and thus his impressions and experiences with poor whites were not nearly as formative to his future career or the writings that defined it. He ends these brief passages of his chronicle of his Mississippi boyhood—merely the first third of *North toward Home*—by stating that only one of the Graball boys ever "made it," and he did so through football—ultimately recruited as a left tackle for Alabama's Crimson Tide. As for the others, he wrote wistfully, "I sometimes wonder what became of them, if they are still hoeing the impoverished red earth or picking the same scraggly cotton deep in the Mississippi backwoods."[41]

Nor is there much sense that this exposure to the "have nots" of Yazoo City's white community had any relevance to an awareness of race, which Morris chronicled even more casually. He related only a single incident that suggests any awareness of the hardship African Americans faced in his community, a story he makes almost chilling by stressing how fleeting an impression it made on him. He was part of a group of high school students who gathered for swimming and a picnic on a Fourth of July afternoon. Across the lake, they watched a black family whose shack had burned down the night before and had moved "into a bare, floorless cabin nearby, alive with crawling things that came out of the rotten wood in the walls." Barely moving, this couple and their small children merely stared at the white teenagers eating and swimming. Finally, Willie and his girlfriend walked around the lake, where they saw their desolation up close. The listless children who had not eaten for two days caused his girl to break into tears. They returned to their group, pooled the money they had on hand—about $15—and took that and their hot dogs and cokes to the family. As they ate, they continued to stare. "Under their stolid gaze," Morris wrote, "I felt uncomfortable; I wanted to head back to [my home on] Grand Avenue."

He ends the story by saying simply: "We packed our things and went to the car, drove through the flat cotton country to town, and resumed our picnic on the back lawn of one of the big houses in our neighborhood." As with his descriptions of the Graball boys and other poor whites, there is no suggestion that this confrontation with poverty and misfortune resulted in any epiphany or had any lasting impact on Morris's sensibilities. In fact, he saw it as an aberration, a rare "moment of pity and sorrow" that contrasted with what he calls "unthinking sadism," the far more common harassment and acts of cruelty that he and his friends inflicted on local blacks.[42]

Only as he closes out the first section of his book, just before leaving Mississippi to embark on a college career at the University of Texas, did Morris assess what he was taking with him into the wider world. Within a lengthy and moving appreciation of family, friends, and community, he claimed to have re-tained "some innocent and exposed quality that made possible, in the heart of a young and vulnerable boy, an allegiance and a love for a small and inconse-quential place." He had nothing explicit to say about either class or race or any sense of social justice having emerged from his childhood or adolescence, but merely stated, more obliquely: "My first seventeen years had been lived rich in experiences — in sensual textures, in unusual confrontations. I had moved easily among many kinds of people."[43]

★ ★ ★

If a heightened sensitivity to racial inequities and injustice often developed in conjunction with or soon after early encounters with poor whites, only rarely did writers prior to mid-century ever acknowledge any causal linkage between Jim Crow and black poverty. It was only in the next generation, as rumblings of change in the South's racial order generated new sorts of qualms among white adolescents, that such connections became more obvious — or that writers con-fronted them more directly.

No one seemed to have reached such dual epiphanies — linking black poverty to racism — during the Jim Crow era; nevertheless, one cannot deny the extent to which the discovery of the inequities and misery of a class-based southern society more often than not led to epiphanies of racial inequities and injustices as well. Of the writers considered here, Katharine Lumpkin came closest to rec-ognizing the linkages in the course of her own transformation. She summarized the theme of her book and the impact of her adolescent discoveries on its last page: "I was a Southerner nurtured in the Lost Cause, who looked upon my people's history and conduct of affairs as scarcely short of exemplary." And yet, she noted, the "glaring incongruities" of southern life began to seep into even her limited childhood perspective and "began to arouse in me a chronic state of doubt." She went on to explain the key to her full conversion:

It is true, this awakened skepticism might have come to very little, even to being stifled by our protecting walls of privilege, had it not been for one thing — the sudden breaking down of my isolation from the realities of Southern life. The Sand Hills intervened, and did so at the very time of my changing teens. Here in actuality was the moment when chance circumstance showed me our native Tree of Life, and had me eat of its revealing fruit. . . . Once my eyes had been opened, it would seem, I never again could return to the comfortable ignorance which would never let me assume as an unfortunate inevitability the destitution, the drabness of life, the spiritual and material exploitation, which was the lot of so many.[44]

And so it was for most of the other writers under consideration here. "Chance circumstance" showed them all "their native Tree of Life," and sooner or later "had them eating of its revealing fruit." Their discovery of poor whites as a coming of age experience, or as an early stage on the road to southern liberalism, seems to have been a phenomenon limited primarily to the decades after the First World War and prior to the civil rights movement. For each of the writers discussed here, the childhood or adolescent experiences they recalled so movingly in later years were crucial steps on the road to defining the ideological perspectives and even career courses they later took. For all but Erskine Caldwell and Willie Morris, these revelations led or were integral to their discoveries of racial injustice, which became priorities in the varied writings—in novels, memoirs, and newspapers—and/or political stances of Styron, Lumpkin, Smith, Carter, and McGill.

Yet there are revealing distinctions between the portrayals of white poverty and black discrimination apparent in these works. It is striking that these writers rarely portrayed poor whites as individuals. With the sole exception of Styron's Dabneys, none of the descriptions of white poverty involve personality or individuality. (And for Styron, it took a fictionalization of his experience to give such vibrant life and depth to his comic characters.) For Lumpkin, Caldwell, Smith, Carter, and McGill, the poor whites they discovered remained faceless composites—generic entities that the authors more often than not observed at a distance or en masse rather than through personal encounters with particular men and women that usually characterize racial conversion narratives. Whether tenants, tramps, remote mountain people, or chain gangs, most of the impressions made came from only fleeting contact between them and those writing about them.

Only Katharine Lumpkin and Willie Morris experienced any extended close contact with their socioeconomic inferiors—she during the course of a single school year in a South Carolina classroom, and he over the course of many years of grammar and high school with the boys from Graball; yet even then he only refers to one of them by name. The result is a curious detachment—more of an intellectual or even sociological observation—toward those about whom they wrote. Even within the same work, such as Lumpkin's *The Making of a Southerner*, such contrasts between the treatment of poor whites and blacks are evident. Lumpkin never identified by name or otherwise individualized the poor white school children or tenants she encountered in the South Carolina sand hills; yet her discovery of racial inequities hinged almost entirely on a single woman and a single incident. It was a Miss Arthur, a black YWCA official who spoke before a group of white students at Brenau while Lumpkin was a student there, whom she credited with her epiphanal moment in terms of race.[45] For Lillian Smith, none of the forty-eight convicts with whom her family shared Christmas dinner are singled out or portrayed in any individual detail. Yet her only other childhood memory as fully realized in print is a very personal one: that of Janie, the light-skinned black girl who was mistakenly assumed to be white and lived for several weeks with the Smith family until snatched away once the error in the girl's racial identity was realized.[46]

Perhaps these different approaches to matters of class and race suggest that the first of these revelations — that those of their own race could be victims of poverty — was merely a precursor to what they found as a more compelling and more personally meaningful discovery: that of Jim Crow and its centrality in making the South distinctive and historically significant, at least in the hindsight from which these authors recalled the youthful shaping of lifelong agendas. Or perhaps it speaks to the different types of circumstances by which affluent southern whites made contact with blacks and poor whites, and thus defies any real pattern in terms of the reasons for which they documented those experiences as they later did.

★ ★ ★

The racial conversion narratives by southerners continued through the 1960s and 1970s, but far fewer included revelations of white poverty as part of that experience. By the same token, Americans' sensibilities toward the poor in their midst became more nationalized in the 1960s. President Lyndon Johnson's quest for a Great Society in part through a War on Poverty revealed to the American people at large what had once been very personal revelations. Perhaps as an aftereffect of that new public consciousness of want and deprivation in the midst of national prosperity, a new type of autobiography emerged in the 1980s and 1990s: southern whites writing about the poverty of their own early years. Adapting what had long been a staple of African American autobiography — graphic descriptions of the meager circumstances and destitution of their early years and their eventual triumph over them — white authors began telling their own such stories.

Beginning with Harry Crews's *A Childhood: The Biography of a Place* in 1978, which documents his first six years on a tenant farm in south Georgia, a growing number of white writers have earned both critical and popular acclaim — and even celebrity status — for their narratives of growing up poor in the modern South. These range from Rick Bragg's *All Over but the Shoutin'*, his best-selling paean to his mother's desperate struggle to survive and keep her family intact in the cotton fields and rented shanties of rural Alabama, to Dorothy Allison's *Two or Three Things I Know for Sure*, a harrowing account of her abuse as a child in the slums of Greenville, South Carolina; from Mary Karr, who finds much humor in her turbulent childhood and adolescence as part of a dysfunctional East Texas Gulf Coast family in two books (*The Liar's Club* and *Cherry*), to Linda Scott DeRosier's *Creeker*, a surprisingly upbeat account of her hand-to-mouth existence deep in a Kentucky mountain hollow; from Janisse Ray's *Ecology of a Cracker Childhood*, recounting her emergence as an environmentalist and writer from roots in a junkyard in the piney woods of southeast Georgia, to Jeannette Walls's best-selling *The Glass Castle*, the central section of which depicts the bleak existence of her family in Welch, West Virginia, a dying coal town in which they were among the poorest residents; and from Dean Rusk's description of his first four years on a not very productive farm in north Georgia to Bill Clinton's often volatile lower-middle-class upbringing in Hope, Arkansas, both of which serve as mere prologues to hefty autobiographies focused primarily on their political careers.[47]

There is now no shortage of vivid firsthand accounts, vividly told, of what it means to be poor, southern, and white in our own times. In most of these cases, the author's childhood or adolescence forms the centerpiece of the book, and the poignancy of youthful traumas accounts for the vast appeal of such accounts to modern readers. As with their more affluent predecessors, it is those revelatory moments at which these authors were hit with the reality of their place in the socioeconomic hierarchy that resonate most fully.

No one has articulated that moment more effectively than Rick Bragg. Bragg claimed that in 1971, at the age of twelve, he "had given very little thought to being poor, because it was the only realm of existence I knew." But that Christmas, living in the bleakest of circumstances with his mother and two brothers in mobile homes and cotton fields in north Alabama, he "got a lesson" in who he was.

A fraternity at Jacksonville State University had a party for the children of poor families in the area. He remembered fondly the presents bestowed on him and his brothers and all the sugar cookies and 7–UP he and his brothers consumed. "I wasn't old enough to be ashamed about being the charity these glowing young people had gathered around, like a Christmas tree," Bragg recalled. "But I was beginning to realize the difference between me and them." He knew these were "rich folks . . . not by Manhattan standards, merely by Possum Trot ones." They were nice rich folks, as demonstrated by all they were doing for these poor children they didn't even know, and yet they "were as alien to people like me as Eskimos and flying saucers."[48]

What follows is a dead-on analysis of class in the small-town South that is as accurate now as it was in 1971, made all the more heartrending because of the twelve-year-old innocence in which Bragg wraps it. "They were Southerners like me, yet completely different. I remember thinking that it would be very, very nice to be their kind instead. And I remember thinking that, no, that will never happen." He reasoned that "we were part of it, of that night, because we were poor and because we were children. . . . But you simply outgrow your invitation into that better world, as your childhood races away from you. You reach the age ultimately when that barrier slams down hard again between you and them, and the rest of the nice, solid, decent middle class." He ends that thought with the most devastating observation of all: "Perhaps it wouldn't be so bad, if it was a wall of iron instead of glass."[49]

For Harry Crews, who along with Bragg, produced an uncommonly emotional and multitextured self-portrait of white southern poverty, it was a Sears Roebuck catalogue that provided him, as a very young boy, with a sense that not everyone lived lives as bleak as his own and that of everyone around him — a conclusion he reached purely on the basis of physical appearances. "I first became fascinated with the Sears catalogue because all the people in its pages were perfect," Crews wrote in *A Childhood*. "Nearly everybody I knew had something missing, a finger cut off, a toe split, an ear half-chewed away, an eye clouded with blindness from a glancing fence staple. And if they didn't have something missing, they were carrying scars from barbed wire, or knives, or fishhooks." But he saw none of that, of course, in the models posing in the catalogue pages. "They were not only whole, had all their arms and legs and toes and eyes on their unscarred bodies, but they were also beautiful . . . and on their faces were looks of happiness, even joy, looks that I never saw much of in the faces of the people around me."

Crews insisted that his childhood would have been radically different without those hefty slick volumes, because they provided him — and his young companions, including a black boy named Willalee Bookatee — with a rich fantasy life. He suggested, in fact, that it was creating imaginary stories about these perfect people that somehow triggered the writer in him. "Since where we lived and how we lived was almost hermetically sealed from everything and everyone else," he explained, "fabrication became a way of life. Making up stories, it seems to me now, was not only a way for us to understand the way we lived, but a defense against it as well." He concluded: "The federal government ought to strike a medal for the Sears, Roebuck company for all those catalogues to all those farm families, for bringing all that color and all that mystery and all that beauty into the lives of country people."[50]

In a far different way, Janisse Ray acknowledged the relevancy of poverty and related how she came to realize that her family's plight was by no means the worst experienced in her world in the 1960s and 1970s. Ray labeled herself, in her title no less, a "cracker," and she stated up front that "it didn't take many years to realize I was a Southerner, a slow, dumb, redneck hick, a hayseed, inbred and racist, come from poverty, condemned to poverty: descendant of Oglethorpe's debtor prisoners." Yet she also reveled in life in the Georgia junkyard that served as a business for her father and a playground for her and her siblings. Despite the financial tightrope on which the family managed to balance precariously throughout her childhood, she devotes a chapter entitled "Poverty" not to their own plight, but to that of others with whom they had regular contact. "We were poor but solvent," she states, "and surrounded by people much poorer."

Ray's father, it seems, was not unlike Erskine Caldwell's or Lillian Smith's fathers, whose concern for the poor in their midst proved so inspirational to their children. "My father fed the poor," she wrote, "especially the wayfaring and those who could never feed him in return." Their junkyard was located on U.S. 1, the primary thoroughfare from New England to Florida, "the road the snowbirds coasted, and the one the vagabonds wore their soles out on," and it was from that vantage point that Ray discovered a far less privileged existence than that she enjoyed.[51]

In what sounds more like the 1930s than the 1960s, Janisse recounted the visits of various hobos and "families like the Joads," seeking either food or some auto part required in order to continue their trek. Mr. Ray always obliged them all, despite the size of the families or the drunkenness of the hobos. His daughter described a typical family breakdown, noting her father's affection for the "children who poured out of the packed car, dirty and tired." For them, "he'd go dig in the freezer for a bag or two of Easter candy he'd bought cheap a week after Easter, and he'd have Mama make them all bologna sandwiches. He'd help the man find the part he needed and get them on the road." Like Caldwell and Smith, Ray told these stories as much to demonstrate her admiration for her father's generosity and compassion as to acknowledge those less fortunate than themselves. "Daddy had a kindness that belied his brusqueness," she wrote with great affection. "His heart was big enough for all of us and a world besides, and put innocent children and very old people at the center of it."[52]

Southern victims of poverty, it seems, no longer need to be discovered, or exposed, by their socioeconomic betters. They can tell their own stories and do so quite adeptly, even as their sense of that poverty and how it defined them and those around them comes across as far more personalized and emotionally engaged than that of earlier generations of southerners who had merely observed their plight from afar.[53] Yet as the works under consideration here suggest, the troubling facets of race and class in southern life were obviously not apparent to those so well insulated from both in the 1920s and 1930s. Even during the Depression years, which raised American awareness of poverty to new heights, we see a number of young people who experienced the shock, discomfort, and revelatory effects of their firsthand exposure to those, white or black, less fortunate than themselves.

Such reactions may have been unusual, but one does not read autobiographies for the typicality of their authors' observations or experience. Nor do we value such work now only for the impact it had on contemporary readerships. For most of these authors, the influence of their testimonials on other white southerners was minimal. These writers were, for the most part, exceptional in their sensitivity to the misfortune they observed around them at the time, and in the fact that such experiences proved transformative enough to create in them powerful social consciences about their communities and their region. It was those consciences that drove many of them, in one way or another, to tell their own stories. The intensity and often compassion with which they did so serve not only as moving reflections of the times, places, and people about which they wrote; they also reveal the inspiration that drove these writers to use their own stories to "tell about the South," to give in to the peculiarly "southern rage to explain."[54]

CHAPTER FOUR

Railroads, Race, and Remembrance

The Traumas of Train Travel in the Jim Crow South

AT THE BEGINNING of *I Know Why the Caged Bird Sings*, her classic account of growing up in Stamps, Arkansas, Maya Angelou told of the journey in 1931 that brought her there. She was a mere three years old when she and her four-year-old brother Bailey, the refuse of divorce, were sent by train from California to begin life anew with their paternal grandmother. The children were left in the care of a porter who got off the train in Arizona, and they continued their journey on their own, with tickets pinned to their coats and tags on their wrists made out "To Whom It May Concern" as their only identification. As they crossed into the South and were relegated to a Jim Crow car, things looked up, as sympathetic "Negro passengers . . . plied us with cold fried chicken and potato salad," until they were safely deposited in "the musty little town" that was to be their home for the next ten years. Angelou concluded her opening vignette by noting that "years later I discovered that the United States had been crossed thousands of times by frightened Black children traveling alone to their newly affluent parents in northern cities or back to grandmothers in southern towns when the urban North reneged on its economic promises."[1]

With that statement, Angelou universalized her earliest memory and revealed what was indeed a central, and often traumatic, aspect of southern black life for much of the nineteenth and twentieth centuries: train travel. Since railroads first appeared in the South in the 1830s, they played key roles in many

African American lives, and they are depicted as such in a striking number of autobiographical accounts of southerners coming of age. Both literally and figuratively, trains represented a means of bringing families together, of tearing them apart, and of escape, both legal and illegal.

But if the journeys themselves often served as means of seeking new horizons or grasping new opportunities for African Americans on the move, trains represented much more than merely the means by which those journeys were made. In both the nature of the trips and the ways in which blacks were treated en route, railroads often served as testing grounds, even battle grounds, between black passengers and white authority figures. These, in turn, led to revelatory moments for the former — either at the time or imposed by memory and hindsight — in which their status came into sharp focus, sometimes quite suddenly, and served as catalysts through which other, more internalized truths surfaced as well. Coretta Scott King stated in her autobiography that "despite efforts by African-American parents to protect their children from the dreadful hurt of segregation and discrimination, sooner or later, all African-American children lose their racial innocence. Some incident suddenly makes them realize that they are regarded as inferior."[2] For numerous children, adolescents, and even young adults, that realization took place on a train. Railroads often provided the first venue in which that innocence was lost, as young people were forced to confront their blackness as defined by the larger society in which they lived.

Black autobiographical narratives are filled with accounts of such incidents, which viewed together reveal much about the vast range of responses segregation elicited on both sides of the "color line." The multiplicity of lessons learned, assumptions questioned or even shattered, and emotions stirred as a result of those remembered confrontations are among the most common features in the self-told life stories of southern African Americans from the late nineteenth through much of the twentieth century. By focusing on this most common — yet specific — example of racial oppression through the words of those involved, we can assess the impact of these traumatic experiences on the individuals who recounted them, often much later in life. Equally integral to the insights, discoveries, and confusions were what these incidents revealed to many of these writers — and to us — in terms of the strengths or weaknesses, the pride or humiliation, the courage or complacency of their parents and other elders forced to cope in an oppressive and dehumanizing system that so perplexed their offspring.[3]

Finally, by placing these many accounts in chronological order, we can see more clearly, if only anecdotally, how Jim Crow's career played out over time. We see in its earliest manifestations a somewhat checkered practice that allowed black passengers to negotiate with conductors or even challenge them successfully in order to remain where they were, even if it wasn't in newly designated segregated spaces. We also see African Americans shocked and defiant when asked to move — that is, in their first encounters with a restrictive new system that all too soon would become a way of life in which such emotional responses gave way to compliance, if not complacency. And by the late 1940s and 1950s, we see signs of new disgruntlement with the practice and ever fewer incidents related in autobiographical work produced in subsequent years.

This chapter thus contends that this cumulative set of memories serves multiple purposes for us historically. While testifying to the universality of Jim Crow's most ubiquitous manifestation and how it evolved from the mid-nineteenth to the mid-twentieth centuries, these remembered incidents also reveal much about the particularities and variables in how it was both challenged and enforced. Yet perhaps what resonates most from these most intimate of sources is the emotional and psychological impact of this very public form of discrimination on those victimized by it at some point during the course of Jim Crow's long and often strange career.

There is no other experience that represented for southern blacks the essence of Jim Crow as often or as strikingly as did a segregated railroad coach. W. E. B. Du Bois declared that there was "no more disgraceful denial of human brotherhood in the world than the 'Jim Crow' car of the southern United States." In 1908 journalist Ray Stannard Baker noted that "no other point of race contact is so much and so bitterly discussed among the Negroes as the Jim Crow car."[4] In his 1944 expose, *An American Dilemma*, Swedish observer Gunnar Myrdal confirmed it to be "resented more bitterly among Negroes than most other forms of segregation," while the white South's most outspoken critic, Lillian Smith, declared in the same year that "transportation has become a symbol of the white man's injustice to the Negro."[5]

The restrictions imposed on rail travel were not a universal problem for southern blacks, if only because it remained largely a privilege of the middle class, with many — perhaps the vast majority — of African Americans lacking either the means or the occasion to travel by railroad.[6] On the other hand, no other aspect of segregation seemed quite as ubiquitous or so blatant as that imposed on train travel. Railroads were accessible to both urban and rural southerners in a way that other businesses or public enterprises were not, and by its very nature their clientele included women as well as men, and children as well as adults.[7] Compared with other Jim Crow practices, "most of the debates about race relations focused on the railroads of the New South," Edward J. Ayers has observed, noting that for other forms of segregation — exclusion from hotels, restaurants, and other businesses — blacks could find black-run counterparts that they actually preferred in most cases.[8]

The racial segregation of public transportation was a reality in both the North and South throughout much of the nineteenth century, yet during Reconstruction and beyond, such practices were carried out in partial, even inconsistent form in most southern states. As even more railroads crisscrossed the South in the late 1870s and 1880s, the spatial bounds on black passengers became more of a concern, and states began to enact laws mandating racial separation on trains, though they did so at different times and in different ways. As historian Barbara Welke has noted, "the piecemeal construction of Jim Crow at the beginning of the twentieth century very much resembled the piecemeal dismantlement of Jim Crow half a century later," a fact fully borne out by autobiographical evidence.[9]

U.S. Supreme Court rulings in 1877 and 1883 overturned or at least undermined the 1875 federal statute guaranteeing racial equality on public transit. Along with the creation of the Interstate Commerce Commission in 1887, these decisions lent support to actions by individual companies and state legislatures that sought to establish segregated policies on trains.[10] Tennessee moved well before that to become, in 1875, the first southern state to legislate separate first-class cars for black and white passengers. Twelve years later Florida mandated a color line within first-class cars that kept black passengers from sitting with whites, followed shortly thereafter by Mississippi and then Texas, which required separate coaches for black passengers, whether first or second class. By the time the U.S. Supreme Court gave full sanction to such restrictions in its *Plessy v. Ferguson* ruling in 1896, Louisiana, Alabama, Georgia, Kentucky, and Arkansas had passed their own segregation statutes. In the decade after *Plessy*, the remaining southern states — Virginia, the Carolinas, Maryland, and Oklahoma — had followed suit, while Tennessee and Florida strengthened their laws to require separate coaches for each race rather than merely settling for divided space within a single car or limiting such restrictions to first-class cars.[11]

Such restrictions were objectionable for far more than mere principle. The sheer discomfort in which blacks were forced to ride spurred much of the opposition to them. Often the first car behind the engine was designated as the Jim Crow car because of the smoke and grime to which it was especially susceptible. It was generally the oldest car on the train and far more sparsely furnished and overcrowded than the coaches designated for whites. In some cases, a single coach served as both the Jim Crow car and either a smoking car for whites or the baggage car, in either case adding to the discomfort level of black passengers. They were denied access to dining cars and often to adequate restroom facilities.[12]

By 1908 the only legal exemptions for black travelers — and only reprieve from these discomforts — seemed to be Pullman cars, where state laws seemed to vary more than for other passenger cars, either first or second class. Catherine Barnes, who has provided the only comprehensive legal history of segregated transit systems, concludes that by the 1930s some companies had loosened their restrictions on Pullmans, particularly for those passengers traveling across the Mason-Dixon line. Soon after Jim Crow tightened his hold on railroad coaches, most states or municipalities imposed segregated waiting rooms and other facilities in train stations, which in themselves became contested spaces often recounted in autobiographical narratives. Mississippi, Louisiana, and Arkansas legalized separate waiting rooms by century's end, with other southern states following suit soon after the turn of the century.[13]

One of the earliest commentaries on Jim Crow cars comes from a somewhat unexpected source: a fugitive slave narrative. Trains figure prominently as means of escape and serve as the central dramatic devices in several such narratives, from Henry "Box" Brown, who had himself shipped in a crate from North Carolina to Philadelphia in 1840, to William and Ellen Craft, whose escape from Macon, Georgia, began with a harrowing train trip to Savannah with Ellen disguised as a white man. Even more familiar is Frederick Douglass's deliberate refusal to comment on his escape by train from Baltimore in 1835 in his two antebellum memoirs (1845 and 1855), though he ultimately provides a full account of that part of his journey north in his final autobiography, first published in 1881.[14]

But it is in Harriet Jacobs's *Incidents in the Life of a Slave Girl*, first published in 1861, that we find perhaps the earliest firsthand account of segregated seating enforced on trains. In 1842, not long after her escape from North Carolina (smuggled aboard a ship), Jacobs first rode a train and recalled being taken aback by the practice of racial segregation. As she embarked on a trip from Philadelphia to New York arranged for her by one of her white protectors, a Mr. Durham handed her a ticket and warned that she was likely to have "a disagreeable ride," since he had been unable to purchase a first-class ticket. When she assumed that she should have given him more money, he was forced to explain that the problem lay elsewhere: "They don't allow colored people in the first-class cars." That statement proved a rude awakening to Jacobs. "This was the first chill to my enthusiasm about the Free States," she wrote. "Colored people were allowed to ride in a filthy box, behind white people, in the south, but there they were not required to pay for the privilege. It made me sad to find how the north aped the customs of slavery." She followed with a graphic description of the overcrowded, smoke-filled, and noisy conditions that made it "a very disagreeable ride."[15]

After the Civil War, railroad cars became key elements in the evolving struggle over black rights in the South and the implementation of racial segregation. Several extraordinary incidents recalled by autobiographers confirm the lack of uniformity that characterized both the Reconstruction era and the years afterward in terms of spatial boundaries and black resistance to efforts to define African Americans by race. The privileges of class and even degrees of blackness often provided extenuating circumstances that allowed some to challenge what were clearly white expectations of black behavior before the passage of strict legal restrictions that were firmly in place by century's end.

Mary Church Terrell's narrative includes what must have been among the earliest post–Civil War memories of such confrontations, revealing much about the fluidity of both class and color at that point in time. Born in Memphis in 1863, she was just five years old when "the Race Problem [was] brought directly home to me." Her father, Robert Church, a former slave who had established himself as a successful businessman, took Mary with him on a train trip to the North. She explained that although there was a separate car for blacks, it was not a legally binding arrangement in Tennessee at that time, and that "self-respecting colored people would not go into the coach set aside for them."

Her father, the son of his former master and nearly white in appearance, was quick to leave his young daughter in the first-class coach and move back to the smoking car, where he socialized freely with the white men gathered there. (She noted, perhaps a little naively, that "so soon after the emancipation of the slave, it seems remarkable that in their relations with each other both the ex-masters and ex-slaves could adjust themselves as quickly as they did in some instances to the new order of things.") A conductor, encountering Mary alone in the car, angrily pulled her from her seat to take her to the coach "where I belonged." In doing so, he asked a man who had been sitting across from her, "Whose little nigger is this?" A white friend of Mr. Church quickly found him and brought him back to confront the conductor. "There ensued a scene which no one who saw it could ever forget," Terrell wrote much later, in what becomes a suddenly truncated conclusion to her story. Her father apparently pulled out a revolver at some point in his altercation with the conductor, and she wrote simply, "Fortunately no one was injured and I was allowed to remain with my courageous father in the white coach."

Like so many children in similar situations, Terrell stated that "this incident agitated my mind considerably," and she plied her father and later her mother with questions about it, and particularly about what she had done wrong to offend the conductor. Her father refused to answer and forbade her to talk about it. Her mother, equally helpless to provide meaningful answers to a five-year-old, broke down in tears. "Seeing their children touched and seared and wounded by race prejudice is one of the heaviest crosses which colored women have to bear," Terrell concluded.[16]

Ida B. Wells, also from Memphis and a longtime colleague and associate of Terrell's, faced a similar challenge nearly two decades later with an equally extraordinary, if very different, form of resistance. A year older than Terrell, Wells was twenty-one years old in 1884 when, as a young teacher commuting from the city to her rural school elsewhere in the county, Wells took her usual place on what she called "the ladies' coach of the train." When the conductor collecting tickets told her that he could not take her ticket there and that she would have to move to another car, she refused. He attempted to drag her from her seat, and she bit his hand. He then enlisted two other men to help him, and with other passengers in the car cheering them on, they succeeded in dragging her out of the car. Rather than allowing herself to be pushed into the smoker, which was "already filled with colored people and those [white men] who were smoking," Wells chose to get off the train.

It was then that Wells's actions took an even more defiant turn. Back in Memphis, she engaged a black lawyer to bring suit against the railroad on her behalf. Though the attorney was eventually bought off by the railroad, Wells remained undaunted and found a white lawyer to take her case. It eventually came to trial and, with an ex-Union Minnesotan sitting on the bench, she prevailed, and the Chesapeake and Ohio Railroad was ordered to award her $500 in damages. She quoted the headline of the *Memphis Appeal* on Christmas Day in 1884, "A Darky Damsel Obtains a Verdict for Damages . . . What it Cost to Put a Colored School Teacher in a Smoking Car." It was her opening salvo in what became a career of actively challenging racial injustices of all sorts.

Yet the ultimate resolution of the case was far less of a triumph for Wells. The railroad company appealed the case, and the Tennessee Supreme Court overruled the original decision, and Wells was not only denied the $500 award but was forced to pay $200 in court costs. (She claimed that she had opportunities to "compromise the case" and would have been far better off financially if she had done so, but she "indignantly refused.") Years later, she wrote, she discovered that hers had been a precedent-setting case that tested the right of state courts to determine the legitimacy of railroads controlling where their passengers sat — the first case decided in the wake of the U.S. Supreme Court's repeal of the 1877 Civil Rights Act the year before.[17]

James Weldon Johnson related two very different encounters with railroad authorities four years apart. In 1890, at a mere sixteen years of age, Johnson took a train from his hometown of Jacksonville, Florida, to enter college at Atlanta University. He was accompanied by his close boyhood friend, Ricardo, who had moved to the United States from Cuba and had convinced his father that he too should attend Atlanta University as part of his quest to become a dentist. Both boys had first-class tickets and embarked on this momentous journey with a lively send-off at the station from friends and family.

Once underway, the two boys were about to open their box lunches of fried chicken (nearly ubiquitous in these accounts from the 1870s through the 1950s) when the conductor approached and told them that they should move to the car ahead, warning that "you'll be likely to have trouble if you try to stay in this car." Johnson was bewildered by this — noting that the Florida law separating the races on trains had been passed that very year, and that he was ignorant of it. In questioning the conductor, to whom "the new law was very new" as well, Ricardo asked in Spanish what the problem was. Johnson, whose Spanish was apparently better than Ricardo's English, responded in kind, and the two boys agreed to stay where they were. But they never had to put their resolve to the test; as soon as the conductor heard them speaking a foreign language, he relented. "He punched our tickets and gave them back, and treated us just as he did the other passengers in the car," Johnson recalled, and the rest of their trip to Atlanta was restful and uneventful. Although a decade older than Mary Terrell at the time, Johnson accorded this incident much the same significance as she had done at age five: "This was my first impact against race prejudice as a concrete fact." He noted, tongue-somewhat-in-cheek, that "the experience with the conductor drove home to me the conclusion that in such situations any kind of Negro will do, provided he is not one who is an American citizen."[18]

Upon his return to Jacksonville from Atlanta after his graduation in 1894, Johnson encountered Jim Crow on far more ominous terms. Traveling again with Ricardo and two other black friends, the four bought first-class tickets (Georgia had still not passed its "Jim Crow car" law, as he called it) and settled into the first-class car. When collecting tickets, the conductor "suggested very strongly" that they move into the car ahead, designated for blacks. Johnson wrote: "I, remembering how things had worked out on the trip from Jacksonville to Atlanta, told him that we were comfortable and preferred to stay where we were." The conductor did not respond, but the white passengers did, as murmurs became more open threats. A white man approached Johnson and whispered in his ear that a telegram had been sent ahead to the next station, Baxley, Georgia, where a mob was forming to remove the unwanted passengers from the train. Having heard of an earlier incident in which a Baxley mob intimidated and forcibly ejected a group of black preachers traveling together, Johnson admitted that he was frightened but still made no move to leave the first-class compartment. Only when the black conductor confirmed the probability of a mob ahead and urged the foursome to comply did "his warnings raise my fright to the point it broke my determination to hold my ground," and Johnson decided for himself and his companions that the time had come to move to the Jim Crow car ahead — the first time he had ever done so, he was quick to point out.

Johnson wrote that "many of the passengers expressed their satisfaction" as they watched the four college graduates make their exit. "If their satisfaction rose from any idea that I was having a sense of my inferiority impressed upon me, they were sadly in error; indeed my sensation was the direct opposite; I felt that I was being humiliated." As the train moved through Baxley, he concluded, there seemed to be no sign of a mob, which led him to wonder if the black conductor had merely served as a tool of the white passengers. "The more I thought of this," he concluded, "the more I regretted that we had moved."[19]

Each of these episodes was exceptional in how it was resolved. Whether by the threat of a revolver, a law suit won and then lost, the accompaniment of a foreigner, or the persuasive powers of a black conductor and rumors of an external mob — all demonstrated the state of flux that characterized the norms of public transportation in the late-nineteenth-century South. Much seems to have been left to the temperament or judgment of individual conductors, and in each case, the African American passenger or passengers had reason to believe that they were entitled to ride in a first-class coach and had bought their tickets accordingly. In telling their stories, Terrell, Wells, and Johnson all felt the need to explain the particular legal circumstances at the time of their encounters. For Terrell, it was simply that "there was no Jim Crow law in the state of Tennessee then"; for Wells, her encounter took place a year after a Supreme Court ruling in 1883 rendered invalid the federal law that would have protected her right to sit wherever she wanted (and could afford); for Johnson, it was the immediate aftermath of Florida's and Georgia's new segregation statutes — developments so recent that he was unaware of either. His success on his first train trip was far more inadvertent than that of Robert Church or Ida Wells, and if the pressures he faced on his return trip four years later were far more intense, there was still no indication that the force of law drove his decision to give in to them. One wonders if any of the same scenarios described by Terrell, Wells, or Johnson would have led to far different outcomes had they occurred even a few years later than they did, when, as Grace Hale has so aptly put it, "the color bar grew, adding the tight adolescent muscles of law to the baby fat of convention."[20]

Yet even if African American writers rarely found such flexibility or laxity in enforcing racial codes after the turn of the century, their first encounters with railroads and Jim Crow continued to be revelatory in one way or another. Although they lacked the same options for challenging what they had to acknowledge as a firmly entrenched reality, the range of their responses suggests anything but uniformity in this or other types of repression that they faced. Multiple contingencies characterize the experiences related so regularly by autobiographers, and the lessons learned had much to do with the personal circumstances, the temperaments of those involved, the timing of those experiences, and the messages they sought to convey in the retelling of these episodes many years — even decades — later.

For those remarkable centenarian sisters, Sadie and Bessie Delany, train travel provided an early indication of their parents' racial and social identity. They were also among the few to make a sharp distinction between the era before and that after the implementation of Jim Crow. Sadie recounted an incident that she had obviously heard from her parents, and which she used to illustrate her mother's mixed-race identity. In 1891 Sadie, only a toddler, traveled home to Raleigh with her mother after visiting her mother's parents (an interracial couple) in Virginia. While waiting to change trains in Greensboro, a white man tried to make small talk to Mrs. Delany and to play with Sadie, a mere toddler. He assumed they were white, and Sadie's mother made no effort to correct him. Sadie took delight in concluding the story: when the next train finally arrived in Raleigh, "that white man was shocked to see this good-looking Negro man — our Papa — jump on the train and squeeze Mama tight. The white man said, 'Well, I'll be damned,'" which much amused the other white witnesses in the car.

More revealing than the simple mix-up her mother's light complexion could evoke is the fact that once her true racial identity was revealed, no one seemed bothered by it or by the fact that they had shared a coach with a black woman. Once Jim Crow laws were imposed a few years later, Sadie took pride in the fact that her parents still had options not available to most black passengers but chose not to take advantage of them. She noted that her father, an Episcopal bishop who traveled a great deal, was often given the option by admiring Pullman car porters to use those facilities (often not off bounds to black passengers who could afford them), but that he always declined, saying that he would rather "ride with my people and see how they're doing." Her mother still had the option of "passing" but insisted on taking "the colored car even though it was dirtier" for the same reason — she wanted to be with her people. Yet on occasion, Sadie noted, "the conductor thought she was white and would make her sit in the white car!"[21]

Another story of mixed-race identity, that of Ely Green of Sewanee, Tennessee, culminated in a train trip that encapsulated the contradictions and frustrations that had so dominated his young life. Green was born in 1893 to a black mother and white father, a housemaid and the son of her employer. Oblivious to the stigmas of both his illegitimacy and biracial makeup in the paternalistic atmosphere of the elitist mountaintop town, the home of the University of the South, he lived a fairly charmed childhood that evolved into a far more confused and even tortured adolescence, as his light skin and red hair made him an anomaly in both the black and white communities to which he only tangentially belonged.[22]

In 1912, at the age of eighteen, Ely found himself the target of a lynch mob, and with the aid of an uncle he fled Sewanee with a harrowing plunge down the mountain on a self-operated handcar — with no brake — to the train stop at Cowan, where he arrived in time to catch the early morning westbound train that would eventually take him to a new life in Waxahachie, Texas. The stationmaster was immediately suspicious when Green asked for a ticket to Texas, snarling, "Nigger, are you running from trouble? What have you done?" He grudgingly sold him a ticket, mumbling that "every time I've sold a ticket to Texas this time of morning they comes looking for them." Equally grudgingly, he flagged the train down, and it slowed long enough for Ely to jump onto the last car. A porter looked at his ticket and led him through a series of Pullman cars to a day coach. "You're a Sewanee boy," he said, recognizing the cadet's hat that Ely wore.

Only as the porter moved on did Ely look around and realize that everyone else in the car was white, and that the porter had obviously mistaken him for white as well, perhaps because of what he wore. "I didn't have any intention of making my identity known just then. I pulled my hat down tight as I could on my head to keep my sandy, curly hair from showing too much. No one would discover I was a Negro. In the morning I would go to the colored coach." But as he thought about what had transpired, he began to think of the possibilities of a new life and a new identity in Texas. "I remembered how quick that agent discovered I was a Negro the minute I walked into the sitting room," he wrote, adding that he recalled the assumed wisdom of a black acquaintance — "that a Southern sager [a derogatory term for poor white mountaineers] could smell Negro blood in a person no matter how white he was." He also noted that the black porter, obviously not a local, had mistaken him for white. He recalled that his foster sister had advised him that when traveling "to act as in Rome," and that she had spent two days riding in a white coach without detection. "I finally decided that I didn't ask to be there," Green concluded. "I had obeyed the porter. I was not trying to pass for white." In a sense, his new identity had been handed to him, and he hinted that due to the experience on the train, he might live life as a white man in Texas. He concluded his book by stating, "As I looked out the window I could see dawn approaching. That had been a sacred hour when I was in the mountains. That was the last time I held any thought of the life I had left behind me. The porter came through, and said: 'Nashville in fifteen minutes.'"[23]

For three nine-year-olds, encounters that began in railroad stations — often as fully the testing grounds as were the trains themselves — provided eye-opening and perplexing truths not just about the Jim Crow regime but about their own racial makeup or that of family members. Pauli Murray described her "first unnerving encounter with the race problem" while traveling with her Aunt Pauline from Baltimore to Durham, North Carolina, and having to change trains in Norfolk. While waiting for Pauline to inquire about their connection at the Norfolk station, Pauli found herself confronted by an agitated white man, and then surrounded by "a circle of white faces, all regarding me intently and turning to look at one another. Not a word was said, just stares, shrugs, and head scratchings." She found the mysterious scrutiny quite frightening, but was soon rescued by her aunt, who moved her quickly onto the Jim Crow car of the North Carolina–bound train. Just as they seated themselves, they were followed by the first man who had drawn such attention to Pauli in the station. He "strode past us, looking us up and down, and Aunt Pauline stared right back at him. Finally he dropped his eyes and hurried from the car."

Only when the train had left the station did Pauline relax and explain to her niece what had happened. Having earlier broken her eye glasses, she had inadvertently left Pauli in the white waiting room. Pauline was light enough not to draw attention to her presence there, but Pauli, who described herself as "a border-line racial type," found that "in the poorly lighted station they were trying to determine whether I was colored, and therefore out of place, or some foreign mixture." When her aunt had appeared to escort her to the train, they became even more confused, "so the ringleader had followed us out to the train to make sure of our racial identity." Murray wrote that they were the only passengers in the Jim Crow car, and the "unspoken threat" so unnerved them both that they remained tense throughout the night, not daring to sleep and responding with a jolt to the conductor's regular passages through the car. "The incident awakened my dread of lynchings," she concluded, "and I was learning the dangers of straying, however innocently, across a treacherous line into a hostile world."[24]

At the same age, James Farmer and Richard Wright learned very different lessons that began at the ticket windows of train stations. In *Lay Bare the Heart*, Farmer claimed to have first "glimpsed something of the complexity and absurdity of southern caste" in Austin, Texas, in 1930, where his father served as registrar and professor of religion at Samuel Houston College. At the end of a lengthy visit from his brother-in-law, Fred, and his family who lived in New York, James Sr. came up with a creative solution to providing his relatives with space on a Pullman car for their return trip north. As an employee of the railroad, Fred had had no problem reserving such space in New York (and had done so in order to avoid having to move to a Jim Crow car when they crossed the Mason-Dixon line). But for a black family to reserve the same space from an Austin ticket agent was more of a challenge, and young James watched his father make the attempt. His ploy — ultimately successful — was to identify himself as the college registrar and to explain that he was purchasing Pullman space for a distinguished visitor to the college, a prominent newspaper editor who could bring unwanted publicity to southern — more specifically, Austin's — mores if he couldn't travel back home in the same way that he had come south. The manager complied on the condition that they leave on a night train rather than a day one.

Young Farmer was puzzled and shocked by his father's lies. Even after his father explained that it was the only way to get the space needed for their relatives, he wrote many years later: "I was deeply troubled by my father's accommodation to a system that made him less than a man. I despised that within him that would not fight, perhaps because I saw the same survival instinct in myself." He recognized the role-playing required of an educated black man in the Jim Crow South, and practiced by James Sr.: "to the black community, a savant and solon; and to the whites, a 'good Negro,' compromising if not subservient, who knew his place." Nevertheless, he declared, "even as a child, I hated the lying, the dissembling, the subterfuge, the pretense — the squeezing of one's soul into a room too small."[25]

For Richard Wright, it was a different sort of encounter that led to his first awareness — and confusion — about racial identity and its implications. In embarking on a trip with his mother from a station in Jackson, Mississippi, in 1917, the nine-year-old noticed two ticket lines, one white and one black. Upon boarding the train, he quickly observed that "we Negroes were in one part of the train and that the whites were in another." Curious as to what he wasn't seeing, Wright asked his mother if he could "go and peep at the white folks." She told him to be quiet, and in so doing set off one of the most revealing dialogues in *Black Boy*, a painful exchange between mother and son in which he questioned her relentlessly not just about the rationales behind segregation ("I wanted to understand these two sets of people who lived side by side and never touched, it seemed, except in violence") but also the racial makeup of his own family members, beginning with his grandmother's white skin. His mother refused to provide adequate answers, and Wright's frustration and confusion grew. "Again I was being shut out of the secret, the thing, the reality I felt somewhere beneath all the words and silences," he wrote. He ended that train trip to Arkansas angry with her refusal to give him straight answers to his questions, and determined to get to the bottom of what it meant to be colored and why the very topic evoked such "a vague uneasiness about it all."[26]

That quest would drive much of the rest of Wright's narrative, and for all of his many confrontations with others — both white and black — as to his place in the repressive society that he found as baffling as it was constricting, never again would train travel serve as the impetus for his frustrations. Curiously, the next train trip he described was the most momentous of his life — that which carried him from Memphis to Chicago in 1927. With that journey he left the South forever; it formed not only a turning point in his life but the conclusion of the truncated version of his book that was published in 1945. Only in the restored full text published in 1991, which added another third to his narrative, do we see him exit the train that he stepped onto in Memphis, and yet he had nothing to say of the journey itself. His first impressions of Chicago and their implications for his future are as poignant as his discourse on the limited options he would have faced had he remained a southerner. Yet the trip itself evoked no emotion, no catharsis, no revealing moments that he chose to share with his readers. It is, in that respect, reminiscent of the void in Frederick Douglass's *Narrative* nearly a century earlier, though without the rationale that Douglass provided about the security measures that prevented a fugitive slave from revealing the particulars of his escape.

John Hope Franklin was three years younger than Murray, Farmer, or Wright when he first experienced "crude, raw racism" while on a train. Growing up in Oklahoma in the 1920s, he traveled frequently with his parents from their home in Rentiesville to the nearby metropolis of Checotah or beyond. Their rural community was so small that they had to flag down the passing train in order for it to stop. In his autobiography, *Mirror to America*, Franklin related an incident in which his mother, traveling with her two small children, flagged down the train and boarded the car closest to where they stood, which happened to be a white car. When the conductor discovered them there, he ordered them to move to the Jim Crow coach, which Mrs. Franklin refused to do, citing the risks of moving two small children from one car to another on a moving train and arguing that it was not her fault that the "Negro coach" had not been accessible from where they had stood on the platform when the train stopped. The conductor then had the train stopped, "not to let us move to the segregated coach, but 'to teach us a lesson,' by ejecting us from the train altogether."

Only six years old at the time, Franklin was "confused and scared" by the incident. "The uselessness of my mother's reasonable refusal to endanger her children," he wrote, "the arbitrary nature of injustice of the conductor's behavior, the clear pointlessness of any objection on our part, and the acquiescence if not approval of the other passengers to our removal brought home to me at that young age the racial divide separating me from white America." Unlike Mary Terrell's encounter fifty years earlier or the Delany sisters' two decades earlier, in which children had witnessed successful outcomes to parental defiance or conscious choice, Franklin had had to watch his mother's impotence to sway not only the authority figure involved but the complicity of other witnesses to her treatment. Like Terrell's mother and unlike Wright's, Mrs. Franklin tried to comfort her son by assuring him "that there was not a white person on that train or anywhere else who was any better than I was." Rather than waste his energy "by fretting," she urged him to save it in order to prove just that point.[27]

For some children, it was what they observed looking out train windows that made such memorable impressions. Sara Brooks, the daughter of a black cotton farmer in central Alabama, recalled her first train trip in the mid-1910s, from the separate waiting areas (even on the outdoor platform) to the lack of any toilet facilities for blacks. She confirmed that blacks had the train's first coach to themselves but noted that if it filled, the only other option was the baggage car, "where we'd be mixed up with the baggage" and had to stand up. But far more chilling was what she saw outside. She recalled one stop, Foxfield, Alabama, where "no colored peoples got off." There was a sign visible from the train that stated "Niggers, read and run." She speculated much later in life: "I guess a lotta poor white people were livin' there and they didn't want no colored people in that place where they were livin', see what I mean?" Neither she nor her father commented on the sign at the time. "We was just so glad to get on the train. We didn't say nothing and we didn't question anything. Nope. We just went." Yet such practices made an impression, and like many black children, her memories of such incidents continued to haunt her. Brooks ends her simple story by stating, "When we start thinking, getting older, then we'd ask each other, say, 'Wonder why?'"[28]

Willie Mae Workman, a Georgia woman who narrated her life story to Elizabeth Kytle in 1958, also remembered more vividly the view looking out of the train than anything she experienced on board. Her first train trip came as she, then fifteen years old, moved with her sisters from Atlanta to Louisville, Kentucky, to live with their father in the mid-1920s. She made no reference to segregated seating or the condition of the coach in which they traveled for two days; only the train's stop in Lexington, Kentucky, evoked any commentary. Very hungry at that point — "growl hungry," as she termed it — she stated that blacks traveling through were not allowed to disembark there. "Some of the colored folks on the train even kept the shades drawn," she recalled, "so none of those white folks would see us. So we just didn't have a bit to eat, because we were scared to try to get out and buy something."[29]

The outspoken Bessie Delany, a North Carolina native, used a similar incident to illustrate her claim that "Georgia was a mean place — meaner than North Carolina. . . . In Georgia, they never missed a chance to keep you down." On her way to her first teaching assignment in Brunswick, Georgia, in 1913, Delany had to change trains in nearby Waycross. As she sat in the small "colored waiting room" with two other teachers traveling with her, a drunken white man stuck his head in the door and leered at her. Disgusted, Bessie told him, "Oh, why don't you shut up and go wait with your own kind in the white waiting room?" What happened next, she said, "was kind of like an explosion." He retreated indignantly to the platform outside, and shouted, "The nigger bitch insulted me! The nigger bitch insulted me!" Delany's two companions quietly slipped out of the room and hid in the nearby woods. A black porter came in to see what was causing the commotion. He whispered, "Good for you!" to Bessie before also retreating from the scene. As a crowd gathered around the offended drunk, she realized she was in "big trouble." "I was just waiting for someone to get a rope," she recalled. "Thousands of Negroes had been lynched for far less than what I had just done." Two things ultimately saved her. "That glorious, blessed train rounded the bend," breaking up the crowd and giving her a means of escape. And, she said, "it helped that the white man was drunk as a skunk, and that turned off some of the white people as well."[30] Like Brooks and Workman, Bessie Delany found that, whatever the conditions of travel on trains, it was sometimes safer to be on them than off.

Although far less frequent, white autobiographers occasionally included revealing incidents regarding segregated train travel as part of their life stories. Unlike African American writers, of course, they were never on the receiving end of the humiliation or vulnerability inherent in such policies, but nor were they necessarily mere bystanders. With perhaps less emotional investment in the incidents they describe, their participation in such incidents or that of their traveling companions offers other perspectives that make even more apparent the range of ways in which racial dynamics affected railroad travel.

Thomas Wolfe wrote more matter-of-factly about what seems to be a mirror image of many of the experiences told from black perspectives. In 1904 Wolfe was a mere three years old when he accompanied his mother and older siblings by train from their home in Asheville, North Carolina, to St. Louis, where Mrs. Wolfe planned to operate a boarding house for the duration of the world's fair there. In *The Lost Boy* (like so much of his writing, a thinly veiled fictionalization of incidents from his youth) Wolfe recounted, through his mother's later retelling, the gallantry of his eleven-year-old brother Grover in the manly responsibilities he assumed on that trip west. She recalled that when the train crossed from Kentucky into Indiana ("of course, they had no Jim Crow there"), Simpson Featherstone, "that big old yellow, pock-marked darky which your father got to go out with us to St. Louis," walked into the railroad car from the car behind and "swaggered right down the middle of the aisle, as if he owned the place." He placed his suitcase in the baggage rack, took off his overcoat, and took a seat, making "himself at home, if you please, as if he owned the railroad." Much offended by his impudence, Mrs. Wolfe tried to suggest to Simpson that he was in the wrong place and should go back to his "own car." He calmly replied that "I don't have to go back there no more; we's in Indiana now and I can ride anywhere I please."

At that point Grover intervened and forbade his mother's employee to remain. When Simpson insisted that "it's the law," the eleven-year-old replied, "It may be their law, but it's not ours. It's not our way of doing, and it's not your way of doing either. No, you know better cause you were brought up different." Mrs. Wolfe could hardly contain her pride in her son in retelling the story. "Of course, like everyone, [Simpson] respected Grover's judgment . . . and he got up, sir, he got right up, sir, without another word" and marched back to his own car "where he belonged." When a fellow passenger remarked to Mrs. Wolfe that her son was "a remarkable boy," she fully agreed. She concluded the story by stating that the stranger had recognized that "Grover had more sense and character than most grown-ups. And he was right."[31]

If this was a story of a courageous young boy protecting both his family and southern mores beyond the bounds of the South, it was a product of its time — the 1930s — and of a writer who never experienced a "racial conversion" as did so many other southern white autobiographers of a slightly later era. One of the foremost of those who did was Georgia native Katharine Du Pre Lumpkin, who wrote movingly of how traveling with a black companion proved to be a key revelatory moment in *The Making of a Southerner*, one of the most definitive of these so-called racial conversion narratives.[32] From a very young age, Lumpkin became aware of Jim Crow and took comfort in the clarity with which the separation of the races was defined and imposed. "I began to be self-conscious about the many signs and symbols of my race position that had been battering against my consciousness since virtual infancy," she wrote in an early chapter of her memoir, titled "A Child Inherits the Lost Cause." "I found them to be countless in number. As soon as I could read, I would carefully spell out the notices in public places. I wished to be certain we were where we ought to be. Our station waiting rooms — 'For White.' Our railroad coaches — 'For White.' There was no true occasion for a child's anxiety lest we make a mistake. It was all so plainly marked."[33]

Yet as she came of age, Lumpkin found the signage that had proved so reassuring when she was a child to be far less comforting. As a national secretary of the YWCA in the early 1920s, she frequently met with colleagues from other parts of the South and on occasion traveled with an African American colleague. On one such trip from Virginia to North Carolina, she detailed how sharply her perceptions changed. In coming into the station, the twosome had to use separate entrances, one "For Colored" and one "For White." Despite her long familiarity with these designations, she suddenly saw them through different eyes. "Every feature of these now peculiar-seeming arrangements thrust themselves against me as something shockingly new," she declared. She explained that she and her companion had to buy their tickets at separate windows and sit in separate waiting rooms. They defied convention only by strolling together on the platform outside (the one space, she wrote, "that must have baffled our Southern ingenuity.") "Then came the train," Lumpkin wrote, and proceeded to describe the same segregated passenger cars. One was next to the engine, with half of the space given over to baggage. Multiple, more comfortable coaches fell behind. All were clearly marked, leading Lumpkin to note, "One knew one sign was meant to stigmatize, the other to assert superiority. But not for frivolous or capricious reasons. Never had I seen so plainly as on this day how deadly serious the white South was in its signs and separations, or understood in clearer focus its single-mindedness of aim."[34]

Curiously, Lillian Smith had very little to say about train travel amid the vast range of class and racial injustices she condemned so vehemently in her semi-memoir, *Killers of the Dream*. It is less surprising, perhaps, that the one incident she does recount was not one she experienced herself, but rather one told to her by an adolescent white Atlantan who spent the summer at the girls' camp Smith operated in the mountains of north Georgia in the 1930s and 1940s. Smith devoted several chapters to the moral and historical lessons she sought to instill in her campers, which led some of them, in turn, to confide in her. One seventeen-year-old girl, according to Smith, told her that in the dining car on a trip to New York with her father several months earlier, she had noticed the president of a black college in Atlanta eating behind drawn curtains. "I said, 'Daddy, did you see that? He's the president of a college!' And Daddy said, 'That's where colored folks are supposed to sit. You mustn't get silly notions, honey.'" But she couldn't let the matter rest, and couldn't finish her dinner. "I know it was morbid," Smith quoted her as saying, "but I kept looking at all those faces wondering why they felt they had to have a curtain between them and the president of a college, just to eat their dinner. And it began to seem so crazy!"

Yet the young Atlantan's response was not as morally clear cut as one might expect, especially coming from Smith, for whom there was often little shading or ambivalence in her own sense of right and wrong. The girl confided that she had real doubts as to whether she could, or should, challenge her father's wisdom — or at least authority — on this and other matters of decorum and social values. "I want so much to go home and be decent about things. Not make folks mad — just live what I believe is right? But how? Tell me how." This was just the opening Smith needed to launch into a discourse on the South's legacy of racial oppression and how it had evolved.[35] Like James Farmer's treatment of his own father's actions in Austin, it was not the inequity itself but rather the doubts raised as to her own father's value system that proved so troubling to Smith's camper. Likewise, the fact that the object of this humiliating position was not just any black man, but one of real distinction, added to her sense of injustice — and to that of Smith as well.[36]

Finally, Jimmy Carter represents one of the few southern whites who came of age in the 1920s who seemed to need no conversion in terms of his racial views, and yet he wrote very simply and matter-of-factly about segregation as he first knew it. In a vivid memoir of his boyhood on his family's farm in Archery in southwest Georgia, Carter devoted a great deal of space to the closest companionship he enjoyed during those years: that of a black boy of the same age named Alonzo Davis (but called A. D.), who lived with an aunt and uncle, tenants of the Carter family.

Among the many activities shared by the two boys in the late 1920s and early 1930s were occasional excursions to the movies in Americus, the closest town of any size, nine miles away. To get there, they had to take the train, which stopped in Archery only if they raised a red leather flag that signaled the engineer of waiting passengers. After paying fifteen cents each, Carter and A. D. parted company to sit in seats marked "white" and "colored." (Carter doesn't indicate whether these seats were in separate coaches or not.) Once in Americus, they reunited and walked together to the Rylander Theater, where they again separated, as A. D. entered from behind and had to climb to the third balcony, while young Jimmy remained below. "Afterward," Carter wrote, "we would go back home, united in friendship, though physically divided on the segregated train." He admits to very little conscious thought about the situation. "Our only strong feeling was one of gratitude for our wonderful excursion; I don't remember ever questioning the mandatory racial separation, which we accepted like breathing or waking up in Archery every morning."[37]

Such an unassuming telling of this practice is a reflection of the former president's low-key style; but the very fact that he chose to reveal it at all, particularly in noting how routine and unquestioned their train and theater separations were, indicates that Carter had, at some point since, realized how wrong such a system was. It is significant as well that within Carter's relatively isolated, innocent, and idyllic rural world, the one manifestation of the greater society's inequities to which he was exposed was that of a Jim Crow train car, coupled with the movie theater to which that train carried him. Had his one companion on those excursions not been black, segregation would have likely escaped his notice altogether for at least several more years.

While the mixed nature of southern white memories of Jim Crow travel is not surprising, the fact that not all black descriptions of their railroad experiences were negative does challenge expectations. Certain accounts are so positive that one suspects that other agendas were behind the stories they told — or chose not to tell. Booker T. Washington, for example, first traveled by train as part of his long and fitful journey from West Virginia to the Hampton Institute in 1872, and yet he had nothing to relate of that aspect of his trip in *Up from Slavery*, commenting instead on the uncertainties of funding his trip and the accommodations he had to settle for along the way. Nor did his even longer trip nine years later from Hampton to Tuskegee, Alabama, evoke any commentary. In fact, the only anecdote Washington offered regarding railroad travel is to make a very different point from any yet described here.

Only in describing the esteem with which he was held by southerners and the support they had given Tuskegee throughout his years there did he choose to reveal more about a train trip. Washington stated that "in all my contact with the white people of the South, I have never received a single personal insult." To illustrate the point, he related an incident that occurred during one of his extensive speaking tours throughout the region in the 1890s. Traveling from

Augusta to Atlanta, Washington said that he had taken the option of a Pullman sleeper. There he encountered two ladies from Boston with whom he was well acquainted. They seemed delighted to see him and insisted that he share a seat with them in their section of the car. "After some hesitation," he wrote, "I consented," though "when one of them, without my knowledge, ordered supper to be served to the three of us, this embarrassed me further." The car was full of southern men, all of whom were watching this unusual threesome intently. Despite his efforts to make an unobtrusive exit, his hostesses insisted that he remain through the meal. Nervous as to how his presence was perceived by the white observers, Washington finally extricated himself from the women's company and went to the smoking car, to which most of them had retired, "to see how the land lay." Upon entering, he wrote, "I was never more surprised in my life than when each man, nearly every one of them a citizen of Georgia, came up and introduced himself to me and thanked me earnestly for the work that I was trying to do for the whole South." "This was not flattery," he added, because these men "knew that they had nothing to gain by trying to flatter me."[38]

Washington must have known that he strained credibility with this story, even in 1901, when *Up from Slavery* first appeared. And yet what could have been better than so unlikely a scenario to illustrate a point that he drove relentlessly through much of the book: that his work in promoting vocational educational opportunities for southern blacks was not only good for the region as a whole, but that it was recognized as such by most southern whites — and that he enjoyed exceptional treatment by most of them, who valued what he was doing. He was hardly subtle in making the point, and by making the setting of his anecdote one of the most familiar sites for the harassment, abuse, and humiliation of so many blacks, he accentuated just how special his treatment was, and, by implication, how special he was.

Zora Neale Hurston was another southern black writer with a unique perspective on the region and its race relations. One of the most accomplished, if less successful, of the Harlem Renaissance authors, Hurston grew up in the nation's only exclusively black incorporated community — Eatonville, Florida. Given the peculiar nature of that insulated environment, she claimed never to have experienced the oppression or abuse that was so common to others of her generation, at least until she left home. ("Jacksonville," where she was sent to school, "made me know that I was a little colored girl."[39]) In an introduction to Hurston's 1942 memoir, *Dust Tracks on a Road*, Maya Angelou expressed her perplexity with this claim, calling it "a puzzling book" in which the author "does not mention even one unpleasant racial incident"; in fact, according to Angelou, Hurston implied that "the nicest people she met in her youth were whites who showed her kindness." Arno Bontemps was even more critical of Hurston's approach when the book appeared in 1942, noting that she "deals very simply with the more serious aspects of Negro life in America — she ignores them."[40] Angelou, like others who have discovered Hurston and her work relatively late, speculated as to this strange distancing of herself both from southern blacks and from southern racism. Whatever the reasons for it, it was in anecdotes about railroads that Hurston makes her stance most apparent.

One of the first passages in Hurston's autobiography in which it becomes obvious that her memories held no room for racial slights involves her first trip on a train. Her father, a Baptist preacher, traveled frequently in his role as moderator of the South Florida Baptist Association. At some point in the late 1890s, he decided to take his young daughter with him on one such trip, but she was utterly frightened of the train that came "thundering" around a curve and "snorting into the station . . . fixing its one big, mean-looking eye on me." Zora found the whole so fearsome that she refused to get aboard, and since the train only slowed at the small station, rather than coming to a full stop, she took advantage of the opportunity to pull away from her father as he stepped aboard. Eventually she was captured and "hauled on board kicking and screaming to the huge amusement of everybody but me." But she wrote, "As soon as I saw the glamour of the plush and metal of the inside of that coach, I calmed down." Her father laughed heartily at her sudden change of heart. After extra pampering by the conductor and porter, who knew her father well, Zora was, by the end of the trip, "crazy about the train," the inside of which "was too pretty for words. It took years for me to get over loving it."[41]

Of course, what's striking about this story is the lack of any racial element. There is nothing in Hurston's telling of this incident that indicates that either she or her father were African Americans or treated accordingly. The beauty of the train's interior and the gracious treatment accorded the Hurstons by its crew suggest that this was not a Jim Crow car or that blacks were in any way discriminated against at any point in their journey, thus making this — like her autobiography as a whole — very much at odds with that of any other black southerner coming of age in the early twentieth century.[42]

Even more revealing of her efforts to distance herself from others of her race is an experience later in life and far from the South. By then, well established as a writer in New York and a graduate of Barnard College, Hurston described in almost parable-like prose an incident on a subway. She and a male companion (she labels the pair Barnard and Yale — "well-dressed, well-mannered, and good to look at") were returning uptown from a concert by Marion Anderson. At the Seventy-second Street station, "two scabby-looking Negroes come scrambling into the coach" and choose to sit next to Yale and Barnard, despite many vacant seats elsewhere. Smelly and dirty, the two "woof, bookoo, broadcast and otherwise discriminate from one end of the coach to the other. They consider it a golden opportunity to put on a show." Barnard and Yale sit there and "dwindle and dwindle." They don't look around at the white passengers' reactions to the commotion beside them, but they know too well what those reactions are. "Some are grinning from the heel up and some are stonily quiet. But both kinds are thinking 'That's just like a Negro!' . . . Feeling all of this like rock-salt under the skin, Yale and Barnard shake their heads and moan, 'My People, My People!'"

That humiliation led Hurston to expound upon similar frustrations regularly faced by accomplished blacks in the South as well, and for the first time in her book she acknowledged the segregation of southern railroads and explained why so many found it offensive:

> Certain of My People have come to dread railway day coaches for the same reason. They dread such scenes more than they do the dirty upholstery and other inconveniences of a Jim Crow coach. They detest the forced grouping. The railroad company feels "you are all colored aren't you? So why not all together?" . . . So when sensitive souls are forced to travel that way they sit there numb and when some free soul takes off his shoes and socks, they mutter "My race but not My taste." When someone eats fried fish, bananas and a mess of peanuts and throws all the leavings on the floor, they gasp, "My skinfolks but not my kinfolks."[43]

Hurston's elitism is never more in evidence than in this passage, and what easier way to rail against the unfair and inaccurate generalizations made on the basis of skin color than to focus on railroad coaches (or subway cars) as the one crucible in which all of these elements were thrown together — blacks, both refined and uncouth, and the whites who passed judgment on them all?

Hurston was not the first to express such class-based disdain for the assumptions behind Jim Crow cars. Fifty years earlier, in 1892, black feminist Anna Julia Cooper made much the same case in her ground-breaking tract, *A Voice from the South*. Protesting the idea that a quest for "social equality" was behind African Americans' desire to ride in the same passenger cars with whites, Cooper explained that "when I seek food in a public café or apply for first-class accommodations on a railway train, I do so because my physical necessities are identical with those of other human beings of like constitution and temperament, and crave satisfaction." She insisted that "I go because I want food, or I want comfort — not because I want association with those who frequent these places; and I can see no more 'social equality' in buying lunch at the same restaurant, or riding in a common car, than there is in paying for dry goods at the same counter or walking on the same street."

Like Hurston, a part of that comfort sought by Cooper concerned with whom she would not have to associate in a first-class car. "I do not, and cannot be made to associate with all dark persons, simply on the grounds that I am dark," she wrote. "And I presume the Southern lady can imagine some whose faces are white, with whom she would no sooner think of chatting unreservedly than, were it possible, with a veritable 'darkey.'"[44] She, like so many African American writers, revealed through her feelings on segregated train travel her sense of self-worth, her social and racial pride, and her sense of injustice based on both.

In a memoir about her husband published just after his death in 1955, Walter White's widow revealed an incident that suggests that he too was accustomed to more privileged treatment on trains than he always received (and which, for all too obvious reasons, he chose not to reveal in his own autobiography). In returning home to New York from Atlanta in 1931, White dropped by the apartment of Poppy Cannon, then merely a friend, to ask for a cup of coffee before he headed on to his office. Looking stressed and tired, he explained to her that he had no cash; he had had to sit up all night on a Jim Crow coach, where someone had stolen his wallet. "They wouldn't give me a Pullman," he said. Cannon explained to her readers: "I understood the stratagems necessary for a Negro to get Pullman accommodations. I knew about what was called 'Upper 13' — the compartment that was sometimes assigned to prominent Negroes to keep their presence from being noted by white passengers." She noted that White was holding something back, that there was a "look of shame and betrayal in his face." She concluded that the likely reason he had not reported the theft to the conductor was that the thief was a Negro, "perhaps the man who sat next to him in the crowded Jim Crow train and in the morning had disappeared."[45] While sacrificing whatever funds he carried to shield a fellow African American from prosecution and perhaps worse, White also seemed to make clear, at least to Cannon, that it was not a situation in which he often found himself or would have put himself in then if his usual option had been available.

Reported confrontations on Jim Crow railroads became increasingly rare after the Second World War, though those few indicated that the war had had little impact on the rigidity of Jim Crow's hold on the South. John Hope Franklin referred only briefly in his memoir to a story he had often told before: that of taking a train from Greensboro to Durham, North Carolina, in 1945, where he was one of many black passengers crowded into the half car designated for their use. A mere six passengers made use of the first full coach for whites only, and despite requests that some adjustment be made, the conductor was unwilling to relent "and stuck strictly to the letter of the Jim Crow law." Only at this point in the narrative did Franklin reveal that the six white passengers were German prisoners of war. He concluded with the simple remark that "even in the face of the demise of Nazism, those African American passengers remained victims of American racism."[46]

Journalist Carl Rowan offered a more ambivalent account of how rigidly Jim Crow restrictions were enforced on trains in the postwar years, when he detected signs that things were changing in terms of segregation's rules and regulations. In a chapter of his 1952 memoir, *South to Freedom*, titled "Night Train to Georgia," Rowan related an incident that had occurred the year before. In moving from Miami to Macon, Georgia, he reserved a seat by telephone on the Florida East Coast Line. When he arrived at the station and asked for the ticket he had been assigned over the phone — car four, seat thirty-seven — the agent tried, in a very quiet voice, to offer him "anything in car 1." Rowan insisted on the car and seat held in his name, and the agent ultimately relented rather than create a scene.[47]

Rowan wrote that he boarded the train a bit warily, but no one seemed to object to his being there. He even went up to the club car for a sandwich and a beer, and despite "a rustle of eyebrows as I entered, no one said a word." He found an ally in the black waiter, who "'sirred' me in a tone that said he was overjoyed to see what was taking place." He even offered Rowan further service after the announcement that the car was closing for the night and retrieved his typewriter from his seat in car four so that this ground-breaking patron could work from the club car. Rowan was surprised, but he soon realized that "word had traveled fast among Negroes on the train that I was 'putting one over on Jim Crow.'"

After working for a time, he looked up and realized that he was alone in the car except for a white woman passenger. "Here I sit," he thought, "riding in a 'white' railroad coach across Florida and into Georgia. And here I am alone with a typewriter, some paper, a white woman, and four cans of beer and a book." The woman seemed no more bothered by that state of affairs than anyone else on the train. Except for a minor incident in which a sleeping white passenger in car four was awakened suddenly in the morning to find himself facing a black man and scurrying away to another part of the car, Rowan was amazed at what he felt he had pulled off on this train. "This incident did not dim my happiness over the whole trip. I was still jubilant when I left the train at Macon. I had visions of a new day in Georgia, and even the Jim Crow waiting rooms that stared me in the face could not wipe out the optimism."

Rowan's mood — and the story's object lesson — changed quickly, however, when he attempted to cross the line to the white side of the room in order to buy a newspaper and was sternly told by the Macon stationmaster that that was not a valid reason for violating the demarcation of "White Only." He challenged the logic of such a rule, especially when told that only a black redcap was authorized to cross the room and bring the paper to him, taunting the stationmaster, "If your segregation system or democracy had to fall, which would you uphold?" The stationmaster responded, "You ain't in New York. You're just another black nigger in Georgia." Despite his anger, Rowan realized that he had probably carried his verbal challenge as far as was safe, and he quickly headed on his way. He concluded the story by stating, "I had been too hasty in my jubilation, in my illusions of a New South. . . . Bigotry isn't nearly dead in Dixie. 'Georgia is essentially a police state,' I mumbled . . . 'and any white man who decides to be is a policeman, where a Negro is involved.'"[48]

Only four years after Rowan's experience, Lillian Smith, of all people, presented a very different depiction of segregated train travel, suggesting that by 1955 such restrictions were not quite as rigorous as they had once been. (Perhaps significantly, she did so in private correspondence, rather than in print.) In a defense of southern progress despite the brutal murder of Emmett Till that summer, Smith used a train trip she took only weeks later to demonstrate to Vermont writer Dorothy Canfield Fisher, who had written her concerned about increased racial tensions in the South, that Till's death was more an aberration than the norm.

In traveling from Georgia to New York in August, Smith boarded the train in Toccoa, where she encountered in "the newly integrated waiting room" an elderly black couple who were putting their two young granddaughters on the train to return home after a summer spent with them on their farm. "But who knows about these integrated waiting rooms in the small towns?" she wrote parenthetically. Once on board, she found herself in a roomette just across the aisle from the girls and invited them to come over and visit with her in her compartment. "We had fun for an hour or two. Then they went back to their roomette and read comic books and played games." Even a white conductor—with a Georgia accent no less—came by and "spoke most pleasantly to them" and asked them about their summer experience with Grandpa and Grandma on the farm. He was very kind, Smith noted, and assured them that he would help them get off the train in Philadelphia the next morning. At supper time, Smith asked the children to join her in the dining car, and despite a few raised eyebrows, no one made a fuss. "I saw not one expression of shock or resentment and everybody in the dining car was probably a southerner."

She concluded her story by stating that, after the girls had returned to their compartment and had gotten ready for bed, Smith—bunking just across the narrow aisle from them—heard "a chanting of little voices." She opened her door and saw the girls "kneeling in the aisle in their pink and blue pajamas with their head on the bed, saying their prayers. 'Now I lay me down to sleep . . . if I should die before I wake, I pray . . . .'" "But you see," Smith lectured Fisher,

> they did not die. They got home safely and they had a pleasant, comfortable trip
> back North. They had also had a fine vacation, a completely secure one, down
> South. There were thousands of these children who came South last summer and
> returned safe and sound. That does not justify the death of the Till boy, nor does
> it make it less cruel or barbarous; but it does help us see the total picture in an
> honest perspective to be reminded that after all, murder came to only one of these
> children.[49]

In short, Smith used this incident not only to refute Canfield's impression that the Till murder was indicative of racial violence rampant throughout the South, but also to suggest that progress was being made—and she found a railroad car the surest way of making her case.

Then there is Henry Louis Gates's nostalgic and almost elegiac remembrance of his childhood in the small African American community within Piedmont, West Virginia, a dying paper-mill town made up of far more Italian and Irish immigrants than blacks. Gates is remarkably forthright about the segregated existence that seemed so entrenched as he came of age in the 1950s and early 1960s, and yet he also acknowledges what few other black writers ever have: the fact that there were certain aspects of Jim Crow that he and others in his community missed when civil rights — belatedly and gradually — were finally imposed on this remote corner of the border South. (The dawn of the movement was no more than "a spectator sport in Piedmont," Gates declared, watched with interest, but no sense of engagement, on television.[50])

In addition to the loss of *Amos and Andy* on television and black-only picnics for mill workers, Gates pointed out an aspect of Jim Crow railroad cars that none of these other writers acknowledged — the sense of security and camaraderie . . . and the cuisine — that came from this racially exclusive enclosure in which blacks traveled. His childhood trips with his family to visit his mother's sister in Charleston entailed a five-hour train ride, followed by a bus ride. It was the first part of that trek that he remembered so fondly and cited as his prime example of the advantages of segregation. "So what," he asked, "if we didn't feel comfortable eating in the dining car? Our food was better. Fried chicken, baked beans, and potato salad . . . and a book and two decks of cards . . . and I didn't care if the train never got there." It became cherished family time: "We'd sing or read in our own section, munching that food and feeling sorry for the people who couldn't get any, and play 500 or Tonk or Fish with Mama and Daddy, until we fell asleep."[51]

Other than Rowan, Smith, and Gates, few autobiographers comment on railroad experiences in the 1950s or beyond. By the time the civil rights movement took on Jim Crow, buses seemed to have supplanted trains as the testing ground for public transportation — from the boycott in Montgomery in 1955 and 1956 to the Freedom Rides in the early 1960s. Most memoirs by civil rights leaders, from Coretta Scott King and Anne Moody to Ralph Abernathy and John Lewis, make no mention either of protests centered on railroad companies or of childhood memories involving segregated train cars, even though they have much to say about other childhood or adolescent exposures to segregated conditions and racial prejudice.[52] This may be due to the fact that the Interstate Commerce Commission, NAACP efforts, and a series of Supreme Court rulings (beginning with *Mitchell v. United States* in 1941) brought about the desegregation of first-class and Pullman cars during and just after World War II and thus precluded the protests that would otherwise have been inevitable a few years later.[53] Another explanation is simply that buses had become for many African Americans an increasingly viable and less expensive option than trains for long-distance travel by the 1950s.

As with almost any aspect of southern life conveyed through personal memory or reflection, the variations are striking. No black writer condoned the practice of Jim Crow and the related abuses, embarrassments, or inconveniences posed by railroad travel for much of the era, though several — mostly young children from Maya Angelou to Henry Louis Gates — found Jim Crow cars to be racial comfort zones. As much as these stories cumulatively reveal about the realities of racism and its codification and systematized implementation throughout the South during the Jim Crow era, the value of these autobiographical accounts lies far more in the range of responses they reveal on the part of the African Americans forced to confront this oppression either for the first time or on a regular basis.

Particularly telling are the ways in which these authors used their memories of those confrontations to reveal character traits — either in themselves or in others. Mary Terrell was as proud of her father's defiance, even at gunpoint, toward officials who sought to deny him his right to first-class seating, as was Thomas Wolfe's mother of her son Grover's courage in ordering their black employee back into "his place" when he attempted to exercise new liberties once their train had moved across the Mason-Dixon line. Bessie Delany revealed the essence of her defiant approach to white abuse in her actions in a Waycross train station, though she quickly realized the danger resulting from such an impulse — an impulse her sister Sadie would never have given into or approved of. Bessie's acknowledgment of their differences speaks volumes as to the range of temperaments and strategies demonstrated in response to the affronts faced by most of the authors represented here: "Sadie said I was a fool to provoke that white man. As if I provoked *him*! Honey, he provoked *me*! Sadie says she would have ignored him. I say, how do you ignore some drunk, smelly white man treating you like trash? She says, child, it's better to put up with it, and live to tell about it."[54]

The Delanys embodied the two basic impulses of most African American autobiographers who were ultimately forced to take positions of either defiance or compliance. (It is hardly surprising that for those who wrote autobiographies — in itself an act of assertiveness — defiant actions appear far more often than do more passive responses.) Yet even those who courageously — or perhaps recklessly — stood their ground faced mixed success. Several accounts of testing the limits of Jim Crow's resolve suggest that it was often subject to local, state, or regional variations, particularly early on or very late in his career. Ida B.

Wells and John Hope Franklin's mother were removed from trains — the latter with her small children — for defying conductors who sought to remove them from their seats. Carl Rowan stood firm at the ticket window in Miami and insisted that he be given the ticket he had ordered by phone. He realized that he was testing the system — and was somewhat dismayed at what he was able to get away with in doing so — until the reality of Jim Crow's entrenchment hit home as he stepped off that train in Macon, Georgia. James Weldon Johnson's two trips four years apart also suggest that timing and railroad personnel were crucial contingencies as he sought to maintain his first-class seating, with very different results.

Some children, such as James Farmer and Richard Wright, discovered that their parents had learned to either outsmart the system or to conform to it, and they expressed uncertainty as to how they felt about what they had observed. Others, such as Pauli Murray, Eli Green, and the Delanys, discovered the extent to which appearances mattered. They came to see that there were loopholes for the privileged and light-complexioned who took advantage of them; and those who chose not to also revealed character and temperament. The Delany sisters wrote with admiration that their parents — due either to appearance or position — had options as to where they could sit that other black passengers did not, and yet they declined such privileges, choosing instead to sit "with our people." Booker T. Washington acknowledged taking advantage of opportunities whites made available to him because of the high regard in which they held him, while Zora Neale Hurston, Anna Julia Cooper, and, less explicitly, Walter White, seemed to think themselves entitled by class and accomplishment to better treatment than other blacks and resented having to share the indignities imposed on all members of their race by sheer commonality of color.

If train travel served as a litmus test or lightning rod of sorts for the responses of southern blacks to the third-class status to which they were so regularly subjected, many of them also acknowledged that train travel was integral to the course of their lives at one time or another. As Maya Angelou noted, railroads were vital elements in bringing families together and in separating them. They transported many into new lives and toward new opportunities, from Frederick Douglass and Booker T. Washington to Richard Wright and the Delany sisters, moving out of the South (or on occasion, as in Maya Angelou's case, deeper into it). For far more black southerners, trains played a more limited but equally important role: they provided a means of reinforcing kinship ties and keeping families in contact with each other. No small number of the incidents related here involved children visiting grandparents or other relatives. In that context, Gates's nostalgia for that aspect of Jim Crow seems more explicable. Trains brought families to each other — and, in his case, kept them together on board.

W. E. B. Du Bois addressed this point in a curious and rather oblique way. In his 1920 treatise, *Darkwater,* he described an interracial social gathering in a Georgia home, in which the topic of travel came up. A white guest in all innocence commented to an African American couple in the room, "I should think you would like to travel." Their response — that "the thought of a journey seemed to depress them" — led Du Bois to launch into a vivid description of the physical and social discomforts of train travel for blacks — the dirty, overcrowded, and uncomfortable coaches and waiting rooms and rude or callous treatment to which they were subjected by white employees and fellow travelers throughout. He concluded with the response of the woman to whom the comment had been directed: "No," she said, "we don't travel much."

Yet Du Bois did not end his commentary there. For as understandable as the couple's lack of enthusiasm for train travel was, Du Bois disapproved of their avoidance of it. "Pessimism is cowardice," he declared. "The man who cannot frankly acknowledge the 'Jim-Crow' car as a fact and yet live and hope is simply afraid either of himself or of the world." As "disgraceful a denial of human brotherhood" as it is, it is just as true that "there is nothing more beautiful in the universe than sunset and moonlight on Montego Bay in far Jamaica. And both things are true and both belong to this our world, and neither can be denied."[55] It was a curious juxtaposition to apply to southern black experience, given that world travel — even to Jamaica — was well beyond the means of nearly all of those he judged as "cowards" for not thinking of the pains of train travel through larger and more positive contexts (not to mention the fact that Jamaica was inaccessible by train). Yet the point Du Bois seemed to be making was that railroads did allow access to other rewarding aspects of life — whether it was mere scenic beauty or the means to seek greater economic opportunity or to bring families together. To embrace the one meant having to endure the other.

Few if any of the other African American authors cited here ever acknowledged that sort of silver lining to the humiliation, inconvenience, and discomfort they were forced to endure. Even with the range of responses to the experiences described by these many southern autobiographers, the overwhelming commonality that links most of them is what Lillian Smith so aptly referred to as "a psychic brutality," or "the quiet killing of self-esteem, the persistent smothering of hope and pride, the deep bruises given the egos of young Negro children; the never ceasing humiliations which Jim Crow imposes upon human beings who are not white."[56]

It is those hard truths that these stories convey in such personal, even intimate terms. What happened to African Americans on train coaches or in waiting rooms and what they saw from train windows or experienced at ticket windows were significant enough as turning points, and they were so vividly remembered that they became notable components of the versions of their lives they chose to commit to print. This is the real power of autobiography as a historical genre and why for southerners in particular their stories so easily transcend the specifics to tell us much more about the demoralization, discontent, and debilitation that so infused African Americans' sense of themselves and their world under Jim Crow's regime.

CHAPTER FIVE

"I'm Better Than This Sorry Place"

*Coming to Terms with Self
and the South in College*

WILLIE MORRIS'S DISILLUSIONMENT with college life came early in his fresh-man year at the University of Texas in the fall of 1952. A Yazoo City, Mississippi, native who went to UT in Austin at his father's urging — "I think you ought to go to school out there. Can't nuthin' in *this* state match it" — Morris had been desperately homesick when he left home at age seventeen. Though dazzled by this new world in which he found himself — noting that "the life I saw about me was richer, and more flamboyant than anything I had known before" — it was not long before he "would grow progressively more lonely, more contemp-tuous of this organized anarchy, more despairing of the ritualized childishness and grasping narcissism of the fraternity life." At a particularly low moment in his social life, wearing a toga and abandoned on a hilltop outside of town as part of an obligatory hazing, Morris got mad, madder than he'd ever been — "at homesickness, at blond majorettes, at gap-toothed Dallas girls, at fraternities, at twangy accents, at my own helpless condition," all of which led him to declare, "I'm better than this sorry place."[1]

Few autobiographers articulated the emotional impact of their transition to college as passionately as did Willie Morris, and yet he is one of many southern white writers who attended southern institutions of higher learning and later wrote about their years there as catalysts or catharses of one sort or another in their struggles for identity and purpose, and in acquiring a sense of the re-

131

gion that often proved so integral to both.[2] While southerners' comings-of-age entailed a number of hurdles, as the essays here have demonstrated, for those who went to college that experience seems to have been the most consistently transformative, if only because it inspired such introspection, self-examination, shifting outlooks on the world, or challenges to long-established assumptions.

In the preface to his wonderful 1958 anthology *The College Years*, A. C. Spectorsky described that period as "a unique adventure which, in each generation, brings together the cream of the crop to spend unforgettable years between the end of adolescence and the attainment of full maturity, in a place of its own, where each day spells growth, excitement, interaction of people and ideas, stimulation — and downright good fun."[3] While much of that range of experience is evident in southern white memoirs, they usually include another, often more meaningful, layer of collegiate life not generally evident in the memories of other Americans: in southern memoirs, the self-examination so integral to the college years is accompanied by another, often more problematic dimension — an examination of the South itself. Many, like Willie Morris, found in campus life the worst of southern values and practices, and they reached the conclusion that they must escape the region altogether or, if they stayed, somehow rise above or challenge the status quo as reflected on their campuses and in their classrooms. Others encountered someone or something that challenged their assumptions about themselves and/or southern mores, and through those encounters they underwent what ultimately became a conversion experience in regard to race, region, or both. In both scenarios, higher education represented a significant turning point in their life stories as they recounted them many years later.

In a recent essay on American universities in crisis, Harvard president and historian Drew Gilpin Faust noted that "universities are meant to be producers not just of knowledge but also of (often inconvenient) doubt. They are creative and unruly places, homes to a polyphony of voices."[4] And so it was for most of the writers to be considered here, though it is the doubt that proves the most universal element in their characterizations of those years and their impact — with much of it directed against the institutions themselves. Their accounts make clear the extent to which southern college campuses were as often bulwarks of tradition and repression as they were crucibles for change and enlightenment. In whichever role they played, higher education in southern settings — and the doubts it raised on a variety of levels — affected these authors in significant and meaningful ways, which often resulted in a social consciousness and activism that would shape their lives and outlooks afterwards.

For southern adolescents, as for those throughout the country, college represented an opportunity to break out of an insulated, tightly proscribed existence and be exposed to facets of southern society not evident on the farms or in the small towns from which most came. It led — sometimes directly, sometimes indirectly, sometimes even subliminally — to new ways not only of seeing themselves, but of seeing and judging the world as they knew it, a world very much defined as southern. In the mid-1970s the president of Amherst College told his student body that "education is a process by which an individual unceasingly strives to arrive at as intense a self-consciousness as possible about the grounds of one's beliefs and actions."[5] If never really as ceaseless or as intentionally strived for as this statement suggests should be the case, much of what these autobiographical accounts of southern campus experiences share is an acute self-consciousness that emerges at some point during those college years, much of which was shaped by their authors' new awareness of themselves as southerners, for better or worse.

Eudora Welty was one of many who recognized the broadening effects as well as the limitations of the student body to which she was exposed. When she enrolled at Mississippi State College for Women at a mere sixteen years of age in 1925, she noted that "I landed in a world to itself, and it was indeed all new to me. . . . This was my first chance to learn what the body of us were like and what differences in background, persuasion of mind, and resources of character there were among Mississippians — at that, among only half of us, for we were all white."[6] She was astute enough to recognize that what was perceived as a considerable expansion of her social horizons could be seen more objectively as still a very circumscribed environment — in her case, she interacted only with other Mississippians, other women, and other whites.

For Anne Braden, the sheer opportunity to discuss what were taboo subjects at home in Alabama made her college years, if not fully transformative, then at least an essential stepping stone on her journey toward becoming a champion of social justice and racial equality later in life in Louisville, Kentucky. In her 1958 memoir, *The Wall Between*, Braden noted that in the social stratum of which she was a part in Anniston, Alabama, in the 1920s and 1930s, "segregation was not discussed; it was accepted." Not until she was in her teens did she know that anyone even questioned its existence or the rationale behind it. "By the time I was in college, however, World War II was in progress . . . and I began to find that people *were* questioning. I found them, paradoxically perhaps, at the fashionable Virginia women's college I attended [Randolph Macon Woman's College]: a few among the teachers and more among the students, and practically all of them southerners. For the first time in my life, segregation became a topic of discussion." As the rest of her memoir demonstrates, Braden emerged a full convert at the end of her years at the college.[7]

No one was more acutely aware of the transformative potential of college life as a crucible for new and life-altering ideas and perspectives than Katharine Du Pre Lumpkin, a full generation before Braden. From 1912 to 1915, Lumpkin attended Brenau College, a small women's school in the town of Gainesville, a thriving marketing center in the Blue Ridge foothills of northeastern Georgia. In describing her coming of age at Brenau, she seemed especially conscious of its significant place in the incremental conversion process that she called *The Making of a Southerner*. Her stay there represented "crucial years in mental development," and yet, she noted, "one would surely have supposed the place and circumstances to be indistinguishable in the Southerness from all I had hitherto known."[8]

When Lumpkin arrived in Gainesville, "there was certainly nothing visible to me to hint that contrary streams of influence were moving into the South," and she had no reason to think that she would encounter these heretical ideas at Brenau or in Gainesville. Unlike both Eudora Welty and Anne Braden, Lumpkin saw or felt little during her first years that challenged her long-held notions of social hierarchy or racial segregation. While there were early instances of interracial cooperation brewing in the years just before the First World War, she and her fellow students remained not only unaware of them but would have found the very term "interracial cooperation" inconceivable. "Here then," she wrote of this new and seeming radical interaction between white and black, "was a feebly breathing, hardly existing South. It could conceivably reach with its puny influence into our campuses. Yet even if it did, why would it not suffocate and die there before it could . . . penetrate the thick overlay of the old-ways-are-right in which we Southern students were encased?"

More analytical than most about her conversion and the conditions that led to it, Lumpkin recognized that she had two decisive advantages in making her receptive to these "feeble, hardly breathing" new trends — especially as they came to Brenau through the student Christian organizations, the YMCA and YWCA. First, she acknowledged her treatment as a girl had led her to "take for granted a lively intellectual interest" when she came to college. "It had not occurred to me," she wrote, "that it was untypical of our South where girl-rearing was concerned and for girls of my background." Indeed, much of her autobiography chronicles the efforts by both of her parents to stimulate reading, discussion, and debate in which their daughters played parts fully as valid as those of any male in the family. Second, Lumpkin found herself to be part of a small group of students at Brenau who, like her, were open-minded and inquisitive and found a single (though curiously unnamed) faculty member who encouraged them all to "use our minds, go to the sources, have no truck with undocumented hearsay, keep our eyes on the vast play of forces," all of which, she said, they tried hard to do. While she never explicitly stated that racial matters were a part of their agenda — referring only vaguely to creating "the Kingdom of Heaven on Earth" — it is clear that this Social Gospel mission also had much to do with paving the way for her further racial enlightenment.[9]

In 1915 and only nineteen years old, Lumpkin finished her formal course of study at Brenau but stayed on campus as a tutor. In the fall, she, along with several other campus leaders from around the South, attended a YWCA conference in Charlotte, and it was there that she faced the first blatantly racial situation to test her new sensitivity and that of her fellow Brenau students. A staff leader announced to the group that an educated, professional African American named Miss Arthur — Lumpkin *did* remember this name, she notes, simply because of the unprecedented Miss applied to a black woman — was in town and that, if they chose, she would be invited to speak to them on the subject of Christianity and race.[10]

Lumpkin laid out the implications, pro and con, of this radical proposal in great detail: "In one sense, was it so out-of-the-way for a Negro to stand before us and speak to us? There was nothing to be *scared* of. . . . We were used to Negroes, weren't we? Who could be more so?" On the other hand, "This really opened the door to thoughts we would like to avoid. 'What would people say? What if they knew? How explain?' For to concur in what was proposed, by no stretch of our imagination, would be none other than breaking the unwritten and written law of our heritage: 'Keep them in their place.'" Turning again to biblical analogy, she wrote that she and her fellow students were "like a little company of Eves" for whom confusion — and also temptation — reigned. "We had been taught that it was wrong to eat this apple. Yet as it was put before us, we felt guilty not to."

The girls ultimately decided to let Miss Arthur speak, and Lumpkin pondered the significance of that decision, both short and long term, on her own convictions. Curiously nothing Miss Arthur had to say about Christianity and race seems to have registered with Lumpkin (she dismissed it as "of no great consequence"; rather, "what mattered was that she entered the door and stood before us" and was introduced as Miss Arthur. During her speech, "how our pulses had hammered, and how we could feel our hearts pound in our chests." It was, she wrote, "of no small moment to hear her low voice sound in the speech of an educated woman, and to have my mind let the thought flicker in, even if it disappeared again immediately — If I should close my eyes, would I know that she was white or Negro?" It was far more profound a moment emotionally than it was intellectually for Lumpkin and perhaps others. She never even mentioned whether she was introduced to Miss Arthur and thus had to shake her hand, as she had worried about earlier. The sum total of the incident's import for her was simply that, in 1915, she found herself in an audience to which the speaker was a black woman.

Returning to Brenau, Lumpkin seemed relieved that "the heavens had not fallen, nor the earth parted asunder to swallow up in this unheard of transgression." Yet she also felt that she "could breathe freely again, eat heartily, and even laugh again" to have this moment behind her. "Back in my Georgia foothills, I put it out of my mind, or better, pushed it down deep in a welter of other unwanteds." To remind us that so dramatic an incident did not represent a full conversion, Lumpkin noted several pages later that *The Birth of a Nation* came to the Brenau campus and that she, who had read the Thomas Dixon novels on which it was based, was eager to see it. The several showings were all packed with students and townspeople, who responded as white audiences had been doing throughout its southern tours: "All around me people sighed and shivered, and now and then shouted or wept, in their intensity." As for what the movie aimed to say, Lumpkin claimed she was not sure, and yet she admitted that "I felt old sentiments stir, and a haunting nostalgia, which told me that much that I thought had been left behind must still be ahead," a remarkably forthright observation for one whose enlightenment came in such fits and starts and would not be complete until well after she left Brenau College.[11]

Regardless of how incomplete Katharine Lumpkin's college-aged conversion had been, she was one of several writers for whom the source of such transformations had more to do with individuals they encountered — black men or women, often peripheral to the academic venue, who in subtle or not so subtle ways led them to perceive the other race in radically different new ways. Ralph McGill, for example, wrote of two African American contacts made during and just after his freshman year at Vanderbilt in his memoir *The South and the Southerner*. McGill entered school there in 1917, hoping to get a year's worth of college under his belt before the draft drew him into military service during the First World War.

As a work-study student, McGill waited tables at the student dining room, where the head chef was Robert Wingfield, "a tall, dignified, elderly Negro who had been in the university kitchen for some thirty years." He was, McGill wrote, "a devout Christian, who felt a responsibility for his boys, the student waiters." Since the dining room was not open on Sunday night, Wingfield often invited the boys under his supervision to his home for a light meal served by his wife. He used these occasions "to ask us about ourselves, what we thought about things, how we were doing in class, and to admonish us against the lures of the devil, who was rather active in Nashville. There was always a prayer before we left." These sessions, McGill noted, along with some firm admonitions and advice from another black university employee, Boland Fitzgerald, the football team trainer and dormitory janitor, "were, as best I can recall, the only university counseling I had that year from anyone connected with Vanderbilt."[12]

Far more moving was the relationship McGill developed as a result of a summer job he held after his year of military service and before returning to Vanderbilt in the fall of 1919. He was hired by an all-black roofing crew that was part of the Chattanooga construction company for which his father worked as a salesman. Ralph already knew the foreman of the crew, Charlie White, whom he described as "a humpbacked man, quite black, of indeterminate age." Over the course of the summer, the two became quite fond of each other. Charlie was protective of Ralph and took him to his home after work on several occasions, where they talked about Ralph's future.

On his last week on the job, Ralph expressed his sadness at having to leave and go back to Nashville; he confided to Charlie the financial burden he faced and the fact that he would have to work while in school and borrow money to cover his tuition. On the day Ralph left for Nashville, Charlie offered to take him to the train station in Chattanooga. Just before he boarded the train, McGill wrote, "suddenly he moved up and put his arms around me and I put mine about him, feeling, with a sort of shock, the hard thrust of the hump on his back. 'Don't forget me,' the old man said." "I'll never forget you, Charlie," McGill replied, all the while fighting back tears. "You are one of the finest men I've ever known." Charlie then handed Ralph an envelope and instructed him not to open it until he was on the train and out of the station. When he did so, he found a five-dollar bill and a note from Charlie that said simply: "For my helper to spend [at] school." "It was then," McGill stated, "I wept."[13]

McGill never claimed that either of these acquaintances triggered a racial conversion, if only because he claimed never to have harbored any racist beliefs or attitudes in need of converting. Having grown up on an East Tennessee farm, with a strict Presbyterian upbringing, he claimed: "I did not see a Negro until I was six years old. I was never taught any prejudice about them since that was not according to the Scripture."[14] As such, these stories amount to little more than affectionate portraits of mentors fondly remembered, though McGill was obviously aware of the irony that what little adult counseling he received during his years at Vanderbilt came from black men.

More than forty years after Katharine Lumpkin's emotional exposure to a black woman at Brenau, Morris Dees described an equally dramatic conversion experience at the University of Alabama, due to another black woman — this one far better known than Miss Arthur. It was the show-down over Autherine Lucy's attempt to integrate the Tuscaloosa campus in 1957 that led Dees to re-think the role of segregation in his native state and throughout the South. Dees enrolled at Alabama in 1955, and in his memoir *A Season for Justice* nearly forty years later, he stated the obvious — that it was all white at the time. While he admitted that the *Brown* decision had not concerned him greatly, what happened in Money, Mississippi, a year later certainly did. That, of course, was Emmett Till's death, and it triggered Dees's first letter to a newspaper. He wrote to the Tuscaloosa paper, presumably soon after he began his freshman year, stating that "Maybe we believe in segregation. But we also believe in justice. If this young man did something illegal, then he ought to be tried and convicted before he is punished, not lynched." He seemed a bit surprised that the letter was published, a positive sign in itself that even in that era, "there were, on occasion, venues for moderation in the South."[15]

Dees was quick to remind his readers that the University of Alabama was not such a venue. The following year, a federal court order brought the first African American student to its campus, Autherine Lucy. Dees described the angry mob that confronted her as she drove onto campus to register, accompanied only by a priest. This confrontation would lead to her suspension and, ultimately, to her expulsion from the university.[16] With hundreds of hostile and increasingly violent whites surrounding the car and attempting to bar her entrance to the administration building, the students had been told to stay in their dormitories. "Some of us," Dees stated, "disobeyed the order." "I was there not out of sympathy for the cause of integration, but out of curiosity," he insisted. He had never seen the Ku Klux Klan in action, nor ever seen a mob. "As it surged, retreated, and surged again like some monster, I felt frightened and disgusted." Observing the action from a hundred yards away, Dees noted that many of those making up the mob were "good, rational folks when they didn't have to think about segregation . . . but once part of the crowd, they were swept up in the frenzy and turned into mean, dangerous aggressors."

In focusing his gaze on Lucy, Dees felt sick to his stomach. "In [her] face, I saw the faces of many of the black people I had known" at the farm he called home near Mount Meigs, Alabama — "Little Buddy, Miss Perri Lee, Wilson, Clarence." Having established what were for him meaningful and very pleasant relationships with these employees of his father's, memories of them now stirred strong feelings. "All my sympathy for the underdog came out at that moment and in my own way I felt as angry as that crazed mob." This was the moment of catharsis for Dees, the moment "I really did question my belief in segregation." Again he expressed his new conviction through a public pronouncement.

Dees and his new bride had joined the campus Baptist church, and he quickly became the superintendent of the married students' Sunday-school program. On the Sunday following the mob scene, he chose to speak to the fifty-some attendees in his Sunday school class. "Something really disturbs me," he told them. "How can we profess to be Christians and really hate our brothers?" The assembly looked perplexed, he noted, and he continued:

> Autherine Lucy tried to be on this campus. We don't know her and we might not have been out there opposing her, but I think all of us didn't want her to be there. So how can we be good Christians? Do you remember when Jesus gave the Pharisee women that "water of life"? What are we to think of the courthouse here in Tuscaloosa where there's one drinking fountain for white folks and one for colored?

Dees concluded this episode by saying that no one in the class spoke up. Later in the week, the minister of the church paid a visit to his apartment and told him that they planned on instituting some changes with the married students' program and needed some more experienced leadership to take charge. The preacher never mentioned "my lesson," Dees noted, "the real reason for his visit." He had "probably pegged me as some kind of radical rabble-rouser," but Dees admitted that he never saw himself in that role. The fact that he was "oc-casionally moved by the injustice suffered by some individual like Emmett Till or Autherine Lucy didn't, in my eyes, make me a civil rights activist." Even the drama of the Montgomery bus boycott that began a few months later "passed me by completely." He insisted that he was simply "too busy trying to make good grades and good money to consider civil rights."[17]

Few white college students were thrust so directly into the racial fray as was Dees, and few served as eyewitnesses to key confrontations such as that on the Alabama campus. And yet he seemed to insist on a degree of detachment — after a brief demonstration of courage and conviction — from much of what he witnessed that day. This is ironic, given both his unusually liberal upbringing and his later courageous quest for social justice through his work with the Southern Poverty Law Center, which he would found less than a decade later. As with Katharine Lumpkin, such an incident, indeed his entire college career, was but a small step on a longer, more gradual road to full commitment to civil rights and social justice.

Occasionally, students who came to college with well-established convictions regarding racial justice ended up leaving school — or being forced out — because of the resistance and/or hostility they faced there. One such case involved Texan Larry L. King, whose experience is distinguished by the fact that his "conversion" came during a stint in the newly desegregated army in the late 1940s. Two months short of his high-school graduation in Midland in 1947, King enlisted in the Army, and his account of the next two years as a soldier on integrated bases in New York in his *Confessions of a White Racist* serves as one of the more intriguing treatises on race relations among the autobiographical works I know.[18] In 1949, feeling himself to be fully enlightened racially, he left the military behind and enrolled at Texas Tech in Lubbock.

King was quick to note that "among the budding engineers, geologists, ranchers, school teachers, shop keepers, football coaches, and insurance agents I knew at Texas Tech were many young veterans of the military." And yet, while "some few had served with black soldiers, as I had," he acknowledges with some understatement that "they had managed better to preserve their original racial attitudes." Though his fellow veterans occasionally complained about the indignities they had endured in having to serve with African Americans, he noted that none commented on the so-called "Negro problem." "Indeed," he wrote, "I recall absolutely no conversations touching on politics, social reform, history, literature, or sociology. Most of the small-town saplings and farm or ranch boys who shared life in Drane Hall [his dormitory] talked almost exclusively of their career ambitions, football, sex, or cars." Frustrated at the immaturity and superficiality of student life (shared by many of the writers discussed here), Larry King, like Willie Morris, concluded in effect that he was better than this "sorry place" where he had chosen to seek a college education.[19]

King described only a single incident that suggested the racial views he confronted on this fully white campus. He attended the Sun Bowl in El Paso in 1950, where Texas Tech took on the College of the Pacific, whose team included a sole black player, half-back Eddie Macon. On the initial play of the game, Macon carried the ball but was quickly laid low by Tech's defense, which led to "great approving roars and whoops" from their fans. Normal enough, King noted, but then followed racial epithets, including "kill the black ape," that clearly disturbed at least one freshman in the crowd. Toward the end of the game, with Tech comfortably ahead, the same fans were willing to cheer Macon for his several long runs, and yet King could not forget their ugly reaction to that opening play — "all their cheers could not erase the original ugliness." His exposure to black people during his army years in New York "had taught me that they had minds, dreams, and hurts like the rest of us, and in no way deserved their automatic exclusion." Despite his newly acquired awareness of the widespread inequities in economic and educational opportunity, "it was the million mindless 'little' humiliations that stirred my tardy rage and soon caused me to be looked on as a little crazy and unreliable."[20]

King acknowledged that "Texas Tech and I discovered a mutual disenchantment early on." He was a disappointment at football and found nothing in the classroom to inspire him. He began cutting more and more classes, remaining in his dorm room, "staring out the windows across the Western landscape, pining for the lost excitements and promises of New York as the more rational might pine over the loss of a particularly talented mistress." By the middle of his second semester, King made no effort at all to attend classes, which led to "dull days of drugged sleep, dominoes, and purposeless space-gazing." One day, he simply packed his "dirty duds and hit the highway," thus drifting with no more goal or sense of direction than a tumbleweed.[21]

A far less voluntary premature end to a college career was that of civil rights activist Joan Browning. Along with eight other white women civil right activists, Browning tells her story as part of a remarkable compilation of firsthand accounts titled *Deep in Our Hearts*.[22] She grew up in a family of seven children on a small cotton and tobacco farm in south Georgia. During her youth in Telfair County, she wrote, "I do not recall a single incident, or report of an incident, or even rumor or gossip of an incident, involving racial animosity." Certainly segregation was fully intact, but with no challenges or strains on its viability; Browning posits that "perhaps racism was in the air, and those, like me, who did not pay close attention somehow just didn't 'get it.'"[23] That, along with pleasant associations with black cotton pickers who worked beside her in her father's fields, meant that she was somewhat more sensitive to racial matters, certainly than most rural south Georgians, when she entered Georgia State College for Women in 1959.

Browning embraced Milledgeville — certainly the most cosmopolitan community to which she had yet been exposed — and college life with great gusto, claiming that it "was full of possibilities, and I was confident that I could muster whatever I wanted." She quickly became an activist in campus politics and service and helped recruit signatures for the Sibley Commission, a state-sponsored attempt to document Georgia residents' attitudes toward school desegregation in 1960.[24] Raised with strong spiritual convictions in the Methodist Church, she found Milledgeville's whites-only congregation far too large for her and missed the intimacy and sense of community of the small rural church in which she was raised.

In the fall of her sophomore year, Joan discovered "the overgrown miniforest" of a retired art professor who lived near the campus, and seeking to renew ties to the natural world back home, she often took refuge there to read and reflect. In walking to and from this "urban wilderness retreat," she met a young black minister, Rev. Mincey, whose home and church — the Wesley Chapel AME Church — were just across the street from the all-white campus. Through casual conversations over several weeks, they became friends and he invited her to come watch a baseball game on TV with him and his family, which she had no compunctions about doing. She also began to attend his church, where she and a classmate, Faye Powell, were welcomed and found the warmth and emotion from services that seemed lacking at Milledgeville Methodist.

A few months later, Mincey, very impressed with the young women, asked if they would lead a program for his church's youth group, but before they could do so Joan and Faye had a phone call from the college president (named Robert E. Lee, she noted with no hint of irony), who said that he had received threats of violence if they gave the program. The girls backed down only when Rev. Mincey asked them to do so, but they continued to attend services there, to the increasing discomfort of the college administration. President Lee considered their attendance there both "irregular, and increasingly dangerous." He seemed especially worried that Roy V. Harris, the publisher of the *Augusta Courier* and one of Georgia's most rabid racists, would get wind of the girls' activities and condemn the college for tolerating them.

Somewhat baffled by the "increasingly hostile place" she felt the college to be and seeking "to understand why attending a Methodist church caused anonymous threats of violence and Dr. Lee's fears," Browning learned of an interracial Christian conference to be held in Augusta at Paine College in the spring of 1961 and felt that this could serve as an opportunity to seek answers to these and other questions. When the dean denied Joan and Faye permission to attend, they defied his order and took a bus to Augusta. At Paine, a historically black college, they found themselves in the midst of a host of student and other activists and ministers, black and white, and thus became committed to and fully immersed in the Freedom Movement. But that moment proved transformative in more than one way — it would cost Browning her third and final year at Georgia College. (Due to financial limitations, she had planned to complete her degree in pre-med in three years and was close to doing so.)[25]

Roy Harris became aware of the girls' presence at demonstrations that accompanied the conference in Augusta, and he reported his displeasure to President Lee. When heavy-handed threats from the dean of students about Browning's campus job and scholarships failed to dampen her resolve, she first encouraged Joan to leave school and join the military and then told her more forthrightly that she was not welcome at GSCW, and that if she tried to return she would be expelled and her permanent record so marked. Joan thus took the other option offered: a chance to leave quietly with nothing noted on her record.

In assessing her experience, Browning wrote that she had "stumbled innocently, unaware, across southern racism's dividing line." She acknowledged that her naiveté fully matched her determination during those two years in Milledgeville and concluded that "my search for the warmth and friendliness of a small community meant ostracism from the very thing I sought." Only eighteen years old at the time, she moved to Atlanta — telling only her mother why she had to leave Milledgeville. Although she would take a few courses at Georgia State University, being in Atlanta drew her ever more deeply into civil rights activism on multiple fronts. (She noted wryly that for all the organizations Georgia College officials had accused her of belonging to — the Urban League, the Southern Regional Council, the NAACP — she had never heard of any of them until she came to Atlanta.) And it would be thirty years later and at a historically black college — West Virginia State College — that she would finally earn the college degree she had been so close to obtaining in 1961.[26]

Campus epiphanies were not always related to race. Southern identity could prove constricting in other ways and led to struggles on other fronts that also reveal much about regional values and traditions. To return to Willie Morris's years at the University of Texas, his is among the most perplexing of such accounts in that, for all the significance he attributed to his experience there in terms of his new consciousness about what it meant to be a southerner in those turbulent times, his transformation had little or nothing to do with race. Yet we are certainly led to expect one: He acknowledged the campus impact of the *Brown v. Board of Education* ruling that came at the end of his sophomore year, noting that it did little to alter "the mindless self-satisfactions of most of the students," other than perhaps a political "hardening of the arteries." He continued to condemn fraternities and sororities as "the great hotbeds of philistinism in the 1950s," which at the University of Texas, as elsewhere, "reach unprecedented heights of carefully planned frivolity — anything, in fact to do something meaningless with all that energy."[27]

At the same time, we see glimmers of a new racial consciousness slowly emerging in Morris. He was among those who cheered when a black second-team half-back from Washington State scored a touchdown against Texas — the first black ever to play in Texas Memorial Stadium. He acknowledged — and admired — the "Y" and other Christian campus life organizations, noting that they, and the "good people" who made them up, "were the repositories of whatever liberalism existed on a conscious level at the University of Texas at the time." Yet he remained detached from these groups, claiming that "I had ceased to be the torrid activist I had been before," having become "chiefly interested 'in the panorama.'" Yet in the spring of 1955 he decided to put himself squarely back into the fray and ran for the editorship of the campus newspaper, the *Daily Texan*, for which he had served as sports editor the year before. It was an elective post, and in the midst of a campaign rally where students questioned all candidates, Morris was asked about his stand on integration. His response as he records it: "There's an inner turmoil in the United States, there's an inner turmoil in me. The Supreme Court decision was inevitable, but I don't think any universal rule can be applied to the entire nation when the time for integration comes. I don't think Ole Miss is ready for integration. I think the University of Texas is."[28] He doesn't suggest that that answer won him the election, but it's clear that it didn't prevent him from winning.

At home in Yazoo City that summer, before he began his year as editor, Morris went with his father to a town "meeting," whose purpose it was to form a local chapter of the White Citizens Council in response to recent NAACP activity in the area. In listening to the hate-mongering and retaliatory measures against their black employees and others who had signed an NAACP petition, Morris "felt a strange and terrible disgust" and a strong urge to leave. "*Who are these people?*" he asked himself. "What was I doing there? Was this the place I had grown up in and never wanted to leave? I knew in that instant, in the middle of a mob in our school auditorium, that a mere three years in Texas had taken me irrevocably, without my even recognizing it, from home."[29] He returned to Austin and finally found the courage to speak up when, as a finalist for a Rhodes Scholarship, he chose to respond to a more general question about Mississippi politics from the interviewing committee by bringing up the Emmett Till trial; he quoted William Faulkner, saying that "if we in America have reached the point in our desperate culture when we must murder children, . . . then we don't deserve to survive, and probably won't." Again, such a stance could well have lost him any chance of receiving the Rhodes, but it didn't.

Given these key incidents along a seeming path of racial conversion, one would assume that Morris was preparing his readers for the sorts of issues with which he would struggle as editor of the *Daily Texan*. His lead-in for that section of his narrative finds him on a soapbox, preaching against the contradictions inherent in American campus culture of the era. (It's notable that he saw this as an American issue, not merely a southern one.) The university "allows and at its best encourages one to develop critical capacities, his imagination, his values; at the same time, . . . it can become increasingly wary of the very intent and direction of the ideals it has helped spawn." More than hypocrisy, Morris insisted, it was actually schizophrenia—"the splitting of a university's soul."[30] This is a reality sensed by many of the other writers here—though few articulate the paradox so clearly, either at the time or in describing it many years later.

All of this serves as prologue to Morris's account of the strictures imposed on his freedom of the press and the shattering of his dream to make the newspaper "a living thing, distinctive and meaningful, in both its own tradition and the tradition of hard-hitting, outspoken American journalism." These were goals instilled in him by the University of Texas: "the necessity of the free marketplace of ideas was apparently high on its list of formal priorities." Given his newly awakened sensitivity to racial injustice and oppression just as the civil rights struggle took shape, one would assume that these would be the causes that he would champion — and the principles he would fully embrace and push through the pages of the paper he would edit.

Yet strangely, they were not. Race never again comes into play during Morris's account of his senior year at Texas. Rather, it was "those twin deities, oil and gas" and monetary scandals related to both in the capital city of Austin that he editorialized about, thus "committing the crime of being vigorous and outspoken, naively idealistic and exuberantly but not radically liberal in a state that had little patience for either." In so doing, he launched a censorship battle between the students and the university's president and board of regents that became, in Morris's inflated view, "one of the greatest controversies in the history of American college journalism." He and other student activists defied mandates from above and continued to publish editorials, while fighting off efforts to oversee and censor the right of students to take on political issues and lawmakers. Ultimately, with members of the faculty mobilized in support of the students, they prevailed. Morris noted that "contempt for an independent student voice trying to engage itself in important issues in that age of McCarthy and silence was reflected in an effort to do lasting damage to a state university's most basic civil liberties."[31] Yet somehow this rings a bit hollow given the fact that the struggle seems far more significant than the issues — state taxation of oil and gas — that spurred it.

Morris's sense of satisfaction with his key role in this test of wills seems to lie more in the fact that, in his final undergraduate year, he found a principled and character-building cause in which to channel his energies, thus salvaging his sense of self-worth after years of drifting without much sense of purpose or direction in an environment of "carefully planned frivolity." If nothing else, he demonstrated that he was "better than this sorry place." But his fight for freedom of the press seems to have put on hold his awakening social conscience about southern racial injustice that had been on the verge of fully blossoming during those years. He would go on to win a Rhodes Scholarship — without any endorsement or support from UT. Only in the early 1960s — after four years at Oxford — did he return to Austin and work for the *Texas Observer*, the state's most liberal journal, where he finally embraced those issues of racial and social justice for which he had been primed during the mid-1950s, but upon which he had never acted.

Another southerner also headed west to Texas for a college education in 1952, the same year Morris entered UT. Shirley Abbott left her home in Hot Springs, Arkansas, to attend the Texas State College for Women in Denton.

In a chapter of her memoir *Womenfolks* titled "Why Southern Women Leave Home," she provides one of the most pointed critiques of the values imposed on female students in the repressive and often suffocating environments of southern women's campuses of that era. While East Texas stood on the "cusp between the West and the South," Abbott felt that the school's mission was clearly driven by southern aims. The western students, she thought, "were a wilder, stronger breed: beside them we Southerners looked positively dainty." Yet as intimidating as they were, "they seem to have earned some magic exemption from the fate the college clearly had in mind for most of us: it wanted to turn us Southern girls into Southern ladies."[32]

Although established as an industrial arts school for poorer girls at the turn of the century, the college had over the years adapted the finishing school model of the elitist women's schools in Virginia, so that "gracious living was our motto and our goal." With its strict rules of dress and conduct fully adhering to the "southern pattern," Abbott concludes, "if we had been the virginal daughters of the finest families in antebellum Savannah, our morals could hardly have been the object of more solicitude." Yet she was quick to note that the student body consisted almost entirely of first-generation students, "the daughters of farmers, white collar workers, and merchants who had sent us to this place because it was cheap and the curriculum practical." Few of them, she was sure, "had any chance of becoming a lady," even as they submitted to a course of study designed to prepare them for what the dean of women called — as late as 1953 — "woman's only true career — marriage and motherhood."[33]

Abbott was a skeptic from the start and became increasingly frustrated and disengaged from practices — such as beauty pageants, eight or nine a year — that she found as pointless as they were frivolous, especially on an all-women's campus. She even found lesson plans on *Macbeth* pointless, describing them as something she "was to foist off on a hypothetical roomful of students as a work relevant to their daily concerns, unless we all intended to become assassins." "I couldn't imagine passing off such a fraud," she declared. "That surely couldn't be steady work." The cumulative effect of all this was that she grew increasingly pessimistic about her chances of finding a place for herself in the South. "Somehow my once-comfortable environment had been sucked through a black hole and turned into a foreign land."

Abbott confided these frustrations to her mother, aunt, and female cousins during summer vacation before her senior year, which led to "a loud and angry discussion" that brought her mother to tears. Realizing that her values and aspirations were not those of the other women in her family, she concluded at that moment that the only solution was to leave them, "these women I loved in my body and bones — and seek my people in another country." And so she did. The following spring, after finishing her last exam, "I packed up and headed out on a round-trip plane ticket, the other half of which I promptly cashed in as soon as I got to New York."[34]

As she does throughout this combination of memoir and meditation on gender in southern history, Abbott uses her own experience to reflect on the many other white women, most notably Sarah and Angelina Grimké, who left the South rather than be smothered by it. Quoting blues singer Bessie Smith's song — "I ain't good-lookin', and I doan dress fine, but I'm a travelin' woman with a travelin' mind" — Abbott notes that the South has long "produced its small quota of travelin' women who dread the high cost of living and dying in Dixie and find they have to depart."[35] But of all those women who did make that escape, I know of no others for whom the mere frustrations of a college education proved to be the impetus that drove them away.

Perhaps the most successful college career that I have come across in a southern autobiography, and certainly the one told with the greatest self-satisfaction, is that of a Jewish student who attended the University of North Carolina in the mid-1950s. Eli Evans took pride in his achievements of those years, even titling the chapter on his college years "Big Wheel on Campus" in *The Provincials*, a mix of personal memoir and broader commentary on southern Judaism. Evans recounts his family's somewhat ambivalent relationship with the Jewish community in nearby Durham. His parents were not "religious people" but were politically and socially active in that community and beyond, so much so that E. J. Evans, Eli's father, served as the mayor of Durham from 1951 to 1963. Eli too became an activist in local and regional Jewish causes and at high school, having served as student body president his senior year. Thus he entered UNC in the fall of 1954 with far more confidence and sense of purpose than did many of his classmates.

Nevertheless, Evans was very conscious of his Jewish identity as he moved the eight miles to Chapel Hill, and he made much of the distinction between southern and northern Jews. His mother had insisted that he specify "Jewish" for his roommate preference on the housing application for UNC. He did so reluctantly, fearful that he would be matched with a "bunch of loud-mouthed Yankees," and was much relieved when he learned that he had been assigned to room with two Jewish boys from Virginia. He had no trouble meeting others, both Jew and Gentile, noting that he hung around with other North Carolina boys he had met at a state meeting of student body presidents the year before, thinking that they might run as a team for political office at UNC.[36]

Fraternity rush led to Evans's first real confrontation with the limitations imposed by his Jewishness. He found, somewhat to his surprise, that he had five first-night invitations — one from each of the three Jewish fraternities on campus, one from a non-Jewish house that was so strapped financially that they issued blanket invitations to everyone, and then, most surprising to him, one from the Sigma Chis. Evans wrote that "I had been so conditioned to think in terms of Jewish fraternities that, until titillated by the card in that envelope, I had never considered any alternative. I let my imagination soar and toyed with the possibility of pledging Sigma Chi. But of course it was not to be. Accompanied to the house by one of his non-Jewish acquaintances named Kelly, they were quickly separated upon their arrival, with Kelly escorted into "the inner sanctum" of the house, while Evans "was maneuvered skillfully to a corner of the living room for a short face-off with another brother." He introduced himself as a friend of Kelly's but, he wrote, the gig was up. "Uh, uh — not here," he was told. "You'll probably want to go TEP or ZBT or Pi Lam, being Jewish and all," and was escorted back to the front door and told "please forgive the mistake." He made his way to the TEP house, where he was greeted warmly — his father had helped found the chapter thirty years earlier — and asked by someone with a "grating Yankee accent" why he hadn't arrived sooner. When he "sheepishly" admitted that he had gone to Sigma Chi first and explained his very brief stay inside, the brothers roared with laughter. One asked, "Hey, man, don't you know that Sigma Chi means Sign of Christ?" and another commented that he "was probably the first 'Yid' they ever let in that place." Evans winced, noting that "Yid" was a word no Southern Jew would use to describe himself.[37]

In maneuvering through the intense competition to rush him among the three Jewish houses, Evans found himself confronting more of the northern brothers he found so offensive. He offered several pages of commentary on what separated southern Jews from their New York and New Jersey counterparts — differences of maturity, temperament, culture, and geography. "We southerners," he claimed, "were still attached to the world of high school and parental approval; they were cut loose and flying on a four-year lark, and could lose themselves in the knowledge that no one would know and care." He accused them of camouflaging their "Yankee provincialism" by calling us "brown-baggers" and "grits," although they'd never traveled anywhere beyond "the city." Just because they knew the difference between the Brooklyn Bridge and the IRT, they thought they knew it all. Yet sectional reconciliation ultimately prevailed. Evans acknowledged that over time, "I went home with the Yankees and invited them home with me and we came to know and like each other. Chapel Hill softened them over the years as it sharpened me or maybe I began to see them in less stereotyped terms. They learned how to get along with Southerners and I learned to love the Yankees."[38]

With those issues seemingly settled, Evans jumped forward to provide a vivid account — nearly a dozen pages worth — of his campaign for student body president three years later. It was there that he found himself confronting the times and racial issues as they played out in relatively innocuous terms on the UNC campus. Always forthright about his political ambitions, Evans wrote that his goal of being the first Jewish student body president stemmed from his having been "Mister Jew in Durham," and, he admitted, "I am sure that, subconsciously, I wanted to emulate the first Jewish mayor of Durham," his father.

Evans was one of several student government activists who anointed themselves "new southerners." "We were deeply perturbed," he wrote, "that the South was entering an era profoundly different from anything we had grown up with, but were determined to listen to the voices of reason and restraint." In part, the residue of McCarthyism reined in any radical impulses, such as demonstrations or other overt acts of defiance, given the risks of arrest or expulsion on postcollegiate aspirations; thus students so inclined saw student government as the only viable outlet through which to voice their concerns. "We treated the smallest risk as a sign of our courage," Evans acknowledged, "especially any signal of sympathy for the cause of Negro advance." Nine African American undergraduates, all male, were enrolled at UNC by 1957, Evans's senior year, but were largely segregated on campus, most notably by being assigned the top floor of a dormitory that they had to themselves — "a commentary on the sad impact of tokenism," Evans called it. He visited the students there and learned firsthand of the frustrations they faced in being denied service in local restaurants and barber shops; while Jim Crow policies had long been in place, the fact that such restrictions could be applied to Carolina boys made it a far greater indignity in Evans's eyes.[39]

The UNC student body was politicized enough to be divided into two parties — and although Evans remained an active member of TEP, he decided, on the advice of his fraternity brothers, to run as the presidential candidate from the non–fraternity and sorority party, knowing he would have little chance of winning the nomination from the more elitist party, both because it was far more conservative and because he was Jewish. A single debate between him and his opponent led to questions about the relegation of the black students to their own dormitory floor. Evans's opponent predictably said that he would not "agitate" for change and thought their segregated housing was no problem. Evans, though, felt no qualms about criticizing the university's housing policy and insisting that "the purpose of student government is to see that each student is treated equally." He won vigorous applause for that statement, and his northern fraternity brothers cheered him on, saying "That's telling those rednecks!" But others felt that he had probably ruined his chances of winning the election.

Yet win he did, and in the closest student election anyone remembered. But the jubilation of his victory serves as the end of his chapter, "Big Wheel on Campus."[40] He has nothing to say about what he did as student body president or whether he made any attempt to desegregate the boys' dormitory, which his account had made the central issue in the campaign. The bottom line, as even Evans portrayed it, was that, far from a clarion call against racial segregation, his victory was in effect a successful coalition of non-Greek students, social misfits, and Jews, whether fraternity members or not. It was ultimately a personal success story he chooses to tell, and not a triumph of social justice. In the dozen or so pages in which it takes to lay out all the particulars of the election, no more than a couple of paragraphs have anything to do with the plight of nine black students isolated on the top floor of Steele Hall. (In that sense, it offers a striking parallel to Willie Morris's fleeting bid for racial justice, which seemed to evaporate when he won elective office at UT.)

Edward Cohen offers a far different account of a southern Jew adjusting to college a decade or so after Evans. His 1999 memoir, *The Peddler's Grandson*, is a particular favorite of my students, in part because of his disarming portrayal of himself as far more naïve and misguided in his adjustment to college life, and because of how well he articulates his eventual coming to terms with both his southern and Jewish identities — either in spite, or perhaps because, of those early missteps. Cohen was anything but a "big wheel on campus," and his college choice was more random and uninformed than that of any other writer here — or at least that any ever admitted. (Even the utterly passive — and nearly as clueless — William Alexander Percy had parental dictates behind his selection.) Largely due to that naiveté, Cohen provides an especially insightful testimonial as to how he stumbled his way from confused southern teen toward a strong sense of self and the South.

Growing up as part of a large family network but very small Jewish community in Jackson, Mississippi, in the 1950s and early 1960s, Cohen wrestled throughout his adolescence with the dual identities he faced, wryly noting that "one can hardly hail from two more historically losing causes than the South and Judaism. Both my cultures have long, tragic pasts, and not one jot of it has been forgotten."[41] He had been just enough of an outcast in high school, and just enough of a rebel, to have determined that he would not attend college in-state, noting that "few Jackson Jews ever went to state schools." His grade point average was so low that none of the schools to which he applied — from Tulane, his father's alma mater, to several California junior colleges — accepted him. Just as he thought he would have to consider his fallback option, attending a Mississippi school, he received "something novel," an acceptance letter from the University of Miami, to which he had randomly applied and claimed to have forgotten about. "About the school I knew nothing," Cohen admitted, "except that it met my two criteria: it wasn't in Mississippi and it would let me in."[42]

Given his total lack of knowledge about the school he would be attending — "I wondered what kind of people went to the University of Miami and whether there would be any Jews there" — it was only upon meeting his roommates and other freshmen that Cohen faced the hard reality that being from Mississippi in itself posed a serious challenge to his ability to fit in. When he met his roommate, a surfer from New Jersey, "I had the first intimation of the feeling I would struggle with for the rest of my time in Miami: that I was a rustic, a rube, a bumpkin." In typically wry fashion, he added, "Everybody in Mississippi was, only they'd had the good sense not to have to realize it." As he met other students, he concluded that "the nameless faceless alien world I had feared now had names and faces, and they were far more exotic than anything I could have imagined from my eighteen years in the pine-speckled suburbs of Mississippi."[43]

Cohen sensed right away that getting into a fraternity would be essential to avoiding outsider status for the next four years. Like Eli Evans, how that happened dominates his narrative, though unlike Evans, he approached the process with far more trepidation, noting that "I'd never done well in groups, had in fact rebelled against them." Nevertheless, "I began to worry that I wouldn't get in what I didn't want." He bumbled his way through rush, and somehow — miraculously, from his perspective — he got a bid from ZBT, perhaps as a legacy, since his father had been a ZBT at Tulane. "A life of belonging was at last begin-ning. . . . I had found my tribe." Or so he thought.

Like Evans, Cohen soon found that the fraternity was made up of Jews very different from him, "Jews plugged into the main line of Jewish culture and identity, Jews who had no cultural dichotomy." There were a few southerners in the club, "soft-spoken courteous boys from Memphis and Atlanta and New Orleans," but Cohen quickly decided that for his friends he wanted "the real thing." "I knew what I wanted to be when I grew up — a New York Jew." And so his "mutation into a northern Jew" began, and with it an astute self-analysis of the angst triggered by that quest.

Cohen realized just how vast a gulf he would have to cross in acquiring his new identity. "The landmarks and memories that these Jews shared were as alien to me as the altar at Jackson's First Baptist Church," he noted. It also hit him what a radical choice he had made compared with that of his high-school classmates. "Most freshmen," he realized, "had fixed references in the enemies and friends they'd known for twelve solid years. They might've wished to be anonymous, pastless, like me, but they had chosen the familiar evil. And I'd chosen the unfamiliar. I was a lost tribe of one. Everyone else knew holidays like Simchas Torah, and I knew Confederate Memorial Day." He compared his current plight to that of his earlier years: when, as a child, "I had stretched my concept of reality to encompass the gigantic southern Christian universe, it was as much of an accommodation as I thought I could ever make." And yet, he continued, "my view was expanding again, this time to take in an equally enor-mous northern Jewish world, and it was no less unsettling than the first time." He had assumed that being Jewish was all it would take to enter that world, but for "these purebred northern Jews" he realized that he was seen as "an exotic half-breed, an object of curiosity, amusement, and scorn."[44]

Yet he was determined to fit in, or as he put it "not to be different." "To join the tribe, I annihilated my southern self," he acknowledged. "It was no different from what the converts to Christianity, the ones I'd thought were forever lost, had done." Ultimately, Cohen realized that the ZBT's were not the answer to his search for identity, and he abandoned the fraternity and drifted aimlessly for a year or more. Returning home was not an option. After Miami, he found Jackson to be "suffocating, primitive. Everything seemed small and everyone seemed slow." He felt like "an imposter and an intruder" during his visits there, and felt both liberated and lost when he returned to Miami, "as if I were suffer-ing from self-imposed amnesia." His dilemma, as he saw it, was that "home was where you went when you finished school, and though, by now, I felt northern, my transformation was not so complete as to provide me with a past. My real past, Mississippi, seemed to belong to another person, someone I'd once known, then outgrown and forgotten."[45]

Graduating in 1971 — only a semester late — Cohen sought gainful employment in Miami, still determined to "pull free from the gravitational grip" of his home state, but after he failed to find more than menial — even humiliating — employment, he gave in to that pull with great reluctance. He rationalized his decision, noting that while the South was a "conservative, constraining, and unglamorous home to few Jews and no haven for rebels or artists," it was also a region with "its own solid identity" at that point in his so-called "free fall" that in itself seemed important. "Most of all," he declared, "the South was by its nature welcoming, and a welcome was what I needed most."[46]

Arriving in Jackson, Cohen admitted that "if I still didn't know who I was, at least I knew who I wasn't." After several years there, he went to law school, became a corporate lawyer, and moved to Los Angeles, where he found to his satisfaction that "everyone seems to be an immigrant, and no one is excluded or thought to be any different." Yet "in this rootless city, I treasure my history, and this time, I know not to change. Out here, if you don't know who you are, you won't be that way for long." In the final paragraphs of his memoir, he states that he knew his Judaism was so deep that he would never lose it, but that it had taken two exiles to see how much of the South he carried with him. "It seems that a few generations in the South [his grandfather and great-uncle had arrived in Mississippi in the 1920s] exert almost as much pull as an Old Testament of time, and I'm hard put to say where the southern leaves off and the Jewish begins. I may be a man without a country," he concludes, "but I carry two passports."[47]

Cohen was not alone in claiming either such transformative revelations or the struggles with his ethnic identity that preceded him during his undergraduate years. Sonia Sotomayor stated in a 1996 speech at her alma mater that "My days at Princeton . . . were the single most transforming experience I have had. It was here that I became truly aware of my Latina identity — something I had taken for granted during my childhood when I was surrounded by my family and their friends." Likewise, Michelle Obama acknowledged in her senior thesis in 1983 that she had never felt more aware of her "blackness" than during her years at Princeton.[48] They, like so many Americans, have found college campuses to be a crucible in which their identities are sharpened, redefined, or more intensely felt than had been the case earlier in their lives.

But in the South, such self-revelation could be — and usually was — complicated by or juxtaposed with a sense of regional identity. This is what makes Edward Cohen's description of his struggle all the more compelling; it is his attempt first to shun, and then accommodate, his southernness — with his years at the University of Miami merely the culmination of a quest that began with childhood — that distinguishes *The Peddler's Grandson* from Eli Evans's somewhat more superficial confrontation with a similar duality, and it is what ultimately makes Cohen's story the far more meaningful of the two.

Finally, it is worth noting that not all college-educated white southerners found their undergraduate years to be transformative or even influential in leading them toward the causes and ideals they would at some point come to embrace. Pat Conroy, whose moving account of his year teaching black children on South Carolina's Yamacraw Island in 1969 and 1970, *The Water Is Wide*, has next to nothing to say about his years at the Citadel in the mid-1960s, despite the fact that he was there during the height of the civil rights movement. He devoted only two sentences to his four years there, stating simply: "I marched to breakfast, saluted my superiors, was awakened by bugles, and continued my worship of the jock, the basketball, and the school fight song, 'Dixie.' For four years I did not think about the world outside the gates."[49] His enlightenment would begin only as a teacher at Beaufort High School, his alma mater, and come to full fruition during that remarkable year he spent as the only white teacher — indeed the only white person — in the all-black community on Yamacraw.

More common are the few conservative voices that we find among southern autobiographers who have little or nothing to say to about their college educations in terms of personal growth or relevance or meaning to their subsequent lives. William Alexander Percy offers the most direct — and oft quoted — of such sentiments in his classic 1941 memoir, *Lanterns on the Levee*. Percy had just turned fifteen when he was sent to the University of the South, where he arrived in the fall of 1900 "in short trousers, small, weakly, self-reliant, and ignorant as an egg." He wrote with great nostalgia about this mountaintop "Arcadia" of Sewanee, Tennessee, but had nothing to say about any substantive revelations or self-enlightenment experienced during either his four years there, a subsequent year touring Europe, or three years at Harvard Law School.

This most self-effacing of writers (who identifies himself in his subtitle not as a planter but as a planter's son, even though at the time he was in his mid-fifties and his father had been dead for two decades), Percy gleaned little of tangible value from the abundance of schooling bestowed upon him. With his tongue somewhat in cheek, he described his return home to Greenville, Mississippi, after all that education: "For eight years — in fact, for twenty-three, a great number of people have been pouring out money, skill, time, devotion, prayers to create something out of me that wouldn't look as if the Lord slapped it together absent-mindedly. Not Alexander the Great nor Catherine II had been tended by a more noble corps of teachers." Yet Percy found little in all that training that had inspired a career choice. "Obviously," he continued, "I was cast to justify the way of man to God, as it were. But how? What does one do with a life, or at any rate, intend to do?"[50] Certainly nothing cathartic about his college years!

A fellow writer of Percy's generation, Thomas Wolfe, was equally disparaging of the value of his college education. In the closest he came to a nonfictional autobiography, an essay titled "Writing and Living," Wolfe provided a full and seemingly positive description of his years at the University of North Carolina during and just after the First World War. Most of his biographers feel that it was in Chapel Hill that Wolfe found himself as a writer — he wrote two plays that were produced by the famous Carolina Playmakers while there — and yet he concluded, much as Percy did, upon his graduation in 1920, when he was a mere nineteen years old: "I don't suppose it would have been possible to find a more confused or baffled person than I was. I had been sent to college in order to 'prepare myself for life' — as the phrase went in those days — and it almost seemed that the total effect of my college training was to produce in me a state of utter unpreparedness."[51]

Not nearly as introspective as Wolfe, Dean Rusk attributed the times to the limitations of what southern college life offered in the 1920s. An Atlantan, Rusk entered Davidson College in 1927. In a chapter of his 1990 autobiography titled "The Poor Man's Princeton," Rusk described his years there in very positive terms. Thrilled to be attending his father's alma mater, a small but prestigious liberal arts school just north of Charlotte, North Carolina, he recalled Davidson "as an exciting place intellectually, a broadening place," but acknowledged that it was on the whole quite provincial. Yet he didn't hold that against the college or its faculty, for he insisted that "the twenties in general were quiescent years: Warren G. Harding's 'return to normalcy'; isolationism; public indifference to overseas events. . . . Nor were the youth of my generation in a searching mode; few students challenged social values; there was little agitation for reform. We were not encouraged to think critically about the workings of

American democracy and domestic and world events, as were the young people of later generations." He obviously overcame that complacency and credited a political science professor, Archibald Currie, with inspiring him to go on to graduate school — he left Davidson for a Rhodes Scholarship — and a career in government.[52]

Most striking of all is journalist Ben Robertson's 1942 memoir, in which he extolled the pleasures and traditional values of rural life as he came of age in upland South Carolina. In *Red Hills and Cotton*, tellingly subtitled *An Upcountry Memory*, Robertson made no mention of his education at Clemson University, where he followed in his father's footsteps, or of his transfer two years later to the University of Missouri's School of Journalism. Instead, he stated unequivocally that his values were firmly established well before his college years — which for most young men fell in their mid-teens.

Born in 1903 and brought up in the foothills of the Blue Ridge Mountains near Clemson, in a valley claimed by his ancestors since before the American Revolution, Robertson noted that he never traveled much or felt the need to. "I never bothered about going anywhere before I started college," he wrote. "My parents, both college educated themselves, did not care whether I saw an opera or understood a statue; all that could be considered in time, in the future. . . . My kinfolks did not believe in a broad education for a small child." They were, he explained, more interested in character than culture. The latter could be acquired, but "character had to be formed . . . had to be molded in the most exact and unrelenting form." In short, "what they wanted to do was to set me in the mold — to make me a Carolinian, a Democrat, and a Baptist. Once they had accomplished that — well, hell and high water could try as they liked." The implication is, of course, that nothing Robertson encountered in college altered any of his ideas, assumptions, or sense of who he was and where he was from.[53] (While perhaps it is not unusual that he faced little that was new, different, or unexpected during his Clemson years, so close to home, and where his father served on its agricultural extension staff, the fact that nothing at Missouri affected his "unrelenting," "exact," and fully formed mold is less easy to accept.)

T. H. Huxley observed in 1868 that "education is the instruction of the intellect in the laws of Nature, under which name I include not merely things and their forces, but men and their ways; and the fashioning of the affections and of the will into an earnest and loving desire to move in harmony with those laws."[54] From a somewhat broader context than what the agnostic Huxley may have had in mind, that conformist function of higher education — as well as public education at lower levels — would no doubt have been embraced by the majority of twentieth-century southern educators and administrators. Nor is there any reason to think that these more conservative memoirists like Thomas Wolfe, William Alexander Percy, or Ben Robertson would have objected to Huxley's basic premise, or that the educational environments at Chapel Hill or Sewanee or Davidson or Clemson during the early twentieth century represented anything but conventional attempts to have students "move in harmony" with the laws of nature and man. (Perhaps it also explains why these men, and Robertson in particular, had so little of consequence to say about their college years.)[55]

But it is the very questioning of that conformity — and the complacency behind it — that all of the other writers discussed here share. Most would have seen Huxley's formula for a college education's purpose as the very root of the frustration and discomfort they felt on their campuses. In fact, they would likely have defined their real education — or enlightenment — as stemming from their newly discovered doubts about the strictures of white southern society as reflected by collegiate policy, atmosphere, attitudes, and values, whether imposed by authorities or exhibited by their fellow students. Thus, the focus of so many of their narratives lies in describing the sources of those frustrations and their attempts to challenge them to one degree or another. It took a college setting for that to happen, and most acknowledge significant differences in the home life from which they had come and the ideas, values, and opportunities to which they were exposed at college.

Yet it was also in those settings that these writers discovered or developed new ways of thinking about themselves and their worlds — most often defined as the South. As marginalized or alienated from the mainstream as they may have been, it was nevertheless the exposure to other people or movements during those years and in that environment that allowed them to see themselves and their region differently. It is striking how few of their revelations or conversions involved faculty members or classroom experiences. There is little mention of books or lectures or even ideas (at least abstract ideas) as the source of their shifting sentiments.

Gerald W. Johnson, a historian and journalist at the University of North Carolina, made this point more generally. In a critique of American higher education written in 1927, he bemoaned the fact that students seemed to gain far more from their extracurricular activities than they did from the academic curriculum to which they were subjected, though in the end he acknowledged a silver lining. "They come out of college woefully ignorant of books. But they get their money's worth, because they come out much more apt than they were when they went in to live like civilized men, and much less apt to join the Ku Klux Klan."[56] How curious of Johnson to posit the Klan as the antithesis of civilization, and yet it offers a number of implications that apply quite aptly to most of the writers under consideration here. While such a comparison may well suggest that class distinctions still very much delineated college graduates from those less educated, it also suggests the greater degree of tolerance and civility toward others that could be gained by four years on a college campus, given that the Klan (even in the 1920s when it wasn't quite as ruthless as were both its past and future incarnations) still embodied intolerance and incivility.

Yet Johnson's bigger point — that most of what students gained from four years of collegiate education had little to do with what went on in their classrooms — also seems to be supported by the narratives here. More often than not, the transformative moments these writers experienced took place off campus — at conferences or in town or during summers away from school. In large part this is because those moments involved encounters with African Americans, which in itself would have precluded their own all-white campuses as the sites for such contacts. But it is apparent as well that those confrontations involving issues of racial justice and civil rights did not involve faculty members, nor were classrooms or professors' offices the sites of either inspiration or enlightenment. Of all of the testimonials dealt with here, only Katharine Lumpkin makes any reference to a faculty member on her campus — and even she neglects to name him.

A few cases involve student organizations on campus, but those — as reflected in the fleeting activism and political ambitions of Willie Morris or Eli Evans — seem to have been among the more superficial and ineffective of such transformations. Others like Lumpkin and Joan Browning found purpose and validation in what may have seemed more subversive and certainly less mainstream organizations, such as the YWCA (during both the 1910s and 1950s), while Shirley Abbott, Larry King, and ultimately Edward Cohen found any such trappings of student life disdainful and off-putting, and they came to terms with their southern selves by consciously rejecting them all — in effect, declaring themselves, like Willie Morris, to be "better than this sorry place."

A. C. Spectorsky offered some apt insights into the role of memory and reminiscence in his anthology on college life. In introducing a lengthy section of the book devoted to autobiographical accounts of undergraduate years, he suggested that a child's sense of self and others can be recreated in the imagination "but cannot be revisited in recall." Not so with "the world of [older] youth. In the college years the personality, the brain, the body and the psyche of the fully mature adult are prefigured. They will be modified — perhaps more radically and more rapidly than ever again — but they are there, quickened, fresh, responsive."[57] Such certainly seems to be the case for the vast majority of the southern autobiographers we've considered here, most of whom made clear through the chapters they devote to their college experiences — often the longest and most meaty in their books — that they saw them as either turning points or culminations of their efforts to document or assess the trajectories of their struggles for identity as southerners.

But then follows Spectorsky's next sentence: "For most, remembering, those years were full and happy and only too soon over."[58] There is not a single one of these writers for whom that description holds true (except maybe Dean Rusk). For all the nostalgia, pleasant memories of fun, frivolity, and sense of accomplishment and satisfaction that do indeed characterize so many reminiscences of college life, the accounts presented here — especially those of the 1950s, an age on the cusp of dramatic change for the region — are far more sobering, serious, even troubling. As a result, they offer us far more of substance and meaning than, of course, mere nostalgia for good times could ever do. That is why, both individually and collectively, they merit our attention and appraisal today, and why we can understand what it meant to be part of a small minority — southern white youth full of doubts, questions, and aspirations for themselves and their region — during an era and in a region characterized by conformity, conservatism, and consensus.

CHAPTER SIX

Sense of Place, Sense of Being

Appalachian Struggles with Identity,
Belonging, and Escape

IN A RECENT COLLECTION of autobiographical essays titled *Moving Out, Finding Home*, Bob Fox, a Brooklyn native, reflected on the intellectual and psychological impact of his decision to give up an academic career to become a farmer and independent writer in Appalachian Ohio. "On the farm, a grounding in the region gradually overtook my metaphysical interests," he wrote. "The red clay hills, its people and their destiny, infiltrated my writing. In southeast Ohio, the hills, woods, and the unchanged lifestyle taught me that place defines one's sense of being in the world." Until this point in his life, Fox notes, he "had not known how geography can nurture the spirit."[1]

Perhaps more than in most parts of America, place has always defined Appalachians' sense of being, and the linkage between geography and spirit often seems particularly acute in terms of how southern highlanders — and even Ohio highlanders — identify themselves and define their life experiences. If there is any thematic link among the very different works of memoir, autobiography, and self-reflection under consideration here, it is just that — the power of place in shaping one's sense of self.

Yet equally apparent in juxtaposing these works is that the impact of geography is not always as nurturing as it was for Bob Fox. For a number of Appalachian writers, both natives and transplants, their experiences proved oppressive and constraining to spirits that they believed could only soar when and if they left the region. For others, it was only in returning to the mountains — or coming to them for the first time — that they felt fulfilled. Whether it was the lay of the land, its flora and fauna, or even its rural character, each found something therapeutic, calming, even redemptive about the highland South, and their sheer presence in a mountain environment proved nurturing to their spirits in both simple and more profound ways.

While each of these authors engages the region itself and his or her place within it in very different ways, taken together, their work reflects one of the great paradoxes of Appalachia and a recurring theme in its history and literature: that so glorious a natural environment can, and long has, bred such miserable or unfulfilled lives for so many and yet offers such healing and restorative powers for so many others. In her book, *When Memory Speaks: Exploring the Art of Autobiography*, Jill Ker Conway notes that "whether we are aware of it or not, our culture gives us the inner script by which we live our lives. The main acts for the play come from the way our world understands human development; the scenes and key characters come from our families and socialization . . . ; and the dynamics of the script comes from what our world defines as success and achievement."[2]

If Appalachia represents such a world, there is no single "inner script" to which the nine authors whose work is explored here conform. Of these, four have West Virginia roots, two are native Kentuckians, one is a western North Carolinian, and two are transplants to the region — one from Pennsylvania, the other from Brooklyn. Four are poets (most of the male authors), six are academics, one is a journalist, one an independent writer and environmentalist, and one a housewife and mother. Five are married; one is single; one is gay, and the sexual orientation of the others remains unknown and irrelevant.[3] Yet none of those factors defines what Conway calls their "archetypal life scripts" or allows for categorization and commonalities nearly as much as does the relation of each to place. Far more than human development, family and socialization, even success and achievement, it is their attitudes toward Appalachia that are at the core of their "inner scripts" and thus provide the basis for their self examinations and the most fruitful terms for comparative analysis.

★ ★ ★

For Jeanette Walls's father, it was only as a last resort that he brought his family back to his hometown of Welch, West Virginia. It is easy to see why her 2005 memoir, *The Glass Castle*, became such a long-running best-seller. Walls's quirky, but deeply affecting saga of her extremely bright, capable, but utterly eccentric and ultimately dysfunctional parents and the ordeal they put their four children through makes for compelling reading, and how those children — if not their parents — triumphed over that ordeal makes for a story as unique as it is poignant.

Only the central third of Walls's autobiography is set in Appalachia. Her brilliant, high-spirited, but unstable father led his devoted wife and four children from town to town, job to job, in a nomadic, hand-to-mouth existence throughout the American Southwest for most of Jeannette's childhood years. Full of ambition and dreams — his "glass castle" — he admitted defeat in capitulating to his wife's pleas that they abandon his increasingly futile plans ("You know you're down and out when Okies laugh at you," she said), and return home to live with his mother in Welch, West Virginia. Always the optimist, she assured the children they would love it there. "We'd live in a forest in the mountains with the squirrels and chipmunks. We could meet our grandma and grandpa Wells, who were genuine hillbillies."[4]

Only the last part of that prediction proved true. Her grandparents proved so strange and off-putting when they met their long-estranged grandchildren that Jeanette thought that "maybe this was one of Dad's pranks." He "must have arranged for the weirdest people in town to pretend that they were his family."[5] She provides an incisive portrait of this dying coal town in the mid-1970s and makes readily apparent why her family's life so quickly spiraled downward into an even bleaker existence there than what they had known out west. Her first impressions came in entering Welch on the main road, which "was narrow, with old brick buildings crowding in close on both sides. The stores, the signs, the sidewalks, the cars were all covered with a film of black coal dust, giving the town an almost monochromatic look, like an old hand-tinted photograph. Welch was shabby and worn out." Her father told them that this road led farther up into "wet, forbidding mountains and on to other dying coal towns." In a typically succinct encapsulation of the region's economic state of affairs, she quotes him as saying that few strangers came through the town anymore, "and almost all who did came to inflict one form of misery or another — to lay off workers, to shut down a mine, to foreclose on someone's house, to compete for a rare job opening."[6]

Thus setting the scene of their new home, where she would spend her adolescence, she and her siblings find the local social scene just as alienating. "We fought a lot in Welch," she writes:

Not just to fend off our enemies but to fit in. Maybe it was because there was so little to do in Welch; maybe it was because life there was hard and it made people hard; maybe it was because of all the bloody battles over unionizing the mines; maybe it was because mining was dangerous and cramped and dirty work and it put all the miners in bad moods and they came home and took it out on their wives, who took it out on their kids, who took it out on other kids.

She sums up these confrontations as "street brawls, bar stabbings, parking-lot beatings, wife slappings, and toddler whalings," and concludes in typically succinct form: "We had lived in some pretty scrappy places back in the desert, but Mom said Welch was the fightingest town she'd ever seen."[7]

Her father retreated into alcoholism, petty theft, and long absences from home; her mother increasingly absolved herself of any responsibility for her family's care; and her grandparents offered curiously little support or sympathy. Meanwhile, Jeannette and her siblings learned to fend for themselves and each other. Walls captures the power of place in imposing futility and despair — in this case, on a family that had little more than its hopes, dreams, and a remarkable esprit de corps until it landed in West Virginia. What had seemed, from a child's perspective at least, a grand adventure in the constant mobility and variety during those early years out west became in Welch a devastating decline, both economically and psychologically, as the Wallses found themselves trapped in lives of claustrophobia, stagnancy, and hopelessness.

Geography can kill spirit as much as it can nurture it, and no other writer I know applies that hard truth to Appalachia as forcefully as Jeannette Walls, if only because of the contrasts — in place and in fortune — of her family's lives before and after their West Virginia sojourn. One by one, she and her siblings sought escape for themselves and each other, and all but one achieved success in New York City. She described the morning when, at age seventeen, she became the second child to head north. In glancing from her bus window back at her father, the only family member who had come to see her off, she wondered "if he was remembering how he, too, had left Welch full of vinegar at age seventeen and just as convinced as I was now that he'd never return. I wondered if he was hoping that his favorite girl would come back, or if he was hoping that, unlike him, she would make it out for good."[8]

The third act in Walls's story is in some ways the most remarkable of all, for as she and her siblings grow to become mature adults and at last take control of their own destinies, their parents' decline continues unabated, until they too follow their children to New York, not to live with them or even to rely on their financial resources, but rather to exist, quite by choice, as homeless people living on Manhattan's sidewalks and empty lots and in abandoned warehouses. Unlike many such sagas, this is not one of triumph or even redemption. If applying Conway's "inner script" of what defines success or achievement, the plight of Jeannette's parents precludes any possibility for a happy ending for either her or her siblings, if only because their parents were ultimately beyond salvation in any traditional sense of what success means in American society.

★ ★ ★

Allison Glock's *Beauty before Comfort* is another coming-of-age story of an adolescent girl stifled by the limitations of small-town West Virginia. Yet it is of a different era — the 1930s and 1940s — and a different autobiographical approach. In the tradition of secondhand memoirs by Rick Bragg, Mary Lee Settle, Linda Scott DeRosier, and others who made a parent or grandparent the focus of a book, Glock's is a portrait of her maternal grandmother, a woman she knew well.[9] Through frequent visits as a child — sometimes whole summers spent with her — Glock learned enough from the talkative and self-absorbed Aneita Jean Blair about her early years to enable her to recreate convincingly her life in considerable detail and often through Aneita Jean's own words.

Glock herself, raised in Florida, had a great affinity for the Mountain State. "As a child, West Virginia was my world," she writes. "More specifically, Newell, West Virginia, a sad hump of a town paralyzed by poverty. I loved Newell with an inexplicable ferocity, the way a mother loves a screaming baby." The sole reason for this was that it was where her grandmother lived, and where she came to know this lively, even charismatic woman who "sang songs and made men blush and fed me graham crackers with honey and showed me how to walk in heels and how to braid my hair and how to be more than I thought I was in the world."[10]

Born in 1920, Blair grew up in two adjacent towns, Chester and Newell, both Ohio River towns distinguished by a pottery industry that flourished due to a unique blue-tinted clay imbedded there. A natural beauty whose zest for life included great ambitions, Aneita Jean early on felt stifled by small-town life and made up her mind early on that she would leave. She decided, her granddaughter writes, "that by the time she was sixteen, she'd find a man who would carry her over the mountains to a place where all women lolled about, resplendent in chiffon and diamonds, and the men looked like Errol Flynn before he started drinking so much. Someplace glamorous. Like Pittsburgh."[11]

As the book's title suggests, Aneita Jean was obsessed with her looks, an obsession Glock describes as the primary theme of her grandmother's life. Yet she makes it clear that there was purpose behind the vanity: Blair saw her beauty as her ticket out of West Virginia. It would take a man to realize her escape, and her story is peopled with an array of adolescent boys unable to resist the allure of this flirtatious and relatively uninhibited beauty. Aneita Jean kept a "memory book" made up of numerous snapshots of her life during those formative years, and she used it as a visual springboard from which to regale her granddaughter with reminiscences of that period of her life when hopes were high and the possibilities endless.

Glock teases from her grandmother's self-absorbed stories a wonderfully textured portrait of the Blair family and of the two communities that so shaped their identities and destinies over the course of both the Great Depression and the Second World War. The war took its toll on the wide array of male admirers Aneita Jean had once enjoyed, and in 1944 she married Donald Thornberry, the most stalwart of her prewar suitors, when he returned home on leave from the Pacific. Accepting his proposal, she recalled, wasn't so much a decision as it was instinct. But in so doing, she realized that she would never leave Hancock County. Glock writes that "in the years that followed, my grandmother often revisited that day she and Don took a drive in the holler [where he proposed to her]. It amused and frightened her how abruptly her life changed. How decisions can be like car accidents, sudden and full of consequence."[12]

It is here that this quasi-memoir, this vivid character study, constructed in both the first and third persons, is at its best and most poignant: the mix of nostalgia and regret, of celebrating what was while musing on what might have been, that so preoccupied Aneita Jean Blair in her later years. Her life in Newell, where Don became a potter until the industry dried up, was relatively uneventful by the early standards she had set for herself. She raised three daughters (the oldest of whom was Glock's mother), yet even motherhood seemed to offer little consolation in a life she always felt was meant for so much more. Aneita Jean's memory book holds no photographs after 1945, perhaps the saddest commentary on her later life, and how differently she saw herself once marriage determined the direction it would take and the place in which it would be lived.

★ ★ ★

Even more than Glock's portrait of her grandmother, Jeff Mann's memoir is pre-occupied with his sexuality and its relevancy to place. As is obvious from its title, *Loving Mountains, Loving Men*, Mann is homosexual and, as such, found Appalachia, particularly his hometown of Hinton, an isolated railroad town along the New River in southern West Virginia, a difficult society to fit into. Yet what sets Mann's work apart from the other memoirs of escape is that he carefully differentiates between the small town in which he feels so inhibited and Appalachia as a whole, for which he felt a strong affinity, and where he has managed over time to establish a fulfilling and relatively stress-free life for himself.[13]

Mann yearned to leave Hinton since he became aware that he was gay at the age of fifteen. As an undergraduate and graduate student at West Virginia University in the late 1970s and early 1980s, he found outlets in the few gay bars and experienced a number of brief flings with other men, though he acknowledges that it was hardly the "magically welcoming gay paradise" he had naively anticipated upon leaving home. Assuming that he could only be fulfilled in a truly urban culture, he taught for a semester in Washington, D.C., and later traveled extensively to American and European cities, yet he found that none of them offered him the sense of identity and belonging that he found in his native southern highlands. Mann thus emerged as what he calls a "cultural amphibian, insisting on both worlds, Appalachian and queer."[14] This duality, and the complexities inherent in it, form the core of this most introspective and self-analytical of all of the books under consideration here.

Mann knew that he could never live in Hinton. Despite a strong attachment to his family and frequent trips home, too many memories of high school abuse and ostracism, and an awareness of a perpetual, and potentially violent, homophobia there kept him from feeling either comfortable or safe. He settled on a career in academia, which allowed him to maintain his regional roots within probably the most tolerant of regional environments — its college towns. After thirteen years in Morgantown, he took refuge in the intellectual and relatively liberal atmosphere of Blacksburg, Virginia, where he has spent the last fifteen years. Even his academic pursuits reflected the strong duality of his passions. He double majored in English and forestry at WVU and now teaches Appalachian Studies courses along with gay and lesbian literature at Virginia Tech, and he takes great satisfaction in what he brings to — and derives from — both.

Struck by a botany class definition of a weed as any plant that's growing where it's not wanted, Mann goes on to say that even a rose would be a weed in a tobacco patch. As he moves from the natural insecurities and painful aware-

ness of the fact that his sexual orientation is always going to make him an outsider in the world he chooses to remain a part of, Mann comes to take as much
satisfaction in his country boy identity as in his homosexuality. He seems to
revel in his mixed identities and weedlike status, calling himself "the intellectual
among the provincials, the book-worm among the athletes, the pagan among
the Christians, the poet among the illiterate, the hillbilly among the city folk,
the queer among the straights, the leather jacket among the suits."[15] Even his
family — of whom he provides richly detailed character sketches — plays into
his sense of exceptionalism. His sister Amy married a black man, which their
mother found far harder to come to terms with than with Jeff's homosexuality.
He and Amy used to joke about the double crosses she had to bear, knowing
that Hinton's residents labeled the Manns "nigger-lovers and queers." Add to
that "my father's passionately liberal opinions, his hatred of Republicans, con-
sumerism, fundamentalists, and the NRA," Mann writes bemusedly, "and you
have the most colorfully freakish family in Summers County."[16]

Mann is at his best in articulating the parallels between his regional and his
sexual identities. He notes that the histories of both his mountain ancestors
and his "queer forebears" share much in common: "isolation and siege, hardscrabble survival, both physical and emotional, and bald-faced injustices that
insult that concept of individual freedom on which America is based."[17] While
he acknowledges the sad fact that his fellow Appalachians exhibit as intense an
intolerance of gays as those anywhere in the country, he insists that he will continue to lay full claim to both identities. In teaching Appalachian folk culture
at Virginia Tech, Mann writes, he is always reminded of why he stays in the region: "Folklore creates a kind of comforting group identity, a strong, unbroken
bond. It is hard to leave folks who talk like you, eat like you, sing the same songs
you do, predict the weather the same way you do."[18]

This too renders Mann's memoir a unique testimonial to the role of the region in defining the self. No other author considered here — except perhaps
Linda DeRosier, though only in hindsight — captures both the pain and the
joy of being Appalachian so adeptly, or even tries to. With as many reasons
to resent and rebel against his society as anyone — all of which he fully documents — it is remarkable that Mann ultimately views the region with such generosity and affection. "The same Appalachia that flays us with its strict moral
codes," he reminds us, "also teaches us how to survive what pariahs sometimes
suffer. Self-reliance, toughness, resilience become enviable sources of dignity
and strength."[19] Can anyone else say as much with such conviction?

★ ★ ★

Linda Scott DeRosier's *Creeker: A Woman's Journey* is in some respects, the most conventional autobiography among those considered here. Born in 1941 in her grandmother's log house "on the left-hand fork of Greasy Creek in what is now Boons Camp, Kentucky," she provides a straightforward narrative of her childhood and adolescence, her multileveled education and how it led to an academic career in psychology that took her far from Appalachia and her family there. Yet it is that very journey that forced her to confront what it meant to be Appalachian — both for herself, and for others who identified her as such. As her subtitle suggests, evolving as a feminist is at least as central a theme as coming to terms with her "creeker" past. In weaving both of those themes throughout her narrative, her story, like Jeff Mann's, reminds us that one's identity as a highlander never exists in a vacuum, and that conflicting tensions are always inherent in reconciling the various strands of one's sense of self.

While she is upfront about the depth of her Appalachian credentials, DeRosier insists that as "creekers" she and her family are not to be lumped together with Appalachians who grew up in towns, as demographers, social scientists, and other academics studying the region tend to do. Paintsville, the county seat of 4,500 people, was only eight miles from Two-Mile Creek, and yet "was eons away in terms of class, values, expectations, and anything else that counted for much." In terms of expectations alone, she insists, "a woman my age born in Paintsville . . . would be more likely to find similarity with a cohort born in Plainville, Wisconsin or Carthage, Alabama — or any of a thousand other little towns in the United States — than with me." She stresses that hers is "a story from *rural* Appalachia, recently brought to consciousness, and reported by a creeker."[20]

Yet if she makes that declaration, almost defiantly, on the second page of her first chapter, such awareness comes only gradually over the course of her life. DeRosier chronicles with far more precision just when and how she came to that sense of identity and what it meant to her at that time and since. Her opening chapters provide a vivid and unflinching portrait of both the physical and socioeconomic world of Two-Mile Creek in the 1940s and 1950s, and of the limitations and frustrations of lives dependent on coal mines and those who ran them, whether company officials or union leaders. She writes with great affection of both the people and the place that defined her first seventeen years — and argues that they were equally important in shaping who she was. "I

was not only of a place but of a people; even the most distant of family connections were and are significant to me. To my son I have handed down the sense
of belonging to a clan of people just as surely as I passed along my genetic code."
Yet her sense of belonging was never complete or fully accepted. "My world
never folded around me in the way it seemed to drape itself lovingly and warmly
around everybody else I grew up with," she noted. "All my energies, traits, and
desires kept getting in the way of my carrying out my prescribed role."[21]

At the same time, the natural world in which she grew up evokes far more
mixed responses. She is appreciative enough of the flora and fauna of her childhood to carry with her seeds and bulbs from home that she has planted wherever else in the country she's lived, and she sees in their ability to adapt to new
environments a parallel with her own adaptations to new surroundings and circumstances. Yet there is much she doesn't miss about the early, primitive life she
knew as a child or the harsh conditions meted out by an often unforgiving environment. When many of her academic colleagues longed to return to the land
in the 1960s and 1970s, she suggested that "if they'd ever lived on the land, they
might not have been quite so nostalgic for it." She recalls with great fondness
how much she and her family welcomed the arrival of indoor plumbing and
central heating in their lives. She even takes her "tree-hugger" husband to task.
"He has no idea," she tells us, "how very close to nature some of us were forced
to be," and goes on to explain:

> He grew up in Connecticut. If he wanted to commune with nature, his fam-
> ily drove to the shore or to the Berkshires. Therefore he is concerned for every
> snail darter and tree owl on the planet. . . .Town folk live in places where nature
> has been so long domesticated that they don't know her for what she is. Living
> close to the land taught me that nature can be — indeed usually is — one mean
> mother.[22]

It was only incrementally that DeRosier's own awareness and appreciation
of Appalachia fully took shape over the course of her life; she traces the process as she moves from the creek into town, to college and then on to graduate
school, as she goes from social worker to PhD in psychology, then moves out
of Kentucky and sees her roots and heritage at an ever greater distance as she
settles into a career teaching at Rocky Mountain College in Billings, Montana.
The stigma of being a hillbilly — or creeker — was hard to shake, particularly
among other Kentuckians who defined her first and foremost by her mountain
origins, even after she had earned both MA and PhD degrees. "With a bunch of

letters after your name, folks may still look down on you," she notes. However, she suggests that it became for her a game of one-upmanship. Speaking as the psychologist she became, she explains her somewhat convoluted defense system: "Since *you* know what they think about *you* while *they* don't know what you think of *them*, you win. The key to it all is to know the lower limit of your reputation, because you don't ever want anyone to be thinking you are worse than you *think* people think you are."[23]

DeRosier attended Pikeville College, only fifty miles from home, playing it safe, she felt, since "any other place would have chewed me up and spit me right back up Two-Mile Creek, never to be heard from again." It was for her at age seventeen "every bit as far as I could have stretched socially and economically." She notes that *technically* she didn't fully leave Appalachia until she was thirty-nine years old; but she insists, "I really left Appalachia and the comfort and pain of shared values that early September Sunday when my daddy . . . hauled all bad-haired ninety-four pounds of Linda Sue to Pikeville College."[24]

Her education and career unfolded in fits and starts, along with marriage and motherhood, all of it colored by her quest to "pass for normal — not hillbilly." Each year she claims to have gotten a little closer to that goal until her doctoral work at the University of Kentucky "seemingly rooted out the last vestiges of my Appalachian essence, though I did not know it at the time." But it was not to last. She thought that in earning her PhD in 1972 she had "so thoroughly assimilated into the culture of academe that with the exception of my still distinctive speech patterns, I was well-nigh close to passing for normal." And yet, in her first teaching position at nearby Kentucky State University, a predominantly black institution, she "found the hillbilly girl sequestered since my early days at Pikeville and found that I could use cultural insight, long repressed, as a bridge to understanding more about ways my students came to know."[25]

Thus began for DeRosier a steady if circuitous path back to her roots, and to a new appreciation of her identity and the unique culture that shaped it. Although the majority of the authors considered here are academics, most see their scholarly careers as marginal or even irrelevant to the Appalachian-based issues with which they wrestle in more intuitive or emotional ways. Only DeRosier — and perhaps Mann — place their academic life front and center within the quests for their Appalachian heritage, and she in particular is able to use such disparate elements of her career — from teaching African American students or students at the University of Idaho or Rocky Mountain College to working in psychology (a discipline that, unlike history, sociology, or creative writing, hardly lends itself to a regional focus) — to draw meaning and insight from her mountain roots that she never would have mustered had she never left home. After years of resistance and denial, she was forced to rebuild her connectedness to the world of Two-Mile Creek, which makes her epilogue, titled "Comin' Home Spirit," an almost redemptive statement of all she has gained by embracing in full all that she once rejected, or tried to. "For all the sacks of iris rhizomes from Grandma Emmy's, the yellowed pages of lye-soap-making directions, and the family recipe for hogshead souse that I have carried with me all these years," she writes, "the most valuable commodity I brought from home is my Appalachian consciousness — my spirit, if you will."[26]

☆ ☆ ☆

Although Linda DeRosier might view their missions with some skepticism, Jim Minick and Thomas Raine Crowe were among those who "returned to the land" and in so doing found in their geographical surroundings rich sources of spiritual nurture. Both celebrate in lyrical prose the beauty, wonder, and utility of the natural world that makes up and surrounds the farms on which they live in the Blue Ridge Mountains of Virginia and North Carolina, respectively, and they do so far more unequivocally than DeRosier ever did. In the tradition of Thoreau's *Walden*, Annie Dillard's *Pilgrim on Tinker Creek*, and the *Foxfire* books, both Minick's and Crowe's books capture the intricacies and peculiarities of nature and its hold on their authors' sense of their own identity and purpose. Beyond that, both grapple with the particular joys and burdens of living on the land and living off the land. Both men are poets, and their work reflects that temperament and talent, most notably in their ability to derive universal truths from the microcosms they chronicle so astutely.

Minick's *Finding a Clear Path* is the most loosely structured and least autobiographical of all of the books under consideration here. He and his wife, Sarah, moved into a hundred-year-old farm house in the Lost Bent Creek valley of Floyd County, Virginia (presumably when he took a teaching position in the English Department at Radford University, though he never says as much). He chronicles their ten years of life there through a series of brief essays.

More than most of these authors, but not atypical of many Appalachian residents (including those I grew up with), Minick thinks in spatial terms and articulates the topographical features of his world as vital to his own sense of place and sense of being. He grew up a mountain boy — in Pennsylvania. In an opening essay called "Creases," Minick states upfront that two watersheds have created his life. "I have mapped out the valleys and mountains of these singing waters in the folds of my grandmother's quilt and the creases in the palm of my hand. These wrinkles in the landscape, and the waters that created them, carry me home again and again."[27] He grew up near Three Square Hollow in the Alleghenies, where three mountains come together and the waters from them make up the highest edge of the Susquehanna watershed, and he, like his parents and grandparents, knew where they were because of the physical landmarks these peaks, springs, and creeks provided.

In moving to Virginia, Minick felt that until he had oriented himself to those same features — until he could "get his bearings," as his grandfather had so often instructed him to do — he wouldn't feel at home. Buffalo Mountain, some fifteen miles south of his farm, became the single beacon by which he learned to orient himself as he moved around the county, and a hike to its top with his wife sealed his new sense of where he was. Seeing North Carolina's Mount Pilot in the far distance to the south, Mount Rogers to the southwest, and various other peaks and rivers, including the New River valley, all from atop Buffalo Mountain, he defined his world accordingly — "with help from the sun and a map — the latter a poor substitute for a grandfather."[28] No other writer discussed here describes his or her highland world in terms of topography, latitude, longitude, or otherwise. And if it comes across at one level as a bit academic, Minick never loses his sense of the poetic in expressing the emotional satisfaction of his self-placement and in noting its similarity to the world of his youth several hundred miles to the north.

Once he has so clearly established his physical setting both for himself and for his readers, Minick is quick to move his perspective to ground level and stay there. In mixing his own observations with what he reads or with the shared wisdom of neighbors and colleagues, he provides an abundance of factual data about a vast range of topics — from the social and family life of beavers to shifting patterns of migrating bird species to the growth and shedding of antlers (nature's fastest-growing tissue) and their medicinal value to humans. Many of his essays are more instructional in tone: how to build and stock a pond; how to cultivate medicinal roots, from ginseng to black cohosh, and berries, from blue to wine; how to both hunt mushrooms (morels) and grow them (shiitake); how — and why — to build duck houses and bat houses; and how to distinguish good bugs from bad in one's garden. Minick's strong commitment to the environment comes through particularly in the book's latter sections, where he focuses on the multiple benefits of organic farming, timber stand improvement, mason stoves, and root cellars, just to name a few.

What we miss in Minick's writing is a stronger sense of self. As artful as he is in providing us with fleeting glances — some perhaps more unintentional than others — of who he is and where he comes from, one would like to know so much more about this vague but immensely appealing persona that he provides us. What of his education? To what extent did it shape his appreciation for the natural world, and this place in particular? What led him to Radford? How does his love of nature and the region impact his teaching? To what extent did it lead him to become a teacher? It is, of course, an author's prerogative to choose his parameters and to tell us no more than he wants about his background or his career, and it is very much to Minick's credit that we want to know more about him, and about how the various strands of his multifaceted life intertwine.[29] On its own terms, though, *Finding a Clear Path* is a beautifully wrought example of nature writing and environmental advocacy at its most appealing, in part because he recognizes at so many levels the innate worth of the complex natural world of southern Appalachia and the quality of life it can sustain and define.

☆ ☆ ☆

Thomas Crowe reveals much more about himself and the circumstances that brought him to the small farm in the Green River Valley near Saluda in Polk County, North Carolina, where he spent nearly four years (from 1979 to 1982) — and over two decades later chronicled in his book, *Zoro's Field*. His is a tighter and more focused narrative, perhaps because he's writing of a much more self-consciously Waldenesque experiment in rural living. "It is my goal," he states at the outset, "to live at least twice the time [Thoreau] did at the edge of Walden Pond and to give myself a realistic opportunity to take the *Walden* experience and a life of relative seclusion a step further — two full seasonal cycles deeper into the heart and spirit of self-sufficiency and simple living to discover the soul of the wild. To find firsthand the path to a greater sense of self-confidence, with hopes of replacing an unnatural urban psychological fear with familiarity and serenity based on common sense."[30]

Given this more experimental and purpose-driven experience, he infuses his account with a stronger sense of both time and place. It was an invitation from an elderly acquaintance, Zoro Guice, to come live on his abandoned farm property that spurred Crowe's experiment (and his book's title). He left northern California to "come home," a relative term in that Crowe was born and raised several counties farther west in the Cherokee Snowbird community in Graham County. Like Minick, he writes insightfully about the basic functions of self-sufficiency on a mountain farm — digging a root cellar, collecting honey from a bee hive, planting a garden and preserving and storing its output, hunting, fishing, and making "homebrew" — mere beer, it seems, rather than the far more potent potables produced by most others in the area.

Crowe wrestles with more social matters as well, including, ironically, the virtues of living alone, in his opening and one of his best chapters, titled "Solitude." Despite his quest for "hibernating from humanity" and his insistence that he preferred his own company — and those of the plants and animals that surround his cabin — to social gatherings, Crowe, far more than Minick, also takes a strong interest in the Saluda community in which he found himself, and in the individuals who befriended and helped him, among them Zoro Guice himself, who served as both mentor and muse to Crowe in his efforts to live off the land.

Crowe actively immersed himself in the region's cultural heritage by contemplating Cherokee beliefs and traditions and their relationship to this same land, and by reading Horace Kephart, William Bartram, and Thomas Wolfe. He also befriended the goat keeper on what had once been Carl Sandburg's farm in Flat Rock, about ten miles away. That experience captures a particular strength of Crowe's — his ability to blend the practical realities of farm life with his intellectual engagement with that world. His initial interest in Connemara, Sandburg's home, was the availability there of goat manure, which he collects regularly to fertilize Zoro's field; but when the goat keeper allowed him access to Sandburg's study, he spent many hours perusing the Illinois poet's files, papers, and books. He found a soul mate in this transplanted Midwesterner and writes with admiration of the "ordered and balanced life" of Sandburg's latter years in Flat Rock. "We *must* go home again," Crowe insists. "Take the knowledge, the experience, and the strength gained from all the years of wandering, searching, working, and plant this in the soil of our adopted or native homes — whether the west coast of Ireland [the original Connemara] or the mountains of western North Carolina — wherever they may be."[31]

★ ★ ★

This is a philosophy that Bob Fox embraces as fully as does Crowe, at least for a time. His experience in Appalachian Ohio shares much with both Minick and Crowe in that he finds an agrarian existence so therapeutic and satisfying.

While he lays out his story through discrete essays, Fox ultimately provides a more full-bodied chronicle of his life than do most of these authors, in part, no doubt, because — like Jeanette Walls — he knows that one must understand his earlier non-Appalachian experience to appreciate the transformative effects of his new life within the region. Fox seems the unlikeliest of Appalachian transplants. Born in Brooklyn to Russian Jewish immigrants, he grew up in a carefully circumscribed urban world to which he never fully connected. He was eager to leave home and did so at age seventeen, headed for San Francisco. Within a week of his less than amicable departure from his parents, they died in a hotel fire in the Catskills, and that pivotal event haunted Fox's young adulthood as he drifted through a variety of enterprises in a variety of places before eventually receiving a master's degree in English and taking a teaching assistantship at Ohio University in Athens. (Fox is rather vague in delineating this period of his life, and the chronology remains a bit confusing.)

Disillusioned by the ugliness of both Vietnam-era politics and urban life, Fox and his wife moved shortly thereafter out of Athens and purchased a farm in "Dog Holler" in Meigs County, only a few miles from the West Virginia border. "Settling in the hills of southeast Ohio," he writes, "fulfilled my longing for rural, self-reliant living" and became what he calls an "unplanned apprenticeship as a member of an Appalachian community." It also became the only place in which he fully felt at home since summers spent on a Catskill farm, and he immersed himself in the rigors of farm life and the joys of what a poet acquaintance called "the privilege of living what is the past to most America."[32]

Yet over time this new life proved to be less than idyllic. In a particularly incisive essay titled "Song of an Adopted, Displaced Appalachian: Speculations on Individual and Cultural Identity," Fox explains why, after fourteen years, he and his wife gave up their farm and moved to Columbus. While the farm served as his spiritual base and provided a sense of belonging long lacking in his life, he eventually came to crave the intellectual stimulus he once thought he could nurture on his own. "On the farm," he writes, "my inner life remained private. At potluck suppers or evening chats, the conversation among the men concerned building repairs, machinery, garden pests. . . . My imaginative concerns served no useful purpose. I missed talk of ideas." He discovered, much to his regret, that he couldn't have it all: "My various interests did not fall into the ideal natural balance I once envisioned. How many interests could I commit to? Reading and writing, music, and farming? The more I learned what it would take to succeed as an organic farmer, the less willing I was to invest my entire future in the land."[33]

Fox wrestled with an intriguing dilemma: the extent to which one can maintain a fully productive literary and intellectual life while making a living on the land. Others have managed to do so — both Jim Minick's and Thomas Crowe's works are testimonials to the fact that one can succeed on both fronts. But in articulating the dissonance between these two very different parts of his being, Fox raises important questions about the competing priorities posed by modern life, even as one seeks to escape it, and about whether there are limitations to the spiritual nurturing that geography can provide. It is a provocative and very personal piece of writing that gets at some very basic truths about academic life in Appalachia, and one that I now assign to graduate students in Appalachian Studies.[34]

★ ★ ★

Two recent works focus on returns to Appalachia — Chris Offutt to the place of his birth and upbringing in Kentucky, and John O'Brien to his parents' home state of West Virginia. Their very different reactions to both people and place suggest yet again the ways in which personal ambition, temperament, and sense of self have much to do with shaping one's attachment to or alienation from the region one wants to think of as home. In 1998 Offutt, a novelist and short story writer, accepted an instructorship in creative writing at his alma mater, Morehead State University, and in so doing returned to his home county (he grew up in Haldeman, ten miles away from Morehead) for the first time in twenty years. He declared that he had come back in order "to help young people understand themselves, and provide an example of the potential for life beyond the hills. I had come home to give as much as possible."[35] Yet what was intended to be a long-term commitment to the region turned out to be a mere one-year stint, and his account of that year is the subject of his 2002 memoir, *No Heroes*.

Offutt doesn't think much of the school itself. He declares Morehead to be "a poor school in a poor state" and "more like a high school with ash trays than a genuine college." He's also disdainful of the faculty he was about to join, describing the English Department as "career academics who found themselves at a lousy school. They lived in an Appalachian town of six thousand with no airport, no bookstore, no deli, no record store, one bar, and forty churches. Everyone but me had a PhD. Unlike them, I truly wanted to work at MSU."[36] He is equally condescending toward both the region and its people — his people.

"Eastern Kentucky offers no models for success," he writes, "no paths for ambitious people to follow, no tangible life beyond the county line. Doing well is a betrayal of mountain culture. . . . Most glaringly absent from eastern Kentucky is a sense of pride. I hoped to change that."[37] Given his seeming lack of pride in anything about the area, this is a curious statement when it first appears, and one that rings particularly hollow by book's end.

Neither the region's people nor its culture have much to do with Offutt's nostalgia for home or the impulses that drew him back to Kentucky after two decades of living in the Midwest and West. (It's odd that he reveals so little about where he's returning from or what he did there.) Yet his contempt for home is nothing new in this book. In a previous memoir, the much acclaimed *The Same River Twice*, his early years are referred to in only fleeting and flippant terms. He describes his hometown (which he doesn't even bother to name) as "a zip code with a creek" and notes: "It had a store once but the man who ran it died. Long before my birth, a union invalidated the company scrip, shut the mines, and left a few men dead. Two hundred people live here now." He's equally dismissive of scholarship on the region: "Our hills are the most isolated there are in America, the subject of countless doctoral theses. It's an odd sensation to read about yourself as counterpart to the aborigine or Eskimo." He continues his tirade: "If VISTA wasn't bothering us, some clown was running around the hills with a tape recorder. Strangers told us we spoke Elizabethan English, that we were contemporary ancestors to everybody else. They told us the correct way to pronounce 'Appalachia,' as if we didn't know where we'd been living for the past three hundred years."[38] Much of that cynicism and indifference to home carries over into his second memoir. His parents, still living in Haldeman, play surprisingly minor supporting roles in his story, not the central role we would expect in a memoir about retuning home.

By the same token, Offutt's actual classroom experiences seem peripheral to the story he wants to tell. Given his strongly asserted sense of mission in enlightening and inspiring students, it is striking how few pages he devotes to his role as a teacher, and how little effort he seems to bring to that role. He describes his initial encounter with his students at Morehead:

> I walked into my first class late. . . . I announced the name of the class and asked if
> everyone was in the right room. No one spoke or nodded. . . . I gave each student
> a copy of my course description, read it aloud, and asked for questions. There
> were none. A long silence ensued during which I looked out the window at main-

tenance workers busily primping the president's house. When I returned my attention to the students, everyone looked at me, then away. I dismissed class. They
left swiftly without a word.[39]

This is hardly the approach of a teacher committed to making a difference in
students' lives, and nothing that follows suggests that Offutt's classroom rapport with students ever improved. Except for individual encounters with one or
two students — those he merely advises to go elsewhere to school, to get out of
the area — he doesn't seem to have truly inspired anyone who came under his
tutelage.

If Offutt provides little of substance or satisfaction as an educator, his book
offers other pleasures and rewards. As is the case with most of the books under
discussion here, it is the sense of place and a yearning to return home that in-
spires Offutt's best writing. While there for his job interview at Morehead, he
visited a farmstead with a local realtor. In a powerful passage, Offutt describes
walking through a wooded section of the property, where he was so overcome
with the sights and smells and sounds of early spring in his native hills that he
bought the place on the spot, before he was even offered the job. These sensory
associations seem to have triggered a sense of belonging as well. "Out west I
was one of the perpetual faces with no history, a drifter, a stranger, a man from
the East," he writes. "Here everyone knew my entire line — root, branch, and
fork."[40]

Offutt conveys some affection for certain individuals with whom he becomes reacquainted and shares fond memories for the simple childhood and
sense of community he once knew. He punctuates his narrative with lively vignettes of several of them — former teachers, coaches, and classmates, even the
college maintenance crew with whom he worked during his student days, who
are much amused and a bit dubious that he's now crossed over to faculty status.
But he is hit hard by the deterioration and stagnation of so much of the community he once knew, and much of his book serves as a moving meditation on
the economic and social decline of the region and its effect on those residents
forced to endure it, without the option of going elsewhere. Driving through his
hometown, Offutt writes that he felt like a pilgrim in his own country:

> Haldeman had been abandoned in the name of progress. The feds shut the post
> office and retired the zip code. The grade school was closed. The only store sat
> vacant. . . . The bootlegger was gone, the poolroom burnt down, and the poker
> game moved elsewhere. The steel train rails were peeled from the earth and the

cross-ties hauled away. The rail bed was ideal for trailers, which stretched through the hills like cars tethered to the land. Nothing was left of Haldeman but geography. Time had mown my hometown down.[41]

That melancholic tone pervades much of Offutt's musings, so the reader is not at all surprised at the brevity of his stay. Given his ambivalence toward his homecoming throughout the book and the rather naïve and egotistical goals he set for himself in returning, his departure for a better offer in Iowa makes a natural, if sad, end to his story. He acknowledges his hypocrisy in "abandoning home so soon" and likens his efforts to so many other attempts to help the region — VISTA, the War on Poverty, church groups and missions. He admitted that he too had arrived "full of energy and plans, and swiftly became overwhelmed by the problems entrenching within the hills."[42]

Of his ineffectiveness as a teacher, Offutt notes, "I had long recognized that a colossal problem here was the pervasive sense of shame. Now I felt ashamed for having failed to ease that burden in others."[43] In the end it is his sense of shame that makes Offutt's treatment of Appalachia so unsettling. As much as he claims to love the region and as genuine as his homesickness seemed to be when it drew him home, he obviously found too much that he did not like about his mountain community to make the commitment to stay. We might admire his honesty; he certainly includes himself among those in the book's title. Yet we finish his book rather disheartened that he didn't find enough redeeming qualities about his home, his family, his students, or even the woods he so loved to stick with any of them.

★ ★ ★

John O'Brien treats his move to West Virginia as a return home of sorts, even though he was born and raised in Philadelphia. His parents were both natives of Piedmont, a paper-mill town in West Virginia's northeastern corner; for O'Brien, that was enough to stake his own claim to being Appalachian.[44] He had visited his grandparents in Piedmont in the summer and at Christmas, attended West Virginia University, and married a West Virginian. And in 1984, after several moves across the country and fifteen years raising a family in upper New York State, O'Brien and his wife decided to return south and settle in her hometown of Franklin. About a hundred miles south of Piedmont, Franklin was worlds away from his father's hometown in other respects: it was a far more idyllic small town devoid of any of the economic and social malaise brought on mills and mines that characterized his parents' hometown. It was, he wrote in *At Home in the Heart of Appalachia*, "a picture-perfect farm community" that had escaped the industrial wars of much of the rest of the state, due merely to its good fortune of being built on limestone rather than coal.[45]

This seemingly quiet, bucolic town turned out to be a hotbed of political division, if only because its charms had been discovered, in the 1970s and 1980s, by urban professionals from the Washington area, who arrived with "unfortunate opinions about hillbillies. . . . Needless to say, this struck a local nerve." The Woodlands Institute, a foundation that set up shop in Pendleton County and proceeded with its self-defined mission of "advancing" the community by restructuring everything from the public school system to real estate distribution and environmental standards, led to a showdown between insiders and outsiders that rang an all too familiar chord. "Whether the county's mounting anxiety was warranted or simply more Appalachian counterreality," he writes, "its fears seem less bizarre in light of the region's history. The pattern of outside agents working hand in glove with politicians that began more than a century ago remains a fact of life in West Virginia."[46]

This sets O'Brien off on those age-old tensions that had plagued Appalachia for more than a century and turns much of his book into a treatise on that history and how harmful it has proven to be as industrialists, missionaries, and government intervention exploited resident highlanders and the natural world in which they lived. Those outside agents rationalized much of what they did by denigrating the people on whose land and lives they encroached. Much of the Franklin residents' resentment lay in that latter fact; as one of them stated: "These people are making a lot of money by going outside to describe us as a bunch of damned hillbillies who can't put their socks on in the morning without them." Other locals refused to accept that explanation, wondering "how anyone could walk around in a pristine mountain environment, talk with local people, and then conclude that Pendleton County was a part of woebegone Appalachia?"[47]

If O'Brien uses this community struggle as a parable of the persistence of Appalachian stereotyping in the face of a very different reality, his parallel story of how his own family was haunted by those stigmas resonates even more with the themes explored here. It is apparent from the beginning that he sees his father's and grandfather's struggles as even more emblematic of the identity issues with which southern highlanders struggle and how basic their stories are to his own sense of self and how it has been shaped by the region. Completely alienated from his father for most of his adult life, O'Brien — like many autobiographers — sees his book as both therapeutic and redemptive, a means of coming to terms with whatever it was that so troubled his father and pushed his son out of his life. "The biggest part of that mystery," he writes in his preface, "is Appalachia itself; where does that strange, sad place begin and end? What has being Appalachian meant to my father, to my grandfather, and to me?"[48]

No one ties the personal foibles of family members as directly to their Appalachian identities as does O'Brien. His father could never escape, even in moving to Philadelphia, where he still could not shake the curse of the hillbilly label imposed by outsiders but internalized as well. He bemoans the fact that Appalachian migrants still have to confront the "gene-deficient monstrosities in James Dickey's *Deliverance* or the cartoonish dimwits from *Beverly Hillbillies*." He argues that "there is more to escape and more to deny in these hilly towns. The fact that hillbilly stereotypes make as little sense as black or Native American stereotypes is of no consequence to the people who struggle to escape them." Such was certainly true for both branches of his family tree, neither of which ever "understood the social pressures that affected them, which only made the imaginary distance wider."[49]

Just as his father never shook off the hillbilly label by leaving West Virginia, neither could he escape the poverty he endured as a mill worker there. In southwest Philly he headed "the poorest family in a very poor neighborhood." He struggled to get ahead, but ten children supported on a mere assembly line salary — and the inevitable futility of such efforts — ultimately made him, for his son, "the most thoroughly defeated man I have ever known." His father's despair, O'Brien came to realize, "had a great deal to do with what has been called Appalachian fatalism — a profound sense that you are fundamentally inferior and that life is absurd and hopeless."[50]

As with so many of the testimonials examined here, the O'Brien family's ties to their mountain past were not without silver linings. Despite the bleakness of the life that they had lived there, O'Brien's associations with the region were never totally dark. He recalled fishing with his father during their summer visits to Piedmont, and even more he recalled and reveled in his father's stories of his boyhood hunting and fishing there:

> I thought he was talking about paradise and a time before despair was the center of his personality. A landscape of deep forest filled with white-tailed deer, wild turkeys, whirling grouse, speckled trout, and ice-cold streams grew in my mind.

My dad was happy there, somehow whole, and so was I. That vision of Appalachia became my dream life.[51]

And yet, those memories, or mere visions, could never overcome the later reality of his father's fatalism. Compounding his father's ill-fated relationship to his Appalachian roots is his grandfather's story; only as an adult did John learn of it and come to realize what else it was about Piedmont that so haunted his father. One day he casually asked his father about his grandfather, which led his father, "looking frightened, to turn around and run into the cellar." Only then did his mother tell him the family secret that he had been sheltered from for so long. His grandfather, it seemed, was an angry, discontent drunk who "lived his life in fits and rages, terrorizing his family." After an altercation with his supervisor at the paper mill, he returned home, downed a bottle of whiskey, then "in a burst of manic energy, he drank poison, cut his throat, and shot himself, all within a minute." O'Brien wrote that he still remembers how the hair on the back of his neck stood up and how he had a strange sense that somehow he had always known this story.[52] It took this discovery, along with his father's unhappy fate, to seal O'Brien's firm belief in the existence of that Appalachian fatalism to which he attaches such importance throughout his memoir.

At one point, O'Brien states, "In time I would learn that Appalachia was an imaginary place and that being Appalachian was imaginary but terribly damaging." This may have been a more credible observation coming from a number of other authors here; for O'Brien, both his family's experience and those of the communities — Piedmont and Franklin — that he examines with such penetrating historical and sociological insight have been haunted and handicapped by imagination or perception or stereotype, whether imposed by outsiders or internalized. Yet there are plenty of stark realities from which those myths and misconceptions have stemmed, and they have been at least as damaging as the identities and judgments both his family and their communities have had to endure both as individuals and as a group. Along with Jeanette Walls's *The Glass Castle*, O'Brien's memoir packs the most emotional wallop in its account of both place and family, though the temperaments of their respective parents differ so vastly that one might conclude that the only common denominator in these two compelling stories lies in the places where they occurred.

★ ★ ★

Playwright Thornton Wilder, another midwesterner, once noted that southerners were "cut off, or resolutely cut themselves off, from the advancing tide of the country's modes of consciousness. Place, environment, relations, repetitions are the breath of their being."[53] If such was indeed the case for many southerners when he wrote this in the early twentieth century, it was, in many respects, even truer of southern Appalachians then and, as these works suggest, now. Yet they also demonstrate there is much variance in how and why their authors were cut off from "the country's mode of consciousness." Jim Minick, Bob Fox, and Thomas Crowe deliberately cut themselves off — and they took great satisfaction in the merits of living relatively simple lives far removed from "the advancing tide of the country's mode of consciousness," at least for a while. John O'Brien sought much the same thing, though more complex demons lured him back to a mountain life. On the other hand, Jeannette Walls, Aneita Jean Blair, and Jeff Mann, who found themselves in small, woebegone West Virginia towns, and Linda DeRosier, even more remotely situated up a Kentucky creek, were all fully aware of the world beyond their very circumscribed existences. The internal push factors were as pronounced and as tangible as the external pull factors were vague, intangible, yet nonetheless alluring. (Small-town West Virginia takes particularly hard knocks from Appalachian memoirists — all of the authors born or raised there are eager to leave, and only one of those who return to Appalachia, John O'Brien, settles in the Mountain State, despite the fact that he has as much reason as any of them to be repelled by it.)

Yet, for some, like Crowe, Fox, O'Brien, and Offutt, who had experienced the world beyond Appalachia, the return home represented a refuge, a restorative sense of recapturing a way of life, and a value system lacking elsewhere. If O'Brien and Offutt are ultimately disappointed in the region's failure to fulfill their aspirations, those disappointments have much to say about how realistic their expectations were and whether geography alone is ever enough on its own to nurture the spirit or resolve internal discontent. Thus we encounter the contradictions and diversity of the testimonials presented here — and the socioeconomic, emotional, and psychological variables that shaped those relationships to land, community, and region.

Appalachia as both place and experience is ever apparent in juxtaposing these works, as is the presence of other contingencies. One wonders how different Jeannette Walls's or James O'Brien's (John's father) lives might have been if they had been raised on farms in Polk County, North Carolina (like Crowe), or Floyd County, Virginia (like Minick), or Meigs County, Ohio (like Fox), rather than in the oppressive West Virginia environments of Welch and Piedmont, respectively. Had Aneita Jean Blair found herself in a college town like Blacksburg or Morgantown (or for that matter, in one of my favorites, Boone or Berea or Cullowhee), instead of the declining industrial towns in which she was stuck, how much less frustrating would her adolescence have been and how much weaker the impulse to escape? By the same token, would Chris Offutt have been more self-fulfilled and less contemptuous of the region had he chosen one of those other colleges or college towns to "help young people understand themselves . . . to give as much as possible"?

Would Jim Minick or Thomas Crowe have embraced so enthusiastically the farm lives they have lived or exhibited such strong affinities for the natural world had they not grown up in similar environments elsewhere? On the other hand, would Bob Fox have appreciated the bucolic life he and his wife shaped for themselves had it not contrasted so dramatically with the tensions and traumas of the urban life they had known, even if they ultimately retreated back to the latter? How different would Linda DeRosier's sense of her Appalachian identity be, and how much sustenance would that culture have provided her, if she had grown up in Paintsville, a mere eight miles away, or Pikeville, a mere fifty, instead of coming of age in the remote, self-contained world of Two-Mile Creek?

Journalist Joel Garreau once wrote that "the South is more of an emotion than a region." Pat Conroy phrased it even more pointedly through his South Carolina protagonist in *The Prince of Tides*, who saw the South as much of the source of his various hang-ups. "My wound is geography," Tom Wingo muses. "It is also my anchorage, my port of call."[54] Again, these are truths perhaps even more applicable to Appalachia, as nearly all of these works testify. For Appalachians in particular, such feelings — whether love or hate, wounds or anchors — are integrally tied to place, often driven by a sense of tension between existence within the region and the possibilities of life beyond it.[55] While felt and expressed by these authors in a wide range of ways, it is inherent in all of their works, both those seeking to escape from the region and those finding refuge within it.

That paradox is perhaps best conveyed in one of my favorite memoirs of mountain life, *Dorie: A Woman of the Mountains*, in which a daughter extracts from her mother, over the course of nine years of interviews and story-telling, a remarkable re-creation of a life spent in the logging camps of the Great Smoky Mountains in the early twentieth century. After an unsatisfying — even stultifying—stint in a textile mill village in Spartanburg, South Carolina, Dorie's parents returned the family to the much harder life they had known high in the Smokies. "Times will be hard," Pa warned the family as young Dorie gloried in the beauty of the mountains up ahead. "Well, if we starve to death, we'll be in a place worth dying for," her mother replied.[56]

Not one of our authors combines quite so succinctly that love of a place and what one must endure to eke out a life there, and Dorie's story, as moving as it is, is far more oriented to the physical and materialistic aspects of the life she both endured and thrived upon than are the more introspective treatments of what it means to be a southern highlander dealt with here. Nevertheless, each of these very personal testimonials reflects some variant of that paradox. They convey what it means to link one's identity and fortune to a particular piece of this varied landscape and culture we know as Appalachia, and while both place and culture provide the "inner script" by which they live their lives and write about them, each does so on his or her own terms. John O'Brien wisely notes that "no one fits his or her culture exactly." In musing about his father's Appalachian identity, he says that his life "was a complicated web of inherited traits, personal experiences, fears, frustrations, memories and thoughts. . . . To suggest that his life, or mine, can be explained by a single fact of biography [their Appalachian heritage] is to reduce both of us to stick figures in a child's drawings."[57]

Yet O'Brien and the authors here chose to make that place and their relationship to it the central thrust of their autobiographical reflections and the primary impetus for telling their stories (as most of their titles alone suggest). He could have added family ties, ambition, self-esteem, and social status to the list of other factors that shaped one's life or perception of it, but however he and these other authors chose to complicate their self portraits, the land and the culture built upon it are never far from the core of who they think they are and choose to describe for us in print. Thus we can appreciate the individuality and intimacy that render autobiography such a powerful and appealing form of expression while it also reveals far greater truths about the region that, in one way or another, defined them all.

"Getting Pretty Fed Up with this Two-Tone South"

Moving toward Multiculturalism

IN HIS ESSAY COLLECTION *Beyond the Binary*, my friend and former colleague Timothy Powell called for a new paradigm for American cultural studies. It is time, he wrote in 1999, to move beyond the long-established theoretical binaries of Self/Other, Center/Margin, and Colonizer/Colonized that "helped scholars to delineate the inner workings of oppression and to establish a new critical paradigm that would allow minority voices not only to be heard but to be esteemed as a critically important point of view."[1]

At a more elemental level, one could argue that for historians of the South, the central binary of White/Black—along with others such as Haves/Have Nots, Urban/Rural, and even North/South—has been just as integral in how we see and explain the structure and tensions inherent in southern society over the past century or more. Certainly the essays here lend themselves to those dualities—along with whatever variations, complexities, and subtleties I may have entwined within them.[2]

Yet, even as Powell and his compatriots have been among those advancing a more multicultural American past, both historically and literarily, as an academic field, multiculturalists have been slow to embrace the South as an entity worthy of special attention or to acknowledge those southerners whose ethnicity or national origins do not adhere to the basic Black/White binary that has so dominated analysis of the region. In Powell's *Beyond the Binary*, for example, not one of its eleven essays is set fully in the South, and only one even incorporates a southern component—post-removal Cherokees in East Tennessee.[3] That void seems equally apparent in the vast and growing scholarship on autobiography. In the fullest treatment of the topic, an essay collection titled *Multicultural Autobiography: American Lives*, editor James Robert Payne acknowledges the South as the first to embody the "notion that distinctive cultures of American regions or sections may produce distinctive autobiography"; yet only one of eleven chapters deals with the work of a southerner — Payne's own examination of an unpublished memoir by New Orleans writer George Washington Cable.[4]

Given the dearth of scholarly attention to southern multiculturalism as reflected in autobiography and memoir, I conclude this volume with a brief sampling of work, most of it recent, that helps move us beyond the traditional southern binary or binaries in a variety of ways. The fact that we don't have more works by Native Americans, Asians, or Latinos living in the South makes the few we do have all the more valuable and worthy of serious attention by both scholars and teachers.

Despite their lengthy and integral role in southern history, it is particularly striking that we have so little autobiographical work by southern Indians (not including those from Oklahoma). Several life narratives by Cherokees, some quite unconventional in form, offer particularly rich testimonials to the unique struggles many face in terms of identity and status in a post–civil rights South.

Marilou Awiakta, a Cherokee poet who grew up in Oak Ridge, Tennessee, has written extensively, if somewhat obliquely, about her life as an Indian, an Appalachian, and as a part of a closely guarded scientific community in two multigenre works, *Abiding Appalachia: Where Mountain and Atom Meet* (1978) and *Selu: Seeking the Corn-Mother's Wisdom* (1993). In both, she incorporates poems, stories and legends, and nonfictional essays to explore issues of Cherokee history, spirituality, and identity, including her own Cherokee-Celtic heritage. She quips that she had "grown up in the 1940s on a government reservation — for atoms, not Indians" and explores the tensions and contradictions between those two worlds, or three, as she notes in *Selu*.[5]

Returning home from an extended stay in France in the mid-1960s, where her husband was assigned, Awiakta wrote that she had struggled there with finding herself and her place among people of different cultures, but that "by the time I returned to America, I knew I was a Cherokee/Appalachian poet. I was determined to sing my song." The turbulence of identity politics in the mid-1960s proved a challenge, and that "outer turmoil" forced her to seek harmony "from my three heritages: Cherokee, Appalachian, and scientific." The atom, she insisted, was a part of her, and the new technology brought with it its own culture — "its own worldview, value system, and language."[6] Awiakta's simultaneous embrace of tradition and cutting-edge modernity may seem more extreme than most people's, but it is a pattern that plays out to varying degrees in the work of most Native American writers — perhaps more for those based in the South and Appalachia than elsewhere. One yearns for an even deeper exploration of those themes in a full autobiography from her someday.

More recently, another poet, Allison Adelle Hedge Coke, with both Cherokee and Huron blood, wrote a more conventional narrative of an anything but conventional life. She was born in 1958 in Amarillo, Texas, where her father regaled her and her sister with stories of their dual Indian heritages and of the rich spiritual culture that continued to make both meaningful. The first sentence of Coke's narrative declares: "I descend from mobile and village peoples, interracial, ingenious, adventurous, and bold. . . . In this great ancestral river thoroughly bloodstreamed true, I am born from those . . . devoted to their beliefs and ways of living." She concludes that opening paragraph with a simple statement: "I understood all this by the age of three."[7]

In 1971 the family moved to North Carolina, the source of much of that heritage, which for Coke was a journey in reverse "across the terrible Trail Where They Cried." Even though her family didn't settle in the beautiful mountains of its Cherokee ancestors, but rather in the Research Triangle in the center of the state, Coke felt that this would be close enough to those ancestors to serve as a fresh start. Hers was a troubled life, and much of her story is of a schizophrenic mother, a troubled and sometimes violent marriage, and drug and alcohol abuse, yet her Native identity remained a constant — sometimes a steadying force, sometimes a source of prejudice and discrimination, for as she is quick to note: "North Carolina in the early 1970s was not an easy place to be an Indian or a mixed blood." She goes on to demonstrate the many ways in which that was indeed the case.

Among the most engaging narratives by a Native American is Jerry Ellis's *Walking the Trail*. Ellis, a self-proclaimed failed Hollywood screenwriter, is the son of a Cherokee father, and he grew up in Fort Payne, Alabama, the site of one of thirteen detention camps into which the military forced his ancestors in 1838 before leading them off on the catastrophic Trail of Tears. Tracing that route in reverse, Ellis called his trek a "spiritual journey." "I long to know more about the man I am, where I came from, and where I am going," he insisted. His was as much a collective mission as it was an individual one. He borrowed camping equipment for the trip from a friend whose grandmother was actually born on what he calls the "death march," and whose Cherokee mother hid the newborn with a white family to keep her from having to battle the elements that proved so deadly to so many other children and adults. En route over the two-month trek, he sought out and learned much about fellow Indians, who provide a vast array of opinions, perspectives, and life stories that complicate the meanings of Native and southern identity. In the end, Ellis concludes that "I walked nine hundred miles and entered into an odyssey that will feed me the rest of my life."[8]

Novelist Lisa Alther provides one of the most eye-opening recent accounts of Native American ancestry and, in the process, one of the most astute commentaries on multicultural identity and the challenges it poses. Born and raised on a tobacco farm in East Tennessee, Alther grew up thinking that the most multicultural aspect of her gene pool was that her father was from Virginia and her mother from New York. That combination alone, she says, in her tart, tongue-in-cheek memoir, *Kinfolks* (a take-off on her first and best-known novel, *Kinflicks* [1976]), inflicted her with a "chronic identity crisis." She writes: "I rationalized my penchant for protective coloration by reviewing what I knew about my hapless ancestors, who were usually in the wrong place at the wrong time. They were Huguenots in France after Catholics declared open season on heretics; English in Ireland when the republicans began torching Anglo-Irish houses; Dutch in the Netherlands during the Spanish invasions; . . . Native Americans in the path of Manifest Destiny; Union supporters in Confederate Virginia." She concluded that she had "inherited genes that condemned me to a lifetime of being a stranger in some very strange lands."[9]

Only when her cousin, Brent Kennedy, the leading scholar of the Melungeons, informed her that some of their shared ancestors were in fact Melungeon did she seriously begin to pursue her ethnic lineage. Her memoir consists of her quest to determine if in fact she had Melungeon ancestors, and just what that controversial, and somewhat suspect, label actually means. As she aptly explains early on, there are two hostile camps on the matter of Melungeon identity: "The Romantics ascribe Melungeon origins to Portuguese sailors shipwrecked on the Carolina coast, to survivors of Sir Walter Raleigh's Lost Colony, to deserters from sixteenth century Spanish expeditions, to other exotic sources too far-fetched even for someone as gullible as me." On the other hand are "the Academics," who claim that "the Melungeons are mere one of some two hundred groups of 'tri-racial isolates' . . . found throughout the eastern United States." Most were concentrated in the nearby community of Newman's Ridge,

Tennessee, and Alther had grown up hearing the local lore that they lived in caves, kidnapped mean children, and were born with six fingers per hand. "Regarded as wannabes by Indians, whites, and blacks alike," Alther concludes, "they were raceless in a racist society."[10]

After nearly a decade of searching for the truth behind this folk wisdom and these rival claims, much of which Alther relates, often irreverently, in chapters with such titles as "Chief Sit 'n' Bull," and "All-American Stir-Fry," she concludes with the results of a DNA test she took to establish her own makeup. While it included no proof of Melungeon "blood," it did explain, she says, "why a sense of belonging had always eluded me. . . . I learned that I'd been walking around for six decades in a body constructed by DNA originating in Central Asia, the eastern Mediterranean, the Indian subcontinent, the Middle East, and sub-Saharan Africa," all of which was "in addition to the contributions from England, Scotland, Ireland, France, Holland, and North America."

She claimed that after receiving these results, she wandered around in a daze, humming "We Are the World." But eventually the realization struck: she had at last found the "long-sought group" to which she belonged. "It consists of mongrels like myself who know that we belong nowhere — and everywhere." She'd made the journey from "bemused Appalachian misfit to equally bemused citizen of the world."[11]

Linda Tate also made a recent quest to seek out and validate her Native American ancestry, though with far different results — and far different lessons learned than Alther. In *Power in the Blood*, Tate states that from childhood on, she was convinced that her maternal grandmother Fannie came from Cherokee stock in Appalachian Tennessee, due to fleeting references she made to Fannie's mother having "been a little Indian" and her own love of the Smoky Mountains. Unable to verify those Cherokee roots, Tate traces her family only to the "Land Between the Rivers" in western Kentucky, where they eventually settled with other Indian and mixed-race refugees in the 1870s and remained for at least two generations, before they were forced out by the federal government when the TVA turned that stretch of land into the "Land Between the Lakes" and allocated it for recreational use.

It is a very different migration story than that with which we're far more familiar, and unlike most such family sagas her efforts to verify her Native American roots never fully succeed, in large part due to the enormous pressures on displaced Indians to hide their racial identities and assimilate into white society. She is left with strong, but still only circumstantial, evidence that the preponderance of families there who claimed Cherokee ancestry may well have been descended from those pushed west out of the mountains by their forced removal in 1838, or those who merely "slipped off the Trail [of Tears] along the way." Yet Tate ultimately realized that what she could tell — indeed was compelled to tell — was "a story of silences, gaps, denial, not knowing, a tale of severed connections to the past," and that these confusions, gaps, and uncertainties actually *were* the story, and thus that they work as well as a testimonial to the restorative powers of the quest itself as much as to any discoveries made along the way.[12]

There's some irony in the fact that the best known and certainly most popular Cherokee memoir can no longer be counted as a memoir at all. For a brief period, I enjoyed teaching Forrest Carter's *The Education of Little Tree* as part of my course on southern autobiography — as did many others both at the college level and in high-school and middle-school classes — not when it was first published in 1976, but in the late 1980s, after the University of New Mexico Press reissued it in paperback in 1985.[13] Carter's so-called memoir recounted a boyhood growing up with his Scottish-Cherokee grandfather and full-blood grandmother in the mountains of East Tennessee in the 1930s, and the lessons he learned from them of the natural world of Appalachia, of moonshine production, and of coping with the prejudices of the white highlanders among whom they lived.

After the 1985 reprinting, the book quickly became a cult favorite, in part because it was appropriate for young readers from middle school on; in 1991 it won the American Booksellers Association's award as the best book of the year. Later that year, historian Dan Carter, while working on a biography of George Wallace, exposed Forrest Carter — and his book — as a fraud. The author was actually Asa Earl Carter, an Alabama white supremacist, Ku Klux Klansman, novelist, and one-time speech writer for Wallace, with nothing in his past that bore any resemblance to the "self" he claimed for himself as "Little Tree." This news broke during a semester in which I had assigned the book, and I chose to wait until after we had read and discussed the book in class before disclosing the fact that it was pure fiction. My students felt betrayed both by the book and by me, though it led to a lively discussion about what had been lost in terms of the lessons conveyed by the book when it turned out to be a novel rather than a memoir. I haven't assigned it since. Yet this revelation hardly seemed to affect *Little Tree's* popularity. It has continued to sell remarkably well, with the UNM

Press making no alteration to it other than removing the words "A True Story" from its cover.[14]

Fortunately, an authentic — and much richer — memoir of growing up Cherokee in Southern Appalachia is on the horizon. Theda Perdue has shared with me the manuscript of a wonderful memoir that's forthcoming in the University of Nebraska Press's American Indian Lives series. In *Up from These Hills: Memories of a Cherokee Boyhood*, Michael Lambert records his father Leonard's oral narrative of his early years on a small farm in Birdtown, adjacent to the Eastern Band reservation in North Carolina's Smoky Mountains in the 1930s, and of their move in 1943 to a larger farm south of Knoxville, Tennessee, where his father sharecropped for several years until he moved back to North Carolina to join his brother as a maintenance worker at Mars Hill College.

Leonard Lambert offers not only a full chronicle of his mixed blood ancestry from the early antebellum period up until his birth in 1932, but also meticulous descriptions of daily life on the small mountain farm he shared with his parents and siblings, and of a remarkable grandmother who lived nearby. Though his father detested FDR, he took on work assignments for both the CCC and TVA dam construction that helped the family through the Depression years, and then he moved to Tennessee as much to avoid the draft during the Second World War as to improve his family's economic plight. Leonard ends his memoir with his college education, first at Mars Hill, then at North Carolina State; he was the first in his family to earn a college degree. Fully grounded within the contexts of his Appalachian and Cherokee heritage, Leonard uses his own and his father's lives to do what the best autobiographical work does so well — to capture an era of history and the impact of larger historical forces on particular people and places, regardless of how remote or removed their lives may seem from the larger world.[15]

★ ★ ★

There are a handful of firsthand accounts of Asian immigrants in the South. One of the most intriguing is that by John Jung, whose Chinese parents operated a laundry and raised a family in downtown Macon, Georgia, from 1928 to 1952, when the cultural isolation proved too much for them and they moved to San Francisco, so that their children could be part of a Chinese community. Kwoi Fui migrated from Canton in 1921 and settled with cousins in Augusta, Georgia, where he worked until 1928, by which time he had made enough money to return to China, find a bride, and bring her to Macon, where they established their own business (and where he renamed himself Ben Jung) and raised three children over the next two and a half decades. One of their children, John, provided a nostalgic memoir of his childhood in Macon, titled *Southern Fried Rice* (2005).

As the only Chinese family in Macon, they never fully assimilated into southern society. Jung's mother, in fact, never learned English, but she was a remarkable woman in her own right and in the lessons in tolerance and identity that she instilled in her children in the midst of this rigidly segregated society. The Jungs were considered "white" in terms of their access to schools, businesses, and other facilities; yet they were also decidedly "second-class citizens ... who were sometimes objects of curiosity and targets of ridicule." They only left Georgia to resettle in San Francisco in 1952, when Mrs. Jung grew concerned that their children were losing any sense of their Chinese heritage and culture as they became adolescents.[16]

Koji Ariyoshi, a Japanese-American raised in Hawaii, recounts a far briefer, even more curious sojourn in Georgia. Born to coffee workers on a Kona plantation in 1914, Ariyoshi eventually became a prominent labor activist and then journalist in Honolulu, earning national notoriety when arrested by the FBI in 1951 for his Communist associations both in the United States and in China. In his "political memoirs" published in 2000, he describes a crucial step in his "radicalization" that took place in 1940 and 1941. In a chapter called "Georgia: Tobacco Road Explored," he writes about a visiting year he spent at the University of Georgia. Having been awarded a YMCA scholarship to study at any college in the country, he chose Georgia because he had read Erskine Caldwell's novels and was deeply interested in the South and in "the Negro people."[17]

What follows is a unique perspective on racial segregation as Ariyoshi discovered it and recognized strong parallels with forms of discrimination against Asians that he and his parents had known in Hawaii. (His first evidence of southern segregation came when the black passengers on the Greyhound bus on which he traveled east were crowded into the rear seats once it crossed the line into Texas). He found there to be only a single Chinese family in Athens, Georgia, and observed that they seemed to be subject to many of the same restrictions as local African Americans. His attempts to befriend African Americans met with uneasiness on their part; this was especially true of a campus janitor who resisted his attempts at casual conversation and insisted on addressing him as "Mr. Koji" despite Ariyoshi's insistence that the "Mr." was not necessary or even desired on his part.

Ariyoshi found that UGA students greatly admired *Gone With the Wind* as a true depiction of their South. He heard Margaret Mitchell speak on campus and was surprised that he alone saw that "she actually portrayed the desperate struggle of a decadent class that went down fighting because it did not wish to give up its privileged position." On the other hand, his fellow students had nothing but contempt for Erskine Caldwell's work and insisted to Koji that "he writes trash" and that there was no such thing as "Tobacco Road" in Georgia. This — along with a basic interest in sharecropping stemming from his own up-bringing on a coffee plantation — made Ariyoshi more determined than ever to see for himself what truth there was in Caldwell's treatment of poor whites. In the spring of 1941, he hitchhiked to Augusta and actually tracked down Caldwell's parents in nearby Wrens, and he concludes his chapter with a rich description of how they convinced him that their son did indeed know whereof he wrote.

When the school year ended Ariyoshi returned to San Francisco, and he was there when the attack on Pearl Harbor took place on December 7. He would spend the next year in the Japanese internment camp at Manzabar, where he saw even more clearly that "the fight for Negro rights was a fight for my rights also," as "the anti-Negro and anti-Oriental congressmen from the South and the West Coast got together in 'racial alliance' to kick us around."[18]

One of the few accounts of an Indian experience in the American South comes from a doctor, Abraham Verghese, who spent four years (1985–89) at a Veterans Administration hospital in Johnson City, Tennessee, where he found himself having to embrace a practice far different from anything he had expected to be doing there — treating AIDs patients. In his acclaimed memoir, *My Own Country* (1994), Verghese — whose parents were Indians who had immigrated to Kenya, where he was born and raised — chronicles an often wrenching experience in dealing with the increasing number of AIDs cases that began to show up in this conservative and insulated corner of southern Appalachia in the late 1980s. The culture clash makes for a fascinating and surprisingly positive subtheme of his book, as he and his wife embraced both worlds: "The parochial world of Indians in America [he was one of several Indian medical practitioners in the area] and the secular world of East Tennessee." He insists that he felt at peace in Johnson City and eager to settle in — not only to make it home for his growing family, but also to see it as "my own country."[19]

Given the rapidly growing presence of Latinos throughout the South, it is curious how little autobiographical work has yet been produced by those who have lived and worked in the region. My friend and colleague Judith Ortiz Cofer seems to be among the few Latino/Latina writers who have even hinted at elements of their experience in the South through their writings. A Puerto Rican by birth, Cofer spent most of her childhood and early adolescence in Paterson, New Jersey, before she moved at age fifteen with her family to Augusta, Georgia, in 1968. She has remained a Georgian ever since, living on a farm in Jefferson County while serving as one of the most distinguished and popular faculty members in the University of Georgia's creative writing program.

Cofer writes with great insight and humor about her tripartite identities as Puerto Rican, New Jerseyan, and Georgian, most notably in the poems and essays in her book *The Latin Deli*. "I have journeyed across three cultures and three languages," she has said, meaning "Spanish, New Jerseyan English, and Southern English." Of her move to the South, she writes:

> For me it was a shock to the senses, like moving from one planet to another: where Paterson had concrete to walk on and gray skies, bitter winters and an ethnic population, Georgia was red like Mars, and Augusta was green — exploding in colors in more gardens and azaleas and dogwood and magnolia trees — more vegetation than I imagined was possible anywhere not tropical like Puerto Rico. People seemed to come in two colors — black and blonde.[20]

Few writers seem as attuned as Cofer to the physicality and appearances of ethnic identity, which she explores in essays titled "Advanced Biology" and "The Story of My Body." Cofer opens the latter with the statement: "I was born a white girl in Puerto Rico and became a brown girl when I came to live in the Unites States." This led to some prejudice and even rejection when she was a high-school student in Augusta, but in college her foreignness suddenly seemed to attract those males "who had survived the popular wars in high school; they had to act liberal in their politics, in their lifestyles, and in the women they went out with."[21]

Cofer states that she has written about her Puerto Rican and New Jerseyian childhood and adolescence with "the confidence of the historian or the archaeologist reconstructing Rome and recreating the lives of the Romans from artifacts and from whatever records survived time." But she is, at long last, ready to write about her life as a southerner, as she has only recently come to an awareness and perspective of "a new juncture in time and place" in which she can actually think of Georgia as home. She has begun a full-scale treatment of her life as a southerner, to be titled "Peach Pit Corazon." The first piece of it is a playful yet compelling take on the first Ortiz to come to Georgia: her imaginary ancestor, Juan Ortiz, in a "document" she calls "A Brief Account of the Adventures of My Appropriated Kinsman, Juan Ortiz, Indian Captive, Soldier, and Guide to General Hernando de Soto." In this document, she details her forefather's misadventures en route through Georgia — moving through sites where his proud descendant would later live, in Augusta and Jefferson County. "Through you, Juan Ortiz," she declares in an appended "proclamation" in which she asserts her kinship to him, "I claim our part in the creation myth of this land we now call home."[22]

The only other Latino memoir I know of that chronicles a southern experience is a classic of sorts by another Puerto Rican, poet and fiction writer Piri Thomas. In his often harrowing memoir of growing up in Spanish Harlem, *Down These Mean Streets* (1967), Thomas includes a section called "Down South," in which he recounts a trip he and a black friend made to Norfolk, Virginia, in the mid-1950s for no reason other than that Thomas wanted to "go down South to find out what's shaking." In fact, the trip seems an exploratory attempt by Thomas to come to terms with his confusions about racial categories and where he fit within a nation and society that extends well beyond the boundaries of Harlem.[23]

He does not have to wait long for some answers. In wandering through a black neighborhood in Norfolk, Thomas and his companion, Brew, encounter an educated Pennsylvania bartender — a light black man and a scholar who had come south to research a book on what it means to be black in the civil-rights South. In a chapter titled "Barroom Sociology," the three young men engage in a deep discussion of race: how bigotry differs in North and South; their own perceptions of themselves and their mixed-race genealogies; the blurred lines between Latinos and African Americans in many white eyes; and a host of other topics. Together their exchange forms one of the most freewheeling and ultimately profound treatises on race that I have ever seen encapsulated in a memoir.[24]

From Norfolk, Thomas and Brew took jobs as seamen on a freighter that took them to Mobile, New Orleans, and Galveston, all in an attempt to see other parts of the South. Curiously, while in the more racially and ethnically diverse New Orleans, Thomas complains that "I was getting pretty fed up with this two-tone South." Indeed, none of their encounters — even with Mexicans in Galveston — compares in meaning or drama with that great barroom exchange in Norfolk. He eventually returns to Harlem, where he declares simply, "I came back to New York with a big hate for anything white."[25]

Like Piri Thomas, we should reconsider our fixation on "this two-tone South," and the works surveyed in this chapter can help us do so. Through these life stories of southern natives, newcomers, and visitors who are neither black nor white, we can appreciate more fully not only how much and how fast the South is changing in its embrace of multiple cultures and ethnicities, but also the extent to which we have always been much more than simply a biracial society and culture. While historians, sociologists, anthropologists, and journalists have documented this reality, past and present, in both quantitative and qualitative ways, the voices of these "others" themselves can breathe life and humanity into those multihued variables and reveal the psychological, emotional, and often spiritual dimensions of identity that social scientists alone can never fully capture.

To quote Tim Powell once again, he insisted a decade ago that "the time has come to initiate a new critical epoch, a period of cultural reconstruction in which 'identity' is reconfigured in the midst of a multiplicity of cultural influences . . . that more accurately reflects the multicultural complexities that have historically characterized 'American' identity."[26] If it has taken a bit longer to bring into focus the South's multicultural complexities, we are now at a point at which any characterization of the region as merely "two-toned" can be rightly called outmoded. The sparcity of autobiography and memoir by Others suggests that the genre still lags behind other forms of documentation of this reality, both historical and current.

The works surveyed here, as powerful and moving as many of them are, surely form only a first wave of self-narratives by those who see both their genetic and cultural identities as something other than white or black; yet these works bode well for what surely will become in the near future a panoply of testimonials by Native Americans, Asians, Latinos, and others recounting their lives as southerners, or hyphenate-southerners. The many ways in which they see and experience the region will undoubtedly become ever more multifaceted and multicultural over the course of the twenty-first century.

But it is not only those of other ethnicities whose life stories will allow us to see the South differently in the years ahead. What it means to be black, to be white, indeed to be southern, is itself changing in subtle and not so subtle ways. (I can detect this change in my students' expressions of their sense of self and South in recent years.) While journalists and travel writers, sociologists and eventually historians will confront and chronicle the evolving twenty-first-century South in their own particular ways, I for one am eager to see what the next generation of autobiographers, increasingly eclectic but no less southern, is going to make of it all.

NOTES

PREFACE

1. L. S. Inscoe Jr., *Pop Went to War: World War II Memories of L. S. Inscoe, Jr.* (Richmond, Va.: privately published, 1996); and *When Life Stretched Out Before Me Fair: Memories of Growing Up in North Carolina, 1924–1941* (Richmond, Va.: privately published 1999). His four grandchildren all call him "Pop," hence the first book's title. The title of the second is the first line of a poem written by his grandfather Joseph Turner Inscoe.

2. Charles E. Hawkins Jr., "The War from the Wasatch: Recollections of the War in the Pacific: Interviews with Charles E. Hawkins [III]" (unpublished manuscript, Albany, Ga., 2002). Memories of his early years are a work in progress.

3. Susan Inscoe Seaton, *"I Am a Part of All That I Have Met": The Memoirs of Susan Inscoe Seaton* (Richmond, Va.: privately published, 2007).

4. Rubie Ray Cunningham, *Of Days That Are No More* (Charlotte, N.C.: privately published, 1951).

5. John C. Inscoe, "Memories of a Presbyterian Mission Worker in the Kentucky Mountains, 1918–1921: An Interview with Rubie R. Cunningham," *Appalachian Journal* 15 (Winter 1988): 244–58.

6. Joseph Linwood Inscoe, ed., *"These Humble Words I Write": The Poems and Writings of Joseph Turner Inscoe* (Richmond, Va.: privately published, 2008).

7. Ibid., 47–48.

INTRODUCTION

1. Flannery O'Connor, *Mysteries and Manners: Occasional Prose* (New York: Farrar, Straus & Giroux, 1969), 103.

2. Like most current critics and commentators, I tend to use the terms "autobiography" and "memoir" interchangeably. Some scholars distinguish between the two, seeing autobiography as a more formal and more inclusive summation of one's life and memoir as less formal in structure, more literary in style, and more selective in which aspects of one's life an author chooses to relate and reflect upon. For the fullest discussion of these distinctions, see Larson, *The Memoir and the Memoirist*, chapter 1.

3. Rubin, *A Gallery of Southerners*, xiii. For a more expansive treatment of this point, see Cobb, *Away Down South*.

4. In his anthology of autobiographical work, *Southern Selves*, James H. Watkins points out that "'place' can denote a fixed position in a racial or social hierarchy" as much as a geographical locale, and as such, many southern autobiographies are chronicles of the author's "efforts to reject the place he or she has been assigned," be it based on race, class, or gender, as much or more than mere physical space (xiv).

5. Angelou, *I Know Why the Caged Bird Sings*, 15.

6. Pat Conroy, *The Prince of Tides* (Boston: Houghton-Mifflin, 1986), 225.

7. Crews, *A Childhood*, 16–17.

8. Hobson, *Tell about the South*.

9. Lillian Smith, introduction to Green, *Ely: An Autobiography*, ix.

10. Edwin M. Yoder Jr., introduction to Willie Morris, *North toward Home*, xvii.

11. Bragg, *All Over but the Shoutin'*, xi, xxi–xxii.

12. See Yagoda, *Memoir: A History*, 76–82, 150–54, for a discussion of the "democratization" of American autobiography and memoir and of the proliferation of those "life stories being turned out by those hanging on to the lower rungs of the social ladder" (76).

13. Corder, *Yonder: Life on the Far Side of Change*, ix.

14. Bragg, *All Over but the Shoutin'*, xii.

15. Conway, *When Memory Speaks*, 6.

16. Welty, *One Writer's Beginnings*, 6.

17. Morris, *North toward Home*, 78.

18. Lillian Smith, *Killers of the Dream*, 25, 27, 30.

19. Cohn, *The Mississippi Delta and the World*, 180.

20. Wright, *Black Boy*, 267.

21. Franklin, *Mirror to America*, 3. Wright and Franklin were born a mere seven years apart, Wright in 1908, Franklin in 1915.

22. Hurston, *Dust Tracks on a Road*, 248–49; Angelou, foreword to Hurston, *Dust Tracks on a Road*, x.

23. Gates, *Colored People*, xiii, xv.

24. Wallach, *"Closer to the Truth than Any Fact"*, 154.

25. One of the most insightful treatments of many of these facets of autobiographical work is Bjorklund, *Interpreting the Self*.

26. Larry L. King, *Confessions of a White Racist*, vi–vii. For a thorough discussion of the relationship between truth, authenticity, and autobiography, see Yagoda, *Memoir*, 94–112, 168–77.

27. Judith Ortiz Cofer, *Silent Dancing: A Partial Remembrance of a Puerto Rican Childhood* (Houston: Arte Publico Press, 1991), 12–13.

28. Monson, *Vanishing Points*, 32.

29. Hobson, *Tell about the South* and *But Now I See*.

30. Berry, *Located Lives* and *Home Ground*.

31. Boles, *Autobiographical Reflections on Southern Religious History* and *Shapers of Southern History: Autobiographical Reflections*.

32. Jones, *Growing Up in the South*; Watkins, *Southern Selves*.

33. Ritterhouse, *Growing Up Jim Crow*; O'Dell, *Sites of Southern Memory*; and Wallach, *"Closer to the Truth"*.

34. That version of this essay appeared in Richard Godden and Martin Crawford, eds., *Reading Southern Poverty between the Wars, 1918–1939* (Athens: University of Georgia Press, 2006), 145–62.

35. I should note that I have by no means exhausted topics or themes worthy of further exploration and analysis in southern autobiographical work. Politics, religion (aversion seems a far more common thread than adherence to it), sharecropping and tenantry, gender and sexuality, and the relationship between teachers and pupils are all topics that I could have shaped full chapters around and that I may tackle in the future or encourage graduate students to do so.

36. Maxine Hong Kingston, *The Woman Warrior: Memoirs of a Girlhood Among Ghosts* (New York: Alfred A. Knopf, 1994), 8–9.

37. Lillian Smith to George Brockway, June 1949, in Margaret Rose Gladney, ed., *How Am I to Be Heard? Letters of Lillian Smith* (Chapel Hill: University of North Carolina Press, 1993), 126.

38. Lillian Smith, "Letter to My Publisher," in *Killers of the Dream*, 21–22. For a closer examination of Smith's humanism, see a forthcoming essay of mine, "Lillian Smith, Humanist," that will appear in Ann Short Chirhart and Kathleen Clark, eds., *Georgia Women: Their Lives and Times*, vol. 2 (Athens: University of Georgia Press, 2011).

CHAPTER ONE *Lessons from Southern Lives*

1. James W. Loewen, *Lies My Teachers Told Me: Everything Your American History Textbook Got Wrong* (New York: New Press, 1995), chapter 5. The chapter remains unchanged in his 2007 revision of the book.

2. Albert E. Stone, "American Biographies as Individual Stories and Cultural Narratives," introduction to Stone, *The American Autobiography*, 2; Robert E. Sayre, "The Proper Study: Autobiographies in American Studies," ibid., 11.

3. Scholarly work on the role of children and adolescence in history includes Kett, *Rites of Passage*; Palladino, *Teenagers*; and Graff, *Conflicting Paths*.

4. Jamil S. Zainaldin, "Building Vital Communities and Strong Citizens: The Character Education Connection," *The Georgia ASCD Reporter*, Special Theme Issue on Character Education, Winter 2000, 15.

5. Bjorklund, *Interpreting the Self*, 159–60.

6. Ibid. ix.

7. Coretta Scott King, *My Life with Martin Luther King, Jr.*, 31.

8. Lillian Smith, *Killers of the Dream*, 96.

9. Douglass, *Narrative of the Life of Frederick Douglass*, 29.

10. Wright, *Black Boy*, 272.

11. Percy, *Lanterns on the Levee*, 126–27.

12. Angelou, *I Know Why the Caged Bird Sings*, 188–91.

13. Ibid., 111–15.

14. Carter, *An Hour before Daylight*, 32–33.

15. Baker, *Growing Up*, 256–60. Other southern autobiographers whose vivid memories of a Joe Louis fight add even more variations to those presented here include the Delany Sisters, Harry Crews, William Alexander Percy, and Raymond Andrews.

16. Moody, *Coming of Age in Mississippi*, 125–26. Other autobiographers who wrote of being traumatized by Till's murder include Charlayne Hunter-Gault, Morris Dees, Willie Morris, John Lewis, and Florence Mars, who attended the trial of his murderers and described the experience in *Witness in Philadelphia*, 65–69. A number of works deal with the impact of the civil rights movement on young people in the South, black and white. See Palladino, *Teenagers*, chapter 11, "The Content of Their Character: Black Teenagers and Civil Rights in the South," 174–89; Levine, *Freedom's Choice*; and Robert Coles, *Children of Crisis*, vol. 2, *A Study in Courage and Fear* (Boston: Little, Brown, 1967).

17. Spencer, *Landscapes of the Heart*, 288–89, 291.

18. Nordan, *Boy with Loaded Gun*, 79; Nordan, *Wolf Whistle: A Novel* (Chapel Hill, N.C.: Algonquin Books, 1993).

19. Ibid., 80. Nordan devotes a full chapter to "The Boy in the River," which concludes his account by saying that just after the publication of *Wolf Whistle* in 1993 he sought out this classmate, who claimed that he had no memory of having spoken up in the locker room that day.

20. Dees, *A Season for Justice*, 87–88. Anne Moody also describes a strong emotional reaction to the Birmingham church bombing in *Coming of Age in Mississippi*, 316–19.

21. Beals, *Warriors Don't Cry*, 91.

22. Curry, *Silver Rights*, 42–43.

23. Marsh, *The Last Days*, 259–60.

24. Ibid., 271.

25. See, for example, Percy, *Lanterns on the Levee*, chapter 18, in which he recounts his father's being targeted as a Catholic by Klansmen in the early 1920s, leading to a fight he called "a bloodless, cruel warfare, more bitter and unforgiving than anything I encountered at the front [France in World War I]" (229); Moody, *Coming of Age in Mississippi*, 338–39, in which she found herself broken by the movement soon after her

discovery that that she was on a Klan "hit list," a moment she described as "one of the most horrible scares of my life"; Mars, *Witness in Philadelphia*, in which she focuses on the Klan murders of the three civil rights workers who vanished in Nashoba County, Mississippi, in the summer of 1964, and whose business was later boycotted because of her stated sentiments on behalf of local blacks. Charles Marsh and Timothy Tyson recount the moral struggles with which their fathers, both ministers, wrestled along with their congregations and communities in Laurel, Mississippi, and Oxford, North Carolina, respectively in response to local Klan atrocities, and offer contrasting examples of how Christian leadership met the challenge posed by the Movement and the Klan, in Marsh, *The Last Days*, and Tyson, *Blood Done Sign My Name*.

26. Walter White and Stetson Kennedy both infiltrated the Klan and provided harrowing, often sensationalistic, accounts of narrow escapes from detection and other risks they took in their efforts to expose Klan members and activities from the inside. See White, *A Man Called White*; and Kennedy, *The Klan Unmasked*; in *Proud Shoes*, 218–25, Pauli Murray recounts her grandfather's successful standoff with the Klan in Reconstruction North Carolina in defense of the freedman's school he had established in Orange County; Morris Dees recounts the legal strategies by which he crippled several Klan organizations by bankrupting them through civil suits in the 1980s in *A Season for Justice*; and Will D. Campbell, in *Brother to a Dragonfly*, describes a remarkable one-on-one debate he had with a North Carolina Klansman in which the latter actually made the better intellectual argument (239–50).

27. Lumpkin, *The Making of a Southerner*, 90, 92. Lumpkin devoted much of a chapter to the Klan and its activities in Oglethorpe, Greene, and other middle Georgia counties (77–99).

28. Ibid., 136. Although Lumpkin doesn't acknowledge it, the timing of these children's versions of the KKK suggests that they may have been inspired by the southern tour of a stage production of Thomas Dixon's *The Clansman*, which made its way into Georgia early in 1906, when she would have been eight or nine years old.

29. Zellner, *The Wrong Side of Murder Creek*, 17, 20–21.

30. Ibid., 21–22.

31. Ibid., 22–23.

32. McWhorter, *Carry Me Home*, 15, 27, 83.

33. Ibid., 518.

34. Ibid., 580–85.

35. Cobbs, *Long Time Coming*, 52–53.

36. Ibid., 43, 66–67.

37. Ibid., 26.

38. Gates, *Colored People*, 19, 22.

39. Moody, *Coming of Age in Mississippi*, 307.

40. Durr, *Outside the Magic Circle*, 44.

41. Morris, *North toward Home*, 77–78.

42. Lillian Smith, *The Journey*, 146–47.

43. Ibid., 147–49.

44. Bragg, *All Over but the Shoutin'*, 64–66.

45. Styron, *A Tidewater Morning*, 73. Though the book is fictionalized, Styron insisted that the character of Shadrach and his long walk back to Virginia to be buried on home ground was based on an actual incident recounted to him by a childhood friend. James L. W. West III, *William Styron: A Life* (New York: Random House, 1998), 420.

46. McLaurin, *Separate Pasts*, 26.

47. Ibid., 146, 151.

48. Ibid., 151–54.

49. Murray, foreword to *Proud Shoes*, vii.

50. Delany and Delany, *Having Our Say*, 97.

51. Hurston, *Dust Tracks on the Road*, 134–35.

52. Braden, *The Wall Between*, 30–31.

53. Ibid., 31.

54. Conroy, *The Water Is Wide*, 7, 9.

55. Ibid., 9–10.

56. Ibid., 11.

57. Quoted in Elizabeth Schultz, "To Be Black and Blue: The Blues Genre in Black American Autobiography," in Stone, *The American Autobiography*, 120.

58. Murray, *South to a Very Old Place*, 18.

59. Morris, *North toward Home*, 8.

60. Zainaldin, "Building Vital Communities and Strong Citizens," 15.

61. Lillian Smith, 1966 introduction to Green, *Ely: An Autobiography*, xxxiv.

CHAPTER TWO *"I Learn What I Am"*

1. Walter White, *A Man Called White*, 3.

2. Ibid., 10–11.

3. Ibid., 12, 11.

4. Ibid., 12.

5. In his biography of White, Kenneth Janken casts serious doubts as to the veracity of this story, both in terms of the armed defense of the White home and its impact on Walter's racial identity. See Kenneth Robert Janken, *White: The Biography of Walter White, Mr. NAACP* (New York: The New Press, 2003), 15–18.

6. For a concise history and use of the terms miscegenation and amalgamation, see David A. Hollinger, "Amalgamation and Hypodescent: The Question of Ethnoracial

Mixture in the History of the United States," *American Historical Review* 108 (December 2003): 1363–90. I realize that the term "mixed race" is problematic in this context, as is the use of "black" and "white." But I have chosen to use them, both for sheer clarity and because they are the terms used by many of these authors themselves.

7. Lillian Smith, *Killers of the Dream*, 96.

8. Joel Williamson, *New People: Miscegenation and Mulattoes in the United States* (New York: The Free Press, 1980), xi. Williamson takes his title from the self-description of a mulatto character who passes for white in Charles W. Chesnutt's 1899 novel, *The House on Cedar Street*.

9. The first comprehensive overview of mixed-race identity in America was Williamson's *New People*. More recent books exploring the topic of mixed-race identity in America include Gary B. Nash, *Forbidden Love: The Secret History of Mixed-Race America* (New York: Henry Holt and Co., 1999); Scott L. Malcomson, *One Drop of Blood: The American Misadventure of Race* (New York: Farrar, Straus, Giroux, 2000); Gayle Wald, *Crossing the Line: Racial Passing in Twentieth-Century Literature and Culture* (Durham, N.C.: Duke University Press, 2000); David Parker and Miri Song, eds., *Rethinking "Mixed Race"* (Sterling, Va.: Pluto Press, 2001); Elise Lemire, *"Miscegenation": Making Race in America* (Philadelphia: University of Pennsylvania Press, 2002); Steve Talty, *Mulatto America: At the Crossroads of Black and White Culture, A Social History* (New York: HarperCollins, 2003); Ariela J. Gross, *What Blood Won't Tell: A History of Race on Trial in America* (Cambridge, Mass.: Harvard University Press, 2008); and Peggy Pascoe, *What Comes Naturally: Miscegenation Law and the Making of Race in America* (New York: Oxford University Press, 2009). See also an AHA Forum on "Amalgamation and the Historical Distinctiveness of the United States," with an essay by David A. Hollinger, and responses by Thomas E. Skidmore, Barbara J. Fields, and Henry Yu, *American Historical Review* 108 (December 2003): 1362–1414; Catherine Clinton, "Breaking the Silence: Sexual Hypocrisies from Thomas Jefferson to Strom Thurmond," in Bernadette Brooten, ed., *Beyond Slavery: Overcoming Its Religious and Sexual Legacies* (New York: Palgrave MacMillan, 2010); and several essays in Martha Hodes, ed., *Sex, Love, Race: Crossing Boundaries in North American History* (New York: NYU Press, 1999). Curiously, of all the individuals whose writings are the subject of this essay, none are mentioned in these works except for brief and scattered references to Walter White in Williamson's, Nash's, Wald's, and Talty's books, and Essie Mae Washington-Williams, on whom Catherine Clinton focuses in her essay.

10. Douglass, *Narrative of the Life of Frederick Douglass*, 41. See William S. McFeely, *Frederick Douglass* (New York: W. W. Norton, 1991), for the most detailed treatment of his mixed-race identity and quest to identify his father.

11. Ibid.; Jacobs, *Incidents in the Life of a Slave Girl*; and Craft and Craft, *Running a Thousand Miles for Freedom*, quote on p. 4, with discussion of other cases on pp. 4–11.

Other valuable treatments of the long-term implications of slave-master miscegenation include Edward Ball, *Slaves in the Family* (New York: Farrar, Straus, Giroux, 1998); Joshua D. Rothman, *Notorious in the Neighborhood: Sex and Families Across the Color Line in Virginia,1787–1861* (Chapel Hill: University of North Carolina Press, 2003); and Clarence E. Walker, *Mongrel Nation: The America Begotten by Thomas Jefferson and Sally Hemings* (Charlottesville: University of Virginia Press, 2008).

12. For analyses of literary treatments of miscegenation, see Werner Sollors, *Neither Black nor White yet Both: Thematic Explorations of Interracial Literature* (New York: Oxford University Press, 1997); and Toni Morrison, *Playing in the Dark: Whiteness and the Literary Imagination* (Cambridge, Mass.: Harvard University Press, 1992). Even Walter White's experience was fictionalized by Sinclair Lewis in his novel, *Kingsblood Royal*, published in 1947. See Matthew J. Jacobson, *Whiteness of a Different Color: European Immigrants and the Alchemy of Race* (Cambridge, Mass.: Harvard University Press, 1998), 265–71, for a discussion of Lewis's novel and how it was received.

13. Williamson, *New People*.

14. Lillian Smith, *Killers of the Dream*, 34–38.

15. See Hobson, *But Now I See*, chapter 1, for the most detailed analysis of Smith's "conversion."

16. Wright, *Black Boy*, 30–31.

17. Ibid., 55–58.

18. Ibid., 58.

19. Green, *Ely: Too Black, Too White*, 19. This is a much expanded version of *Ely: An Autobiography*, an earlier book that focused only on Green's childhood and adolescence. All subsequent quoted material, including Lillian Smith's introduction, comes from this earlier 1966 version of Ely's

story.

20. Ibid., 9; Smith's introduction, xx.

21. Ibid., 8–9.

22. Ibid., 13.

23. Ibid., 22.

24. Ibid., 73–74.

25. John Reilly, afterword to the 1966 Perennial Classic expanded edition of *Black Boy* (New York: Harper Perennial, 1996), 286.

26. Delany and Delany, *Having Our Say*, 44, 48.

27. Ibid., 10.

28. Ibid., 94.

29. Ibid.

30. Andrews, *The Last Radio Baby*, 8–9.

31. Ibid., 62. For a very different set of familial circumstances in which relative skin tones determined attitudes, see Moody, *Coming of Age in Mississippi*, 57–60.

32. Andrews, *The Last Radio Baby*, 64.

33. Hunter-Gault, *In My Place*, 19.

34. Ibid., 24. For a fuller study of white fathers bequeathing property to illegitimate black sons and establishing them in local businesses in a neighboring Georgia county, see Mark R. Schultz, "Interracial Kinship Ties and the Emergence of a Rural Black Middle Class: Hancock County, 1865–1920," in John C. Inscoe, ed., *Georgia in Black and White: Explorataions in the Race Relations of a Southern State, 1865–1950* (Athens: University of Georgia Press, 1994), 141–73.

35. Hunter-Gault, *In My Place*, 29.

36. Ibid., 135–36. For a full analysis of the racial implications of the film *Pinky*, see Susan Courtney, *Hollywood Fantasies of Miscegenation: Spectacular Narratives of Gender and Race, 1903–1967* (Princeton, N.J.: Princeton University Press, 2005), 174–90.

37. Roger Wilkins, *Jefferson's Pillow: The Founding Fathers and the Dilemma of Black Patriotism* (Boston: Beacon Press, 2002), 114–15. Wilkins knows far more about his paternal ancestry, primarily because of his civil-rights-activist uncle Roy Wilkins's posthumously published memoir, *Standing Fast*.

38. Pauli Murray, *Proud Shoes*, 55–56.

39. Zora Neale Hurston, who claimed no mixed-race identity, expressed her skepticism of the Indian blood claimed by so many southern blacks, such as Pauli Murray, Raymond Andrews, Charlayne Hunter-Gault, and the Delany sisters. She opens an essay titled "How It Feels to Be Colored Me" by declaring: "I am colored but I offer nothing in the way of extenuating circumstances except the fact that I am the only Negro in the United States whose grandfather on the mother's side was *not* an Indian chief." Hurston, "How It Feels to Be Colored Me," *World Tomorrow* (May 1928), reprinted in Andrea A. Lunsford and John J. Ruszkiewicz, eds., *The Presence of Others: Voices and Images That Call for Response*, 3rd ed. (New York: Bedford-St. Martin's Press, 2000), 384. For other treatments of this phenomenon, see Joel W. Martin, "'My Grandmother Was a Cherokee Princess': Representations of Indians in Southern History," in S. Elizabeth Bird, ed., *Dressing in Feathers: The Construction of the Indian in American Popular Culture* (Boulder, Colo.: Westview Press, 1996), 129–47; and Darlene Wilson and Patricia D. Beaver, "Transgressions in Race and Place: The Ubiquitous Native Grandmother in America's Cultural Memory," in Barbara Ellen Smith, ed., *Neither Separate nor Equal: Women, Race, and Class in the South* (Philadelphia: Temple University Press, 1989), 34–56.

40. Pauli Murray, *Proud Shoes*, 33.

41. Ibid., 270–71.

42. Ibid., 56–57, 59.

43. Washington-Williams, *Dear Senator*, 1.

44. Ibid., 12–15, 36–40.

45. Ibid., 41, 45.

46. Ibid., 64.

47. Ibid., 160–61.

48. Ibid., 221–23.

49. Barbara J. Fields, "Ideology and Race in American History," in J. Morgan Kousser and James M. McPherson, eds., *Region, Race, and Reconstruction: Essays in Honor of C. Vann Woodward* (New York: Oxford University Press, 1982), 144, 146.

50. Pauli Murray, 1966 introduction to *Proud Shoes*, xx.

51. Nash, *Forbidden Love*, viii.

52. Pauli Murray, 1978 introduction to *Proud Shoes*, xix, xx. For a more extended analysis of the therapeutic purposes Murray found in coming to terms with her family's past, see her later autobiography, *Song in a Weary Throat*, 298–305.

53. Murray's version of this story appears in *Song in a Weary Throat*, chapter 11. The story is told in a far fuller context in Glenda Gilmore, *Defying Dixie: The Radical Roots of Civil Rights, 1919–1950* (New York: W. W. Norton, 2008), chapter 6. Gilmore plays down Murray's white ancestry as an argument she used in this case, noting that she stressed more (at least in a letter to FDR) that she deserved to be admitted because her grandfather and mother had devoted themselves to southern education (275).

54. Williamson, *New People*, 2.

55. Delany and Delany, *Having Our Say*, 106–7.

56. Goodwin, *It's Good to Be Black*, 244–45.

57. Moody, *Coming of Age in Mississippi*, 60.

58. Pauli Murray, *Proud Shoes*, 60–61.

59. Barack Obama, *Dreams from My Father: A Story of Race and Inheritance* (New York: Times Books, 1995), 11–12.

60. Barack Obama's speech on race, March 17, 2008, transcript from the *New York Times*, March 18, 2008.

61. Ibid. More recently, in October 2009, genealogists revealed a more typical mixed-race ancestry for Michelle Obama. Her great-great-great-grandmother, a fifteen-year-old slave girl named Melvinia, gave birth to a son on a Georgia plantation in 1858. The child's father was either her owner or one of the owners' four sons. Rachel L. Swarns and Jodi Kantor, "In First Lady's Roots, a Complex Path from Slavery," *New York Times*, October 7, 2009.

62. Colbert King, "A Story Much Older than Ol' Strom," *Washington Post*, December 20, 2003, quoted in Clinton, "Breaking the Silence," 19. Clinton's essay puts this case

firmly within the southern tradition of black women's liaisons with white men and how they or others have chosen to tell those stories.

63. Williamson, *New People*, xiii.

CHAPTER THREE *"All Manner of Defeated, Shiftless, Shifty, Pathetic and Interesting Good People"*

1. Styron, *A Tidewater Morning*, 42. The Dabneys appear in a chapter titled "Shadrach," which was first published as a story in *Esquire* in 1978.

2. Ibid., 42–43.

3. Ibid., 58.

4. Ibid., 44–45.

5. Several essays deal with adolescence and southern autobiography, usually within the context of race. See especially Melton McLaurin, "Rituals of Initiation and Rebellion: Adolescent Responses to Segregation in Southern Autobiography," *Southern Cultures* 3 (Summer 1997): 5–24; Francis Smith Foster, "Parents and Children in Autobiography by Southern Afro-American Writers," and Lynn Z. Bloom, "Coming of Age in the Segregated South: Autobiographies of Twentieth Century Childhoods, Black and White," both in J. Bill Berry, ed., *Home Ground: Southern Autobiography* (Columbia: University of Missouri Press, 1991), 98–109, 110–22. See also chapters 1 and 2 of this volume.

6. Hobson, *But Now I See*.

7. Lumpkin, *The Making of a Southerner*, 151. For insightful accounts of Lumpkin's autobiographical writings, see Elizabeth Fox-Genovese, "Between Individualism and Community: Autobiographies of Southern Women," in Berry, *Located Lives*, esp. 28–34; and Jacquelyn Dowd Hall, "'You Must Remember This': Autobiography as Social Critique," *Journal of American History* 85 (September 1998): 439–65.

8. Lumpkin, *Making of a Southerner*, 151–52.

9. Ibid., 156.

10. Ibid., 158–59.

11. Ibid., 160.

12. Ibid.

13. Caldwell, *With All My Might*, 40.

14. Caldwell, *Call It Experience*, 24–25.

15. Caldwell, *With All My Might*, 40.

16. Caldwell, *Call It Experience*, 26.

17. Ibid., 102.

18. Ibid., 102–3.

19. The empowerment of "exile" for writers from the South was not unusual. Caldwell

was one of several southern writers who articulated their feelings about their native region in either fictional or nonfictional form only after leaving it. New York City, in particular, served as the base from which many other writers — including Styron, Morris, and Lumpkin — found perspective and inspiration to write about the South and their lives as southerners.

20. Anne Loveland, *Lillian Smith, A Southerner Confronting the South: A Biography* (Baton Rouge: Louisiana State University Press, 1986), 9–10 (quote on p. 9).

21. Ibid., 10–11.

22. Lillian Smith, "Memory of a Large Christmas," *Life*, December 15, 1961, 90–94. This article was expanded and published as *Memory of a Large Christmas*, the book version cited here, 60–62.

23. Ibid., 62.

24. Ibid., 63.

25. Lillian Smith, *Killers of the Dream*, 27.

26. She came closest to doing so in a childhood memory of a young, very light-skinned black girl, Janie, who briefly lived with her family when it was assumed that she was white and had been kidnapped by a local black family in the community. Ibid., 34–37. See chapter 2 of this book for a discussion of that incident.

27. Jimmy Carter, *An Hour before Daylight*, 270.

28. Ibid., 59.

29. Ibid., 60.

30. Ibid., 60–61.

31. McGill, *The South and the Southerner*, 59–60.

32. Ibid., 61.

33. Ibid., 61–62.

34. Ibid.

35. Morris, *North toward Home*, 20–21.

36. Ibid., 22–23.

37. Ibid.

38. Ibid., 125, 124.

39. Styron, *A Tidewater Morning*, 42–43.

40. Morris, *North toward Home*, 126–27.

41. Ibid., 23–24.

42. Ibid., 90.

43. Ibid., 142.

44. Lumpkin, *The Making of a Southerner*, 239.

45. Ibid., 189–93.

46. Lillian Smith, *Killers of the Dream*, 34–37.

47. Crews, *A Childhood*; Bragg, *All Over but the Shoutin'*; Moss, *Change Me into*

Zeus's Daughter; Allison, *Two or Three Things I Know for Sure*; DeRosier, *Creeker: A Woman's Journey*; Karr, *The Liar's Club: A Memoir* and *Cherry: A Memoir*; Ray, *Ecology of a Cracker Childhood*; Walls, *The Glass Castle*; Rusk, *As I Saw It*; and Clinton, *My Life*.

48. Bragg, *All Over but the Shoutin'*, 96–97.

49. Ibid., 97–98.

50. Crews, *A Childhood*, 58, 62.

51. Ray, *Ecology of a Cracker Childhood*, 30, 157.

52. Ibid., 151.

53. For another perspective on the post–civil rights era shift from race to class in southern autobiographical work, see Hobson, *But Now I See*, 134–47.

54. Quotes are from Hobson's book *Tell about the South*.

CHAPTER FOUR *Railroads, Race, and Remembrance*

1. Angelou, *I Know Why the Caged Bird Sings*, 3–4.

2. Coretta Scott King, *My Life with Martin Luther King, Jr.*, 31.

3. Most scholarly treatments of southern autobiography and memoir emphasize race relations, most notably Fred Hobson, *Tell about the South* and *But Now I See*; O'Dell, *Sites of Southern Memory*; and, especially, Ritterhouse, *Growing Up Jim Crow* and Wallach "*Closer to the Truth than Any Fact.*"

4. W. E. B. Du Bois, *The Autobiography of W. E. B. Du Bois*, 234; Ray Stannard Baker, *Following the Color Line: An Account of Negro Citizenship in the American Democracy* (New York: Doubleday, Page, and Co., 1908), 31. While these statements and the two that follow seem to lump trains and street cars together, the vast majority of southern experiences took place on trains, which remain the primary focus of this study.

5. Gunnar Myrdal, *An American Dilemma: The Negro Problem and Modern Democracy*, 2 vols. (1944; New York: Harper & Row, 1962), 2: 637; Lillian Smith, "Addressed to Intelligent White Southerners," in Helen White and Redding S. Sugg Jr., eds., *From the Mountain: Selections from "Pseudopodia" (1936), "The New Georgia Review" (1937–1942), and "South Today" (1942–1945)* (Memphis: Memphis State University Press, 1972), 124.

6. The major exceptions to these norms were those who participated in the massive migration out of the South in the early twentieth century, a topic that could form another, equally full essay. Other than fugitive slave narratives and a few classic memoirs, such as Richard Wright's *Black Boy*, few black migrants have left firsthand accounts of their trips north. One particularly striking reference to the large numbers of blacks leaving the South by train comes from Sarah Rice, a young black Alabamian, who described in her memoir the scene in Montgomery station as she and her family changed trains

there in 1917. "In the train station, it was just like an exodus of black people traveling, going north to better their lives, because the boll weevil had eaten up all the cotton and ruined their lives," she wrote. "It was pathetic, like you see these people in these countries now, escaping for their lives with the bundles and stuff like that . . . they just had sacks to put their clothes in, headrags on and everything, going north. We ran into all those kinds of those people until we caught the train." Rice, *He Included Me*, 12.

7. Mark Schultz, in the only study devoted fully to southern segregation in a rural context, suggests that the degree of rigidity of Jim Crow regulations and traditions regarding train travel was a function of community size. The train station in Sparta, the county seat of Hancock County, Georgia, was not as systematically segregated as those in Atlanta or other large cities. On the other hand, in the county's "rural villages, the train stations lacked even those segregationist gestures" apparent in Sparta. Schultz, *The Rural Face of White Supremacy: Beyond Jim Crow* (Urbana: University of Illinois Press, 2007), 70–71.

8. Edward L. Ayers, *The Promise of the New South: Life After Reconstruction* (New York: Oxford University Press, 1992), 137. Yet, as will be discussed later in the essay, one complaint by southern black elites was that they were forced to ride with lower-class members of their own race. Of the vast scholarship on racial segregation in the South, only a few works have provided detailed coverage of the importance of railroads as significant reflections of either the Jim Crow regime or the extent to which southern blacks were first made aware of its restrictions on them and their families. Perhaps the most extensive and insightful is Grace Elizabeth Hale, *Making Whiteness: The Culture of Segregation in the South, 1890–1940* (New York: Pantheon, 1998), in a section titled "Training the Ground of Difference," 125–38. In *Growing Up Jim Crow*, Jennifer Ritterhouse adds an intriguing new element in examining the way in which children were acculturated into a segregated society. See especially 119–27 for a discussion of public transportation and other perspectives on some of the same incidents discussed herein. Other valuable treatments of segregated transportation are Ayers, *Promise of the New South*, 137–46; Leon Litwack, *Trouble in Mind: Black Southerners in the Age of Jim Crow* (New York: Alfred A. Knopf, 1998), 230–46; and Mark M. Smith, *How Race Is Made: Slavery, Segregation, and the Senses* (Chapel Hill: University of North Carolina Press, 2006), 60–63, and chapter 4.

9. Barbara Young Welke, *Recasting American Liberty: Gender, Race, Law, and the Railroad Revolution, 1865–1920* (Cambridge: Cambridge University Press, 2001), 272. Welke's book, Catherine A. Barnes, *Journey from Jim Crow: The Desegregation of Southern Transit* (New York: Columbia University Press, 1983), and Charles A. Lofgren, *The Plessy Case: A Legal-Historical Interpretation* (New York: Oxford University Press, 1987) provide the most thorough treatments of the legalities of segregation on trains in the Jim Crow South. For the most accessible state-by-state listings of Jim Crow leg-

islation, see "The History of Jim Crow," www.jimcrowhistory.org. For broader studies of American and southern train travel, see Sarah H. Gordon, *Passage to Union: How the Railroads Transformed American Life, 1829–1929* (Chicago: Ivan R. Dee, 1996); and Joseph R. Millichap, *Dixie Limited: Railroads, Culture, and the Southern Renaissance* (Lexington: University Press of Kentucky, 2002).

10. These cases were *Hall v. DeCuir* (1877) and the *Civil Rights Cases* (1883). The fullest coverage of both is found in Welke, *Recasting American Liberty*, chapter 9.

11. For detailed accounts of how this legislation unfolded, see Barnes, *Journey from Jim Crow*, 10–16; Ayers, *Promise of the New South*, 137–46; and Welke, *Recasting American Liberty*, chapters 7 and 9.

12. Among autobiographers, W. E. B. Du Bois provided the fullest and most graphic descriptions of these conditions, both in *The Autobiography of W. E. B. Du Bois*, 234–35; and *Darkwater*, 228–30. Historians' treatments of these conditions include Hale, *Making Whiteness*, 132–36, 337n22; Ayers, *Promise of the New South*, 137–40; and Mark M. Smith, *How Race Is Made*, 60–64.

13. On separate legislation applied to Pullman cars, see Barnes, *Journey from Jim Crow*, 15, and for one state, Donald L. Grant, *The Way It Was in the South: The Black Experience in Georgia* (Secaucus, N.J.: Carol Publishing Group, 1983), 214–15. On the segregation of waiting rooms, see Litwack, *Trouble in Mind*, 232–33; Barnes, *Journey from Jim Crow*, 10; Welke, *Recasting American Liberty*, 276; and Rabinowitz, *Race Relations in the Urban South*, 188. Rabinowitz suggests that de facto segregation in depot waiting rooms was practiced in southern cities well before it was legally mandated.

14. Henry Brown, *Narrative of the Life of Henry Box Brown, Written by Himself;* Craft and Craft, *Running a Thousand Miles for Freedom.* Douglass, *Life and Times of Frederick Douglass*, section 2, chapter 1.

15. Jacobs, *Incidents in the Life of a Slave Girl*, 162–63, and 283n. Jacobs actually uses the term "Jim Crow car" later in her narrative, noting an incident when she was not forced to ride in one, given that she was in "servitude to the Anglo-Saxon race" as nursemaid to the baby daughter of her guardian and employer, Mrs. Bruce (176). In *North of Slavery: The Negro in the Free States, 1790–1860* (Chicago: University of Chicago Press, 1961), Leon Litwack confirms that segregated railroad cars were well established under northern state law by the early 1840s, when abolitionists actively challenged them (106–11).

16. Terrell, *A Colored Woman in a White World*, 15–16. Coretta Scott King is one of several other autobiographers who reflect on the plight of black mothers in explaining Jim Crow to their children. She writes that when those children pose the question, "Why?, every African American mother says, 'You are just as good as anyone else. It's just the way things are.' With his deep hurt, the child realizes that his mother is trying to

explain without explaining, and that she wouldn't have to tell him that if there weren't some problem." King, *My Life with Martin Luther King, Jr.*, 32.

17. Wells-Barnett, *Crusade for Justice*, 18–20. Wells's autobiography was edited by her daughter, who provides in both her introduction and footnotes valuable context and substantiation of this case and its significance.

18. Johnson, *Along This Way*, 64–65. Johnson also made incidents on trains crucial elements in his sole novel, *The Autobiography of an Ex-Colored Man* (1912; New York: Penguin, 1990), 480–85, in which the protagonist, passing for white, overhears a revealing debate between northern and southern whites in a smoking car en route from Nashville to Atlanta.

19. Johnson, *Along This Way*, 84–86. Johnson follows this story with two other incidents involving Jim Crow train cars, each very different in tone and circumstance from the two recounted here (86–89).

20. Hale, *Making Whiteness*, 131–32.

21. Delany and Delany, *Having Our Say*, 102–3. Several other autobiographers write of mothers or grandmothers whose light complexions allowed them to ride in white railroad or street cars. Pauli Murray, in *Proud Shoes*, offers a remarkably similar story of her two aunts riding on Durham, N.C., streetcars, where they caused "no end of confusion and embarrassment" on the part of men mistaking them for white just after the turn of the century; and Hunter-Gault, in *In My Place*, 15, tells of a 1942 train trip to Florida on which a white woman mistook her mother for white.

22. Green, *Ely: An Autobiography*. In a preface, Bertram Wyatt-Brown described the setting as "an atmosphere of Anglican noblesse oblige," where "Sewanee Episcopalians set a regional example of racial benevolence" (xiii); Lillian Smith, in an introduction to the same edition, described Green's childhood as "spread with a meringue of love — white people's love, generosity, superficial concern: a fluffy, sweet meringue which covered a pie made of ashes and dung and broken metallic bits of 'history.' The slave's history" (xx).

23. Green, *Ely*, 227–31. While Ely was at best ambivalent about his intentions regarding his future racial identity at the end of his book, he later published a much fuller autobiographical account of his life, *Ely: Too Black, Too White*, in which he told of his life in Texas and acknowledged that he continued to wrestle with his partial blackness for several years before moving to California, where he spent most of the rest of his life without trying to pass for white.

24. Pauli Murray, *Song in a Weary Throat*, 38–39. Although Murray only mentions the threat of lynching, the fear of sexual assault on black women traveling alone on Jim Crow cars was also raised by a number of autobiographers. Mary Church Terrell devotes a full discussion to those vulnerabilities in a chapter titled "Traveling under Difficulties" in Terrell, *A Colored Woman in a White World*, chapter 30. Jennifer Ritterhouse uses

this and several of the following examples — which she calls "dramas of social inequality" — to illustrate how black children were first exposed to race as a determinant of their place in southern society. See her *Growing Up Jim Crow*, esp. 118–26.

25. James Farmer, *Lay Bare the Heart*, 63–65.

26. Richard Wright, *Black Boy*, 46–49.

27. Franklin, *Mirror to America*, 20.

28. Thorids Simonsen, ed., *You May Plow Here: The Narrative of Sara Brooks* (New York: W. W. Norton, 1986), 90–91.

29. Elizabeth Kytle, *Willie Mae*, 71.

30. Delany and Delany, *Having Our Say*, 129–31.

31. Wolfe, *The Lost Boy*, 40–42. This is the original text of a novella written by Wolfe in 1937 and first published, in abbreviated form, in 1941. The lost boy in the title is Grover, who would die of typhoid fever later that summer in St. Louis. For more on Wolfe's frequent treatment of train travel in his fiction, see Millichap, *Dixie Limited*, chapter 3.

32. For the fullest analysis of these particular autobiographical works, see Hobson, *But Now I See*.

33. Lumpkin, *The Making of a Southerner*, 133. Lumpkin goes on to say that railroads and theaters offered the most comfort because "one knew" where the "For Colored" coach would be, and "their place" in a theater "was a nook railed off far up in the buzzard's roost." Street cars she found "more troublesome" because of the uncertainty of the sometimes shifting dividing lines between where blacks could sit at the back and whites at the front, and the "delicate rearrangement" of the sitting in the middle imposed by conductors if whites found themselves without a seat.

34. Ibid., 214–15. For insightful accounts of Lumpkin's autobiographical writings, see Elizabeth Fox-Genovese, "Between Individualism and Community: Autobiographies of Southern Women," in Berry, *Located Lives*, esp. 28–34; Jacquelyn Dowd Hall, "'You Must Remember This': Autobiography as Social Critique, *Journal of American History* 85 (September 1998): 439–65; and O'Dell, *Sites of Southern Memory*, chapter 2.

35. Lillian Smith, *Killers of the Dream*, 55–56. This passage forms the end of chapter 2. Chapter 3, "Unto the Third and Fourth Generation," consists of Smith's response to this perplexed teenager. For a full account of Laurel Falls Camp and Smith's relationship with her campers, see Anne C. Loveland, *Lillian Smith, A Southerner Confronting the South: A Biography* (Baton Rouge: Louisiana State University Press, 1986), 12–20, 191; and Margaret Rose Gladney, "A Chain Reaction of Dreams: Lillian Smith and the Laurel Falls Camp," *Journal of American Culture* 5 (Fall 1982): 50–56.

36. This is one of a number of occasions where Smith expressed contempt specifically for the ill-treatment of distinguished black men and women. On more than one occasion, she pled with southern readers to exercise civility and respect toward "Negro

college presidents, teachers, ministers, lawyers, community leaders, and artists," who deserved to be addressed as Mr. or Mrs. or Miss. See, for example, Smith, "Addressed to Intelligent White Southerners," in Helen White and Redding S. Sugg Jr., eds., *From the Mountain: Selections from Pseudopodia, the North Georgia Review, and South Today* (Memphis: Memphis State University Press, 1972), 118–19.

37. Jimmy Carter, *An Hour before Daylight*, 95–96.

38. Washington, *Up from Slavery*, 120–21. Equally revealing is what Washington chose not to relate in his autobiography. In his biography, Louis R. Harlan tells of two harsh — even violent — confrontations that took place on trains, one involving his daughter Portia and a Tuskegee representative confronted by a white conductor in 1895; the other, in 1885, involving a wedding party of Tuskegee faculty members harassed by a crowd of "crackers" on a train bound for Montgomery, about which Washington wrote a formal letter of complaint to a Montgomery newspaper, in which he upheld the principle of separate cars for blacks but urged that they be up to the same standards as first-class cars for whites. Harlan, *Booker T. Washington: The Making of a Black Leader, 1856–1901* (New York: Oxford University Press, 1972), 229–30; 162.

39. Hurston, *Dust Tracks on a Road*, 70.

40. Ibid., foreword by Maya Angelou, x; Arno Bontemps, "From Eatonville, Florida to Harlem," *New York Herald Tribune*, November 22, 1942, quoted in Wallach, *"Closer to the Truth than Any Fact"*, 143. Other insightful treatments of Hurston's detachment from racial context in *Dust Tracks* include Valerie Boyd, *Wrapped in Rainbows: The Life of Zora Neale Hurston* (New York: Scribner's, 2003), 357–60; Priscilla Wald, "Becoming Colored: The Self-Authorized Language of Difference in Zora Neale Hurston," *American Literary History* 2 (Spring 1990): 84–94; and Philip A. Snyder, "Zora Neale Hurston's *Dust Tracks: Autobiography and Artist Novel*, in Gloria L. Cronin, ed., *Critical Essays on Zora Neale Hurston* (New York: G. K. Hall, 1998), 173–89.

41. Hurston, *Dust Tracks on a Road*, 83–84.

42. Hurston was intentionally vague about her age throughout the book. She claimed elsewhere to have been born in 1901, though other evidence suggests she was born a full decade earlier. *Dust Tracks on a Road*, x. See Boyd, *Wrapped in Rainbows*, 354, and Wallach, *Closer to the Truth*, 143.

43. Hurston, *Dust Tracks on a Road.*, 235–37.

44. Cooper, *A Voice from the South*, 110–11.

45. Cannon, *A Gentle Knight*, 4–5.

46. Franklin, *Mirror to America*, 341. Curiously, Franklin recounts this incident only at his book's end, and through its retelling by President Bill Clinton, who awarded him the Presidential Medal of Freedom in 1995.

47. Rowan, *South of Freedom*, 121–27.

48. Ibid., 126–27.

49. Lillian Smith to Dorothy Canfield Fisher, March 10, 1956, in Margaret Rose Gladney, ed., *How Am I to Be Heard: Letters of Lillian Smith* (Chapel Hill: University of North Carolina Press, 1993), 197–98. Equally revealing in this account is Smith's suggestion that the Jim Crow rules on railroad cars — and even in the waiting room in Toccoa — had eased considerably by 1955.

50. Gates, *Colored People*, 27.

51. Ibid., 19.

52. Coretta Scott King, *My Life with Martin Luther King, Jr.*; Moody, *Coming of Age in Mississippi*; Abernathy, *And the Walls Came Tumbling Down*, 29–35; and Lewis, *Walking with the Wind*. Lewis, alone of these authors, recounted the difficulties of automobile travel in the pre–civil rights era, describing a car trip made with his uncle from Alabama to Buffalo, New York, and back in 1951 (38–40). See also Andrew Young, *An Easy Burden*, and Parks, *Rosa Parks*, neither of which make reference to Jim Crow train cars. Perhaps most striking, not one of the thirty African American children whose testimonials make up Ellen Levine's *Freedom's Children* makes any reference to train travel.

53. In *Journey from Jim Crow*, Catherine Barnes provides a book-length study of the desegregation of public transportation in the South, including that of trains and train stations. See esp. chapters 2 and 11.

54. Delany and Delany, *Having Our Say*, 131–32.

55. Du Bois, *Darkwater*, 229–30.

56. Smith, "Putting Away Childish Things," in White and Sugg, eds., *From the Mountain*, 132, 133.

CHAPTER FIVE *"I'm Better Than This Sorry Place"*

1. Morris, *North toward Home*, 143, 153, 156.

2. The focus of this essay is on white southerners attending southern institutions. One could write equally revealing essays on the experiences of white southerners who attended schools outside the South, where they faced even more layers of culture shock and dislocation, or on southern blacks' collegiate experiences, but those experiences come out of somewhat different dynamics — those of outsiders having to adjust to circumstances far more removed from their comfort zones than white southerners attending school in the South with other white southerners, thus making the forces separating them from their peers far more internalized.

Some of the best of white southern accounts of attending school in the North are those of William Alexander Percy's adjustment to Harvard Law School; Bill Bragg's and Larry L. King's years as Neiman Fellows at Harvard; Bill Clinton at Georgetown University and as a Rhodes Scholar at Oxford; Jimmy Carter at the U.S. Naval Academy; Will Campbell at Yale Divinity School; J. Bill Berry at Princeton; Virginia Durr at

Wellesley; Bobbie Ann Mason at the University of Connecticut; James McBride Dabbs and Katharine Du Pre Lumpkin at Columbia University; and Virginius Dabbs at Clark University.

Of African American accounts I've assigned to classes over the years, those that wrestle in most interesting ways with college life, North and South, are Booker T. Washington at Hampton Institute; Sarah and Bessie Delany at St. Augustine College and Columbia University, respectively; Walter White and James Weldon Johnson at Atlanta University; Zora Neale Hurston at Barnard; Coretta Scott King at Antioch College and the New England Conservatory of Music; Anne Moody at Tugaloo and Jackson State; Henry Louis Gates at Piedmont College in West Virginia; Andrew Young at Dillard and Howard universities; John Lewis at Fisk University; Clarence Thomas at the College of the Holy Cross in Worcester, Massachusetts; Essie Mae Washington-Williams (the daughter of Strom Thurmond) at South Carolina State College at Orangeburg — the only instance I know of a nonsouthern black who came south for a college education; and especially Charlayne Hunter-Gault's momentous years as one of the first two black students at the University of Georgia.

3. Spectorsky, *The College Years*, 18.

4. Drew Gilpin Faust, "The University in Crisis," *New York Times Book Review*, September 6, 2009, 18.

5. John William Ward, "Convocation Address," Amherst College, Fall 1976, reprinted in Wilson Smith and Thomas Bender, eds., *American Higher Education Transformed, 1940–2005: Documenting the National Discourse* (Baltimore: Johns Hopkins University Press, 2008), 54.

6. Welty, *One Writer's Beginnings*, 83–84.

7. Braden, *The Wall Between*, 25–26.

8. Lumpkin, *The Making of a Southerner*, 177.

9. Ibid., 185–88.

10. Ibid., 189–90. Lumpkin devoted a full — and fascinating — paragraph to the novelty of calling black people by anything other than their first names, and the troubling implications of what such a break from tradition suggested, both in white and black minds.

11. Ibid., 192–93. *The Birth of a Nation* was returned to theaters throughout the South for several years after its initial tour in 1915. Many southerners have documented their initial exposure to the film from the late 1910s through the mid-1920s.

12. McGill, *The South and the Southerner*, 74.

13. Ibid., 63–64, 67–68.

14. Ibid., 72.

15. Dees, *A Season for Justice*, 76.

16. The fullest account of Lucy's experience is found in E. Culpepper Clark, *The*

Schoolhouse Door: Segregation's Last Stand at the University of Alabama (New York: Oxford University Press, 1993).

17. Dees, *Season for Justice*, 77–78.

18. Larry L. King, *Confessions of a White Racist*, part 2, "The Young Warrior," 33–58. For an insightful analysis of King's "conversion experience," see Hobson, *And Now I See*, 97–104.

19. King, *Confessions of a White Racist*, 67–68.

20. Ibid., 68.

21. Ibid., 69.

22. Curry, et al., *Deep in Our Hearts*. Of the nine, five attended southern colleges — two of them the University of Texas; of those five, Browning is one of only three who trace their activism and commitment to civil rights back to campus contacts or experience. Browning's essay is titled "Shiloh Witness," 37–84.

23. Ibid., 52.

24. See Jeffrey Roche, *Restructured Resistance: The Sibley Commission and the Politics of Desegregation in Georgia* (Athens: University of Georgia Press, 1998).

25. Browning, "Shiloh Witness," 58–60.

26. Ibid., 62–64, 82.

27. Morris, *North toward Home*, 170.

28. Ibid., 171–72, 175–76.

29. Ibid., 179–80.

30. Ibid., 185–86.

31. Ibid., 184–89, 192. For a scholarly account of this controversy and Morris's role in it, see Doug Rossinow, *The Politics of Authenticity: Liberalism, Christianity, and the New Left in America* (New York: Columbia University Press), 33–38.

32. Abbott, *Womenfolks*, 187. Abbott was aware of Morris's memoir when she wrote hers, and she even quotes his "I'm better than this sorry place," noting that "southern women too have come to that same furious conclusion, though for somewhat different reasons" (191).

33. Ibid., 185–86.

34. Ibid., 187–89.

35. Ibid., 189–98; Bessie Smith quoted on 189.

36. Evans, *The Provincials*, 169.

37. Ibid., 169–70.

38. Ibid., 170–72.

39. Ibid., 177–78. Curiously, the story of the University of North Carolina's desegregation has generated very little attention, and nothing that I've seen makes any reference to the protest of dormitory segregation that Evans relates here. The only scholarly history of the university, William D. Snider, *Light on the Hill: A History of the University of*

North Carolina at Chapel Hill (Chapel Hill: University of North Carolina Press, 1992), makes no mention of the lawsuit that brought the first black undergraduates to campus in 1955. The only treatment of it remains Peter Wallenstein, "Higher Education and the Civil Rights Movement: The Desegregation of the University of North Carolina," in Winfred B. Moore, Kyle S. Sinisi, and David H. White Jr., eds., *Warm Ashes: Issues in Southern History at the Dawn of the Twenty-First Century* (Columbia: University of South Carolina Press, 2003), 280–300; brief reference and the full court ruling on that suit, *Frasier v. Board of Trustees of the University of North Carolina* (1955), can be found in Peter Wallenstein, ed., *Higher Education and the Civil Rights Movement: White Supremacy, Black Southerners, and College Campuses* (Gainesville: University Press of Florida, 2008), 48, and appendix 7, 266–69, and an unpublished dissertation, Neal King Cheek, "An Historical Study of the Administrative Actions in the Racial Desegregation of the University of North Carolina at Chapel Hill" (PhD diss., University of North Carolina-Chapel Hill, 1973).

40. Ibid., 183–84. Evans's father would go on to become the president of Carolina's alumni association in the early 1970s and was the recipient of the university's Distinguished Alumnus Award in 1972, achievements never quite matched by Eli.

41. Cohen, *The Peddler's Grandson*, xi.

42. Ibid., 166, 167.

43. Ibid., 168, 170, 172.

44. Ibid., 177.

45. Ibid., 182, 183.

46. Ibid., 186–87.

47. Ibid., 193.

48. Both Sotomayor and Obama quoted in *Newsweek*, July 10, 2009, 43.

49. Conroy, *The Water Is Wide*, 7. A number of other white southerners experienced their epiphanies regarding race either before or after college, including Melton McLaurin, Anne Braden, Will Campbell, Sarah Patton Boyle, James McBride Dabb, and as discussed above, Larry L. King. Conroy provided a fictional version of his college years in *The Lords of Discipline* (New York: Bantam Books, 1982).

50. Percy, *Lanterns on the Levee*, 126–27.

51. Thomas Wolfe, "Writing and Living," in *The Autobiography of an American Novelist*, 107. Wolfe, who wrote this essay in 1938, just before his death, went on to say that at the time he graduated, "I was just beginning to hint gradually to myself that I might one day try to be professionally a writer," though he wrote that it would be another six years before "I ever dared to commit myself boldly and wholeheartedly to the proposition that I was a writer" (106).

52. Rusk, *As I Saw It*, 58–59.

53. Robertson, *Red Hills and Cotton*, 219–21. In a revealing introduction to this edi-

tion, Lacy K. Ford calls Robertson's stance "an improbable blend of cavalier egalitarian and swashbuckling populist" who was "as loyal a son as South Carolina and the South ever produced" (xi).

54. T. H. Huxley, "A Liberal Education and Where to Find It," a lecture delivered at South London Workingmen's College in 1868, reproduced in Spectorsky, *The College Years*, 361.

55. It is also worth noting that these attitudes come from men whose college educations took place in the early twentieth century and whose memoirs were written in the late 1930s or early 1940s. By the same token, for those for whom college life was more life-altering, the 1950s seem to have been a particularly important decade. Nearly two-thirds of those discussed here — McGill, Morris, Abbott, Evans, and Browning — at least began their college careers during this transitional decade, and all but the two Texas students — Abbott and Morris — found that racial incidents spurred what in hindsight they saw as their most meaningful experiences during those years.

56. Gerald W. Johnson, "Should Our Colleges Educate?" *Harper's Magazine* (1927), reproduced in Spectorsky, *The College Years*, 395.

57. Spectorsky, *The College Years*, 422.

58. Ibid. Perhaps one reason Spectorsky could make this generalization is that he included no southerners among the selections he included in this final section of his book, which he titled "And Fond Recall"; all but one are recalling life at midwestern or northeastern schools. The book's publication in 1958 also means that few memoirs of the campus turbulence of the late 1950s and early 1960s yet existed, which makes such a characterization of college memories more typical than they would be for his own times and subsequent eras.

CHAPTER SIX *Sense of Place, Sense of Being*

1. Fox, *Moving Out, Finding Home*, 132.

2. Conway, *When Memory Speaks*, 6.

3. This essay originated as a review essay of the six books published in 2005; I have expanded it here to include three other significant memoirs that came out several years earlier: DeRosier, *Creeker: A Woman's Journey*; O'Brien, *At Home in the Heart of Appalachia*; and Offutt, *No Heroes*, for which I draw on a review of mine that appeared in the *Appalachian Journal* 30 (Winter/Spring 2003): 235–37.

4. Walls, *The Glass Castle*, 129, 123.

5. Ibid., 131.

6. Ibid., 133–34.

7. Ibid, 164.

8. Ibid., 241.

9. Rick Bragg's *Ava's Man* is a character study of his maternal grandfather and his hardscrabble, moonshining life in northwestern Georgia; Mary Lee Settle's *Addie* is a portrait of her maternal grandmother in West Virginia; Linda Scott DeRosier tells the story of her parents' lives in *Songs of Life and Grace*; and my favorite self-portrait of Appalachian life, Florence Cope Bush's *Dorie*, is a transcription of her mother's memories of growing up in lumber camps in the Great Smoky Mountains of Tennessee and North Carolina.

10. Glock, *Beauty Before Comfort*, 11.

11. Ibid., 20.

12. Ibid., 122.

13. Jill Ker Conway provides an insightful discussion of gay and lesbian memoir in chapter 7, "Different Stories," of *When Memory Speaks*, 127–50.

14. Mann, *Loving Mountains, Loving Men*, xiv.

15. Ibid., 98.

16. Ibid., 119–20.

17. Ibid., 137.

18. Ibid., 138.

19. Ibid., 107.

20. DeRosier, *Creeker*, 103, 2–3. In another especially astute commentary on growing up Appalachian, Ed Ayers, who grew up in Kingsport, in northeast Tennessee, takes the perspective of a town resident in making these same distinctions, comparing his small-city (or large-town) experience not only with his grandparents' lives in far more remote Yancey County, North Carolina, just across the state line, but also with the bigger, more sophisticated world of Knoxville, which he came to know as an undergraduate at the University of Tennessee. See Edward L. Ayers, "Borders, Boundaries, and Edges: A Southern Autobiography," in Boles, *Shapers of Southern History*, 311–31. (It is worth noting that Ayers doesn't subtitle his essay "An Appalachian Autobiography.")

21. DeRosier, *Creeker*, 7, 4.

22. Ibid., 95, 99–100.

23. Ibid., 5.

24. Ibid., 122–23.

25. Ibid., 179, 182–83.

26. Ibid., 220.

27. Minick, *Finding a Clear Path*, 6.

28. Ibid., 11.

29. Minick has produced a memoir titled *The Blueberry Years: A Memoir of Farm and Family* (New York: Thomas Dunne, 2010), in which he recounts the eight years he and his wife operated an organic blueberry farm in Floyd County, Va.

30. Crowe, *Zoro's Field*, 4.

31. Ibid., 123.

32. Fox, *Moving Out, Finding Home*, 8–9, 20.

33. Ibid., 136–37.

34. Sadly, Bob Fox died of cancer only a month after the publication of his book. His wife Susan died a year earlier, also of cancer, and Fox wrote movingly of her battle against it in the latter essays of the book.

35. Offutt, *No Heroes*, 42.

36. Ibid., 26.

37. Ibid., 43. *No Heroes* inspired some harsh reviews by Kentuckians and others in the region. See Cheryl Truman, "Memoir Raises Condescension to an Art Form," *Lexington Herald-Ledger*, April 13, 2002; and review by Beth Newell, in *Now & Then*, Winter 2002, 41–42, in which she states with some bitterness that as one concludes the book, "it is difficult to forget the stereotypical portrayal of Eastern Kentuckians. It is these stereotypes that linger, rather than Offutt's account of his journey home and what he learned through his failure to single-handedly change life in Morehead." She also points out several inaccuracies in these denigrating descriptions of the town and the college, cited here.

38. Offutt, *The Same River Twice*, 19.

39. Offutt, *No Heroes*, 86–87.

40. Ibid., 33.

41. Ibid., 228.

42. Ibid., 244.

43. Ibid., 243.

44. O'Brien, *At Home in the Heart of Appalachia*. Another native son of Piedmont is Henry Louis Gates, who provides a very different account of growing up there in *Colored People*.

45. O'Brien, *At Home in the Heart of Appalachia*, 63–65.

46. Ibid., 274–75.

47. Ibid.

48. Ibid., 6.

49. Ibid., 15.

50. Ibid., 23, 24.

51. Ibid., 26. It is interesting that his father continued to hunt game (primarily rabbit) and fish (often for eels) on the outskirts of Philadelphia in order to feed his large family there (21).

52. Ibid., 25–26.

53. Thornton Wilder, quoted in C. Vann Woodward, "The Search for Southern Identity," in *The Burden of Southern History* (New York: Vintage Books, 1960), 23–24.

54. Joel Garreau, *The Nine Nations of North America* (Boston: Houghton Mifflin, 1981), 118. Pat Conroy, *The Prince of Tides* (Boston: Houghton-Mifflin, 1986), 225.

55. For a strong case for southern linkages between self-identity and place, see William Hogarth, "Writing Upside Down: Voice and Place in Southern Autobiography," in Berry, *Located Lives*; and Watkins, introduction to *Southern Selves*, xiii–xvii.

56. Bush, *Dorie*, 32.

57. O'Brien, *At Home in the Heart of Appalachia*, 300.

AFTERWORD

1. Timothy B. Powell, "Introduction: Re-Thinking Cultural Identity," in Powell, ed., *Beyond the Binary*, 1.

2. James H. Watkins, who teaches English at Berry College, read this manuscript for UGA Press and noted in his report that "a somewhat dated black/white binary informs the author's approach to the project." He suggested that some inclusion of work by Native Americans and other Others be incorporated into the text, hence this final essay. I am grateful for subsequent exchanges with Watkins, and for the many specific suggestions he made that have helped shape it.

3. The only southern-based work considered here is Laura Browder's discussion of Forrest Carter's *The Education of Little Tree* in her essay "'One Hundred Percent American': How a Slave, a Janitor, and a Former Klansman Escaped Racial Categories by Becoming Indians," in Powell, ed., *Beyond the Binary*, 107–38. *The Education of Little Tree* will be dealt with later in this chapter.

4. Payne, *Multicultural Autobiography*, xxiii; his own essay is titled "George Washington Cable's 'My Politics': Context and Revision in a Southern Memoir," 94–113. An earlier treatment of American autobiography that emphasizes biculturalism in nonsouthern settings (Native American, Chicano-American, and Chinese-American) is Couser, *Altered Egos*, esp. chapters 8 and 9.

5. Awiakta, *Selu*, 31. See also Awiakta, *Abiding Appalachia*, in which she explores these themes more through poetry than prose; and an autobiographical essay, titled "Sound," in Dyer, *Bloodroot*, 40–51.

6. Awiakta, *Selu*, 31.

7. Coke, *Rock, Ghost, Willow, Deer*, 1.

8. Ellis, *Walking the Trail*, 6, 9–10, 255. Ellis followed this book with two, more gimmicky but equally entertaining, encores: *Marching through Georgia: My Walk along Sherman's Route* (New York: Delacorte Press, 1995), and *On the Trail of the Pony Express* (Lincoln: University of Nebraska Press, 2002).

9. Alther, *Kinfolks*, xi–xii.

10. Ibid., 45–46. The fullest account of the Melungeons and their history is that

by Alther's cousin and his wife: Brent Kennedy and Robyn Vaughan Kennedy, *The Melungeons: The Resurrection of a Proud People* (Macon, Ga.: Mercer University Press, 1997). Another memoir by a Melungeon is Mattie Johnson, *My Melungeon Heritage: A Story of Life on Newman's Ridge* (Johnson City, Tenn.: Overmountain Press, 1997).

11. Alther, *Kinfolks*, xiii, 235.

12. Tate, *Power in the Blood*, 218–19.

13. Forrest Carter, *The Education of Little Tree: A True Story* (1976; rpt. Albuquerque: University of New Mexico Press, 1985).

14. For accounts of the scandal, see Yagoda, *Memoir: A History*, 255–56; and Browder, "One Hundred Percent American," esp. 126–33. Browder included this account in *Slippery Characters*, a full book on fraudulent autobiography by those claiming false racial or ethnic identities. See also Dan T. Carter's announcement of the fraud: "The Transformation of a Klansman," *New York Times*, October 5, 1991.

15. Lambert, *Up from These Hills*.

16. Jung, *Southern Fried Rice*, 124. Jung went on to earn a PhD in psychology and wrote this memoir when he retired after a forty-year teaching career at California State, Long Beach.

17. Ariyoshi, *From Kona to Yenan*, 32. I thank Carey Clinton in the UGA Admissions Office for alerting me to this book.

18. Ibid., 36–37, 41.

19. Verghese, *My Own Country*, 23, 46. The only other southern experience that I know of by a writer of Indian origins is V. S. Naipaul's *A Turn in the South* (New York: Alfred A. Knopf, 1989). Naipaul was born in Trinidad to immigrants from India. His book is more travelogue than autobiography, though among his more intriguing observations of the South are comparisons with Caribbean culture and society.

20. Judith Ortiz Cofer, "Advanced Biology," in *The Latin Deli*, 127–28. The first quote regarding her three languages is from Cofer's speech on the occasion of her induction into the Georgia Writers Hall of Fame, March 23, 2010. Cofer has written a more conventional memoir of her early years in Puerto Rico titled *Silent Dancing: A Partial Remembrance of a Puerto Rican Childhood* (Houston: Arte Publico Press, 1991).

21. Cofer, "The Story of My Body," in ibid., 135, 146. See also her essay, "The Myth of the Latin Woman: I Just Met a Girl Named Maria," in ibid., 148–54.

22. Cofer, "A Brief Account of the Adventures of My Appropriated Kinsman, Juan Ortiz, Indian Captive, Soldier, and Guide to General Hernando de Soto," manuscript shared with me by the author, January 2010.

23. Piri Thomas, *Down These Mean Streets*, 158, 166–67. The issue of race — and of Thomas's relationship with African Americans — is a central theme of his story long before he travels South. An earlier chapter, for instance, is titled "How to Be a Negro without Really Trying."

24. Ibid., chapter 18.

25. Ibid., 185–86, 195. I thank my colleague Reinaldo Roman for alerting me to Thomas's memoir. While he told me of several memoirs by Cuban exiles in south Florida, the only other life story he knew of by a Latino/Latina elsewhere in the South is an audio recording: Carmen Agra Deedy, "Growing Up Cuban in Decatur, Georgia" (2000; audio CD from Atlanta: Peachtree Publishers, 2004).

26. Powell, *Beyond the Binary*, 1–2.

SELECTED BIBLIOGRAPHY

SOUTHERN AUTOBIOGRAPHIES AND MEMOIRS

Abbott, Shirley. *The Bookmaker's Daughter: A Memory Unbound*. New York: Ticknor and Fields, 1991.

———. *Womenfolks: Growing Up Down South*. New York: Ticknor and Fields, 1983.

Abernathy, Ralph David. *And the Walls Came Tumbling Down: An Autobiography*. New York: Harper & Row, 1989.

Allison, Dorothy. *Two or Three Things I Know for Sure*. New York: Dutton, 1995.

Alther, Lisa. *Kinfolks: Falling Off the Family Tree: My Search for My Melungeon Ancestors*. New York: Arcade, 2007.

Andrews, Raymond. *The Last Radio Baby: A Memoir*. Atlanta: Peachtree Publishers, 1990.

Angelou, Maya. *I Know Why the Caged Bird Sings*. New York: Random House, 1970.

Ariyoshi, Koji. *From Kona to Yenan: The Political Memoirs of Koji Ariyoshi*. Manoa: University of Hawaii Press, 2000.

Ashmore, Harry S. *Civil Rights and Wrongs: A Memoir of Race and Politics, 1944–1994*. New York: Pantheon Books, 1994.

Awiakta, Marilou. *Abiding Appalachia: Where Mountain and Atom Meet*. Memphis: St. Luke's Press, 1978.

———. *Selu: Seeking the Corn-Mother's Wisdom*. Golden, Colo.: Fulcrum Publishers, 1993.

Baker, Russell. *Growing Up*. New York: St. Martin's Press, 1982.

Bates, Daisy. *The Long Shadow of Little Rock: A Memoir*. New York: David McKay Co., 1962.

Beals, Melba Pattillo. *Warriors Don't Cry: A Searing Memoir of the Battle to Integrate Little Rock's Central High*. New York: Washington Square Books, 1994.

———. *White Is a State of Mind: A Memoir*. New York: G. P. Putnam Sons, 1999.

Belfarge, Sally. *Freedom Summer*. New York: Viking Press, 1965.

Boyle, Sarah Patton. *The Desegregated Heart: A Virginian's Stand in Time of Transition*. New York: Morrow, 1962.

Braden, Anne. *The Wall Between*. New York: Monthly Review Press, 1958.

Bragg, Rick. *All Over but the Shoutin'*. New York: Pantheon, 1997.

————. *Ava's Man*. New York: Alfred A. Knopf, 2001.

Brooks, Sara. *You May Plow Here: The Narrative of Sara Brooks*. Edited by Thorids Simonsen. New York: W. W. Norton, 1986.

Brown, Henry. *Narrative of the Life of Henry Box Brown, Written by Himself*. 1849. New York: Oxford University Press, 2002.

Brown, Mary Ward. *Fanning the Spark: A Memoir*. Tuscaloosa: University of Alabama Press, 2009.

Bush, Florence Cope. *Dorie: A Woman of the Mountains*. Knoxville: University of Tennessee Press, 1992.

Caldwell, Erskine. *Call It Experience: The Years of Learning How to Write*. New York: Duell, Sloan, and Pearce, 1951.

————. *With All My Might: An Autobiography*. Atlanta: Peachtree Publishers, 1987.

Campbell, Will D. *Brother to a Dragonfly*. New York: Seabury Press, 1977.

————. *Forty Acres and a Goat: A Memoir*. Atlanta: Peachtree Publishers, 1986.

Cannon, Poppy. *A Gentle Knight: My Husband, Walter White*. New York: Rinehart & Co., 1956.

Carter, Jimmy. *An Hour before Daylight: Memories of a Rural Boyhood*. New York: Simon & Shuster, 2001.

————. *Turning Point: A Candidate, a State, and a Nation Come of Age*. New York: Time Books, 1992.

Carter, Rosalyn. *First Lady from Plains*. Boston: Houghton-Mifflin, 1984.

Clinton, Bill. *My Life*. New York: Alfred A. Knopf, 2004.

Cobbs, Elizabeth H. *Long Time Coming: An Insider's Story of the Birmingham Church Bombing that Rocked the World*. Birmingham: Crane Hill Publishers, 1994.

Cofer, Judith Ortiz. *The Latin Deli: Prose and Poetry*. Athens: University of Georgia Press, 1993.

Cohen, Edward. *The Peddler's Grandson: Growing Up Jewish in Mississippi*. New York: Dell Publishing, 1999.

Cohn, David L. *The Mississippi Delta and the World: The Memoirs of David L. Cohn*. Edited by James C. Cobb. Baton Rouge: Louisiana State University Press, 1995.

Coke, Allison Adelle Hedge. *Rock, Ghost, Willow, Deer: A Story of Survival*. Lincoln: University of Nebraska Press, 2004.

Conroy, Pat. *The Water Is Wide*. Boston: Houghton Mifflin, 1972.

Cooper, Anna Julia. *A Voice from the South*. 1892. Reprint, New York: Oxford University Press, 1988.

Corder, Jim W. *Yonder: Life on the Far Side of Change*. Athens: University of Georgia Press, 1992.

Craft, William, and Ellen Craft. *Running a Thousand Miles for Freedom*. 1860. New edition, Athens: University of Georgia Press, 1999.

Crews, Harry. *A Childhood: The Biography of a Place*. 1978. Reprint, Athens: University of Georgia Press, 1995.

Crowe, Thomas Raine. *Zoro's Field: My Life in the Appalachian Woods*. Athens: University of Georgia Press, 2005.

Curry, Constance. *Silver Rights*. Chapel Hill: Algonquin Books, 1995.

Dabbs, James McBride. *The Road Home*. Philadelphia: Christian Education Press, 1960.

Dabney, Virginius. *Across the Years: Memories of a Virginian*. Garden City, N.Y.: Doubleday, 1978.

Davis, Angela. *An Autobiography*. New York: Random House, 1974.

Dees, Morris. *A Season for Justice: The Life and Times of Civil Rights Lawyer Morris Dees*. With Steve Fieffer. New York: Simon and Shuster, 1991.

Delany, Sarah L., and Elizabeth Delany. *Having Our Say: The Delany Sisters' First 100 Years*. With Amy Hill Hearth. New York: Dell, 1993.

DeRosier, Linda Scott. *Creeker: A Woman's Journey*. Lexington: University Press of Kentucky, 1999.

Douglass, Frederick. *Life and Times of Frederick Douglass, Written by Himself*. Hartford, Conn.: Park Publishing Co., 1881; rev. ed. 1892.

———. *Narrative of the Life of Frederick Douglass: An American Slave Written by Himself*. 1845. Reprint, Boston: Bedford Books of St. Martin's Press, 1993.

Du Bois, W. E. B. *The Autobiography of W. E. B. Du Bois: A Soliloquy on Viewing My Life from the Last Decade of Its First Century*. New York: International Publishers, 1968.

———. *Darkwater: Voices from within the Veil*. New York: AMS Press, 1920.

Durr, Virginia Foster. *Outside the Magic Circle: The Autobiography of Virginia Foster Durr*. Edited by Hollinger F. Barnard. Tuscaloosa: University of Alabama Press, 1985.

Edelman, Marion Wright. *Lanterns: A Memoir of Mentors*. Boston: Beacon Press, 1999.

Ellis, Jerry. *Walking the Trail: One Man's Journey along the Cherokee Trail of Tears*. New York: Delacourte Press, 1991.

Evans, Eli N. *The Lonely Days Were Sundays: Reflections of a Jewish Southerner*. Jackson: University of Mississippi Press, 1993.

———. *The Provincials: A Personal History of Jews in the South*. Rev. ed. New York: Simon & Shuster, 1997.

Evers, Medgar. *The Autobiography of Medgar Evers*. Edited by Myrlie Evers-Williams and Manning Marable. New York: Basic Civitas, 2005.

Farmer, James. *Lay Bare the Heart: An Autobiography of the Civil Rights Movement*. New York: Arbor House, 1985.

Fields, Mamie Garvin. *Lemon Swamp and Other Places: A Carolina Memoir*. With Karen Fields. New York: Free Press, 1983.

Foote, Horton. *Beginnings: A Memoir*. New York: Scribner, 2001.

Fox, Bob. *Moving Out, Finding Home: Essays on Identity, Place, Community and Class*. Nicholasville, Ky.: Wind Publications, 2005.

Franklin, John Hope. *Mirror to America: The Autobiography of John Hope Franklin*. New York: Farrar, Straus and Giroux, 2005.

Gaillard, Frye. *Lessons from the Big House: One Family's Passage through the History of the South, a Memoir*. Asheboro, N.C.: Down Home Press, 1994.

Gates, Henry Louis, Jr. *Colored People: A Memoir*. New York: Alfred A. Knopf, 1994.

Gatins, Joseph. *We Were Dancing on a Volcano: Bloodlines and Fault Lines of a Star-Crossed Atlanta Family, 1849–1989*. Satolah, Ga: The Glade Press, 2009.

Glock, Allison. *Beauty before Comfort: A Memoir*. New York: Alfred A. Knopf, 2003.

Goodwin, Ruby Berkeley. *It's Good to Be Black*. Garden City, N.J.: Doubleday and Co., 1953.

Green, Ely. *Ely: An Autobiography*. 1966. Reprint, Athens: University of Georgia Press, 1970.

———. *Ely: Too Black, Too White*. Amherst: University of Massachusetts Press, 1970.

Griffin, John Howard. *Black Like Me*. 2nd ed. Boston: Houghton Mifflin, 1977.

Hamilton, Mary. *Trials of the Earth: The Autobiography of Mary Hamilton*. Edited by Helen Dick Davis. Jackson: University Press of Mississippi, 1992.

Hemphill, Paul. *Leaving Birmingham: Notes of a Native Son*. New York: Viking, 1993.

Huckaby, Elizabeth. *Crisis at Central High, Little Rock, 1957–58*. Baton Rouge: Louisiana State University Press, 1980.

Hunter-Gault, Charlayne. *In My Place*. New York: Farrar, Straus & Giroux, 1992.

Hurston, Zora Neale. *Dust Tracks on the Road: An Autobiography*. New York: Harper Perennial, 1996.

Jacobs, Harriet A. *Incidents in the Life of a Slave Girl*. Edited by Jean Fagan Yellin. Cambridge, Mass.: Harvard University Press, 1987.

Johnson, James Weldon. *Along This Way: The Autobiography of James Weldon Johnson*. New York: Viking Press, 1933.

Jordan, Vernon E., Jr. *Vernon Can Read: A Memoir*. With Annette Gordon-Reed. New York: Basic Civitas, 2001.

Jung, John. *Southern Fried Rice: Life in a Chinese Laundry in the Deep South*. San Francisco: Ying and Yang Press, 2005.

Karr, Mary. *Cherry: A Memoir*. New York: Viking, 2000.

———. *The Liar's Club: A Memoir*. New York: Viking, 1995.

Kennedy, Stetson. *The Klan Unmasked*. Original title: *I Rode with the Ku Klux Klan*. 1942. Reprint, Boca Raton: Florida Atlantic University Press, 1990.

King, Coretta Scott. *My Life with Martin Luther King, Jr.* Rev. ed. New York: Henry Holt and Co., 1993.

King, Florence. *Confessions of a Failed Southern Lady*. New York: St. Martin's Press, 1985.

King, Larry L. *Confessions of a White Racist*. New York: Viking Press, 1971.

King, Martin Luther, Jr. *The Autobiography of Martin Luther King, Jr.* Edited by Clayborne Carson. New York: Warner Books, 1998.

King, Martin Luther, Sr. *Daddy King: An Autobiography*. With Clayton Riley. New York: Morrow, 1980.

King, Mary. *Freedom Song: A Personal Story of the 1960s Civil Rights Movement*. New York: William Morrow, 1987.

Kytle, Elizabeth, ed. *Willie Mae*. New York: Alfred A. Knopf, 1958.

Lambert, Leonard Carson, Jr. *Up from These Hills: Memories of a Cherokee Childhood*. With Michael Carson Lambert. Lincoln: University of Nebraska Press, forthcoming 2011.

Lewis, John. *Walking with the Wind: A Memoir of the Movement*. With Michael D'Orso. New York: Simon and Shuster, 1998.

Lumpkin, Katharine Du Pre. *The Making of a Southerner*. New York: Alfred A. Knopf, 1947.

Mann, Jeff. *Loving Mountains, Loving Men*. Athens: Ohio University Press, 2005.

Mars, Florence. *Witness in Philadelphia*. Baton Rouge: Louisiana State University Press, 1977.

Marsh, Charles. *The Last Days: A Son's Story of Sin and Segregation at the Dawn of a New South*. New York: Basic Books, 2001.

Mason, Bobbie Ann. *Clear Springs: A Memoir*. New York: Random House, 1999.

Mays, Benjamin E. *Born to Rebel: An Autobiography*. New York: Scribners, 1971.

McGill, Ralph. *The South and the Southerner*. 1963. Reprint, Athens: University of Georgia Press, 1992.

McLaurin, Melton A. *Separate Pasts: Growing Up White in the Segregated South*. Athens: University of Georgia Press, 1987.

McLaurin, Tim. *Keeper of the Moon: A Memoir of a Boyhood in the South*. New York: W. W. Norton, 1991.

McWhorter, Diane. *Carry Me Home: Birmingham, Alabama: The Climactic Battle of the Civil Rights Movement*. New York: Simon & Shuster, 2001.

Mebane, Mary E. *Mary, Wayfarer*. New York: Viking Press, 1983.

Minick, Jim. *The Blueberry Years: A Memoir of Farm and Family*. New York: Thomas Dunne Books, 2010.

———. *Finding a Clear Path*. Morgantown, W.Va.: Vandalia Press, 2005.

Mitchell, H. L. *Mean Things Happen in This Land: The Life and Times of H. L. Mitchell, Co-founder of the Southern Tenant Farmers Union*. Montclair, N.J.: Allenheld, 1979.

Moody, Anne. *Coming of Age in Mississippi*. New York: Dell, 1968.

Morris, Willie. *Good Old Boy: A Delta Boyhood*. New York: Harper and Row, 1971.

———. *North toward Home*. Boston: Houghton-Mifflin, 1967.

Moss, Barbara Robinette. *Change Me into Zeus's Daughter*. New York: Scribner's, 2000.

Murray, Albert. *South to a Very Old Place*. New York: Random House, 1971.

Murray, Pauli. *Proud Shoes: The Story of an American Family*. Edited by Patricia Bell Scott. 1957. Reprint, Boston: Beacon Press, 1999.

———. *Song in a Weary Throat: An American Pilgrimage*. New York: Harper & Row, 1987.

Nordan, Lewis. *Boy with Loaded Gun: A Memoir*. Chapel Hill, N.C.: Algonquin Books, 1999.

O'Brien, John. *At Home in the Heart of Appalachia*. New York: Alfred A. Knopf, 2001.

Offutt, Chris. *No Heroes: A Memoir of Coming Home*. New York: Simon & Shuster, 2002.

———. *The Same River Twice: A Memoir*. New York: Simon & Shuster, 1993.

Painter, Nell Irvin. *The Narrative of Hosea Hudson: His Life as a Negro Communist in the South*. Cambridge, Mass.: Harvard University Press, 1979.

Parks, Rosa. *Rosa Parks: My Story*. With James Haskins. New York: Dial, 1992.

Paterson, Judith Hillman. *Sweet Mystery: A Book of Remembering*. New York: Farrar, Strauss & Giroux, 1996.

Percy, William Alexander. *Lanterns on the Levee: Recollections of a Planter's Son*. Baton Rouge: Louisiana State University Press, 1941.

Powell, Arthur G. *I Can Go Home Again*. Chapel Hill: University of North Carolina Press, 1943.

Price, Reynolds. *Clear Pictures: First Loves, First Guides*. New York: Atheneum, 1989.

Rawlings, Marjorie Kinan. *Cross Creek*. New York: Scribners, 1942.

Ray, Janisse. *Ecology of a Cracker Childhood*. Minneapolis: Milkweed Editions, 1999.

Rice, Sarah. *He Included Me: The Autobiography of Sarah Rice*. Edited by Louise Westling. Athens: University of Georgia Press, 1989.

Robertson, Ben. *Red Hills and Cotton: An Upcountry Memory*. 1942. Reprint, Columbia: University of South Carolina Press, 1991.

Rosengarten, Theodore. *All God's Dangers: The Life of Nate Shaw*. New York: Alfred A. Knopf, 1974.

Rowan, Carl T. *South of Freedom*. New York: Alfred A. Knopf, 1963.

Rubin, Louis D. *My Father's People: A Family of Southern Jews*. Baton Rouge: Louisiana State University Press, 2002.

Rusk, Dean. *As I Saw It*. With Richard Rusk. New York: W. W. Norton, 1990.

Sellers, Cleveland. *The River of No Return: The Autobiography of a Black Militant and the Life and Death of SNCC*. With Robert Terrell. New York: Morrow, 1973.

Settle, Mary Lee. *Addie: A Memoir*. Columbia: University of South Carolina Press, 1998.

Silverstein, Clara. *White Girl: A Story of School Desegregation*. Athens: University of Georgia Press, 2004.

Smith, Lillian. *The Journey*. Cleveland: World Publishing Co., 1954.

———. *Killers of the Dream*. Rev. ed. New York: W. W. Norton, 1961.

———. *Memory of a Large Christmas*. 1962. Reprint, Athens: University of Georgia Press, 1996.

Speer, Allen Paul. *From Banner Elk to Boonville: The Voices Trilogy, Part III*. Johnson City, Tenn.: Overmountain Books, 2010.

Spencer, Elizabeth. *Landscapes of the Heart: A Memoir*. New York: Random House, 1998.

Styron, William. *A Tidewater Morning: Three Tales from Youth*. New York: Random House, 1993.

Suberman, Stella. *The Jew Store: A Family Memoir*. Chapel Hill, N.C.: Algonquin Books, 1998.

Tate, Linda. *Power in the Blood: A Family Narrative*. Athens: Ohio University Press, 2009.

Taulbert, Clifton. *Once Upon a Time when We Were Colored*. Tulsa, Okla.: Council Oak Books, 1989.

Terrell, Mary Church. *A Colored Woman in a White World*. 1940. Reprint, New York, Arno Press, 1980.

Thomas, Clarence. *My Grandfather's Son: A Memoir*. New York: Harpers, 2007.

Thomas, Piri. *Down These Mean Streets*. 1967. Reprint, New York: Vintage Books, 1997.

Twain, Mark. *The Autobiography of Mark Twain*. Edited by Charles Neider. New York: Harper, 1959.

———. *Life on the Mississippi*. 1883. Reprint, New York: Modern Library, 1994.

Tyson, Timothy B. *Blood Done Sign My Name: A True Story*. New York: Crown Publishers, 2004.

Verghese, Abraham. *My Own Country: A Doctor's Story*. New York: Simon & Shuster, 1994.

Walls, Jeannette. *The Glass Castle: A Memoir*. New York: Scribner's, 2005.

Washington, Booker T. *Up from Slavery*. 1901. Reprint, New York: W. W. Norton, 1996.

Washington-Williams, Essie Mae. *Dear Senator: A Memoir by the Daughter of Strom Thurmond*. With William Stadiem. New York: Regan Books, 2005.

Wells-Barnett, Ida B. *Crusade for Justice: The Autobiography of Ida B. Wells*. Edited by Aldreda M. Duster. Chicago: University of Chicago Press, 1970.

Welty, Eudora. *One Writer's Beginnings*. Cambridge, Mass.: Harvard University Press, 1984.

White, Walter. *A Man Called White: The Autobiography of Walter White*. 1948. Reprint, Athens: University of Georgia Press, 1995.

Wilkins, Roy. *Standing Fast: The Autobiography of Roy Wilkins*. New York: Da Capo Press, 1982.

Williams, Cratis D. *Tales from Sacred Wind: Coming of Age in Appalachia*. Jefferson, N.C.: McFarland and Co., 2003.

Wolfe, Thomas. *The Autobiography of an American Novelist*. Edited by Leslie Field. Cambridge, Mass.: Harvard University Press, 1983.

———. *The Lost Boy*. Chapel Hill: University of North Carolina Press, 1992.

Woodward, C. Vann. *Thinking Back: The Perils of Writing History*. Baton Rouge: Louisiana State University Press, 1986.

Wright, Richard. *Black Boy (American Hunger)*. 1945. Restored text ed. New York: Harper Perennials, 1993.

Young, Andrew. *An Easy Burden: The Civil Rights Movement and the Transformation of America*. New York: HarperCollins, 1996.

Zellner, Bob. *The Wrong Side of Murder Creek: A White Southerner in the Freedom Movement*. Montgomery, Ala.: New South Books, 2008.

ANTHOLOGIES AND AUTOBIOGRAPHICAL ESSAY COLLECTIONS

Ayers, Edward L. and Bradley C. Mittendorf, eds. *The Oxford Book of the American South: Testomony, Memoir, and Fiction*. New York: Oxford University Press, 1997.

Boles, John B., ed. *Autobiographical Reflections on Southern Religious History*. Athens: University of Georgia Press, 2001.

———. *Shapers of Southern History: Autobiographical Reflections*. Athens: University of Georgia Press, 2004.

Curry, Constance, et al. *Deep in Our Hearts: Nine White Women in the Freedom Movement*. Athens: University of Georgia Press, 1999.

David, Jay, ed. *Growing Up Black*. New York: Morrow, 1968.

Dyer, Joyce, ed. *Bloodroot: Reflections on Place by Appalachian Writers*. Lexington: University Press of Kentucky, 1998.

Harris, Alex, ed. *A World Unsuspected: Portraits of Southern Childhood*. Chapel Hill: University of North Carolina Press, 1987.

Jones, Suzanne W. *Growing Up in the South: An Anthology of Modern Southern Literature*. New York: Mentor, 1991.

Levine, Ellen, ed. *Freedom's Choice: Young Civil Rights Activists Tell Their Own Stories*. New York: Avon, 1993.

Mayfield, Chris, ed. *Growing Up Southern: Southern Exposure Looks at Childhood, Then and Now*. New York: Pantheon Books, 1981.

Spectorsky, A. C., ed. *The College Years*. New York: Hawthorn Books, 1958.

Swann, Brian, and Arnold Krupat, eds. *I Tell You Now: Autobiographical Essays by Native American Writers*. Lincoln: University of Nebraska Press, 1987.

Watkins, James H., ed. *Southern Selves: From Mark Twain and Eudora Welty to Maya Angelou and Kaye Gibbons: A Collection of Autobiographical Writings*. New York: Vintage, 1998.

White, Deborah Gray, ed. *Telling Histories: Black Women Historians in the Ivory Tower*. Chapel Hill: University of North Carolina Press, 2008.

CRITICISM AND COMMENTARY

Adams, Timothy Dowd. *Telling Lies in Modern American Autobiography*. Chapel Hill: University of North Carolina Press, 1990.

Andrews, William L. *To Tell a Free Story: The First Century of Afro-American Autobiography, 1760–1865*. Urbana: University of Illinois Press, 1986.

Berry, J. Bill, ed. *Home Ground: Southern Autobiography*. Columbia: University of Missouri Press, 1991.

———, ed. *Located Lives: Place and Idea in Southern Autobiography*. Athens: University of Georgia Press, 1990.

Bjorklund, Diane. *Interpreting the Self: Two Hundred Years of American Autobiography*. Chicago: University of Chicago Press, 1998.

Brantley, Will. *Feminine Sense in Southern Memoir: Smith, Glasgow, Welty, Hellman, Porter, and Hurston*. Jackson: University Press of Mississippi, 1993.

Browder, Laura. *Slippery Characters: Ethnic Impersonators and American Identities*. Chapel Hill: University of North Carolina Press, 2000.

Butterfield, Stephen. *Black Autobiography in America*. Amherst: University of Massachusetts Press, 1974.

Cimbala, Paul A., and Robert F. Himmelberg, eds. *Historians and Race: Autobiography and the Writing of History*. Bloomington: Indiana University Press, 1996.

Cobb, James C. *Away Down South: A History of Southern Identity*. New York: Oxford University Press, 2005.

Coe, Richard. *When the Grass Was Taller: Autobiography and the Experience of Childhood*. New Haven: Yale University Press, 1984.

Conway, Jill Ker. *When Memory Speaks: Exploring the Art of Autobiography*. New York: Alfred A. Knopf, 1998.

Cooley, Thomas. *Educated Lives: The Rise of Modern Autobiography in America*. Columbus: Ohio State University Press, 1976.

Couser, G. Thomas. *Altered Egos: Authority in American Autobiography*. New York: Oxford University Press, 1989.

Cox, James M. *Recovering Literature's Lost Ground: Essays in American Autobiography*. Baton Rouge: Louisiana State University Press, 1989.

Culley, Margo, ed. *American Women's Autobiography: Fea(s)ts of Memory*. Madison: University of Wisconsin Press, 1992.

Graff, Harvey J. *Conflicting Paths: Growing Up in America*. Cambridge, Mass.: Harvard University Press, 1995.

Hobson, Fred. *But Now I See: The White Southern Racial Conversion Narrative*. Baton Rouge: Louisiana State University Press, 1999.

———. *Tell about the South: The Southern Rage to Explain*. Baton Rouge: Louisiana State University Press, 1983.

Kett, Joseph F. *Rites of Passage: Adolescence in America, 1790 to the Present*. New York: Basic Books, 1977.

Larson, Thomas. *The Memoir and the Memoirist: Reading and Writing Personal Narrative*. Athens: Ohio University Press, 2007.

Lee, A. Robert, ed. *First Person Singular: Studies in American Autobiography*. New York: St. Martin's Press, 1998.

Long, Jeffrey L. *Remembered Childhoods: A Guide to Autobiography and Memoirs of Childhood and Youth*. Westport, Conn.: Libraries Unlimited, 2007.

Monson, Ander. *Vanishing Points: Not a Memoir*. Minneapolis: Graywolf Press, 2010.

O'Dell, Darlene. *Sites of Southern Memory: The Autobiographies of Katharine Du Pre Lumpkin, Lillian Smith, and Pauli Murray*. Charlottesville: University Press of Virginia, 2001.

Palladino, Grace. *Teenagers: An American History*. New York: Basic Books, 1996.

Payne, James Robert. *Multicultural Autobiography: American Lives*. Knoxville: University of Tennessee Press, 1992.

Powell, Timothy B., ed. *Beyond the Binary: Reconstructing Cultural Identity in a Multicultural Context*. New Brunswick, N.J.: Rutgers University Press, 1999.

Ritterhouse, Jennifer. *Growing Up Jim Crow: The Racial Socialization of Black and White Southern Children, 1890–1940*. Chapel Hill: University of North Carolina Press, 2006.

Rubin, Louis D., Jr. *A Gallery of Southerners*. Baton Rouge: Louisiana State University Press, 1982.

Smith, Sidonie. *Where I'm Bound: Patterns of Slavery and Freedom in Black American Autobiography*. Westport, Conn.: Greenwood Press, 1974.

Smith, Sidonie, and Julie Watson. *Reading Autobiography: A Guide for Interpreting Life Narratives*. Minneapolis: University of Minnesota Press, 2001.

Stone, Albert E., ed., *The American Autobiography: A Collection of Critical Essays.* Englewood Cliffs, N.J.: Prentice Hall, 1981.

Wallach, Jennifer Jensen. *"Closer to the Truth than Any Fact": Memoir, Memory, and Jim Crow.* Athens: University of Georgia Press, 2008.

Yagoda, Ben. *Memoir: A History.* New York: Riverhead Books, 2009.

Zinsser, William, ed. *Inventing the Truth: The Art and Craft of Memoir.* Rev. ed. Boston: Houghton Mifflin, 1998.

INDEX